D0964242

# BAROQUE TIMES IN OLD MEXICO

# BAROQUE
# TIMES
# IN OLD
# MEXICO

*Seventeenth-Century Persons, Places, and Practices*

by Irving A. Leonard

Ann Arbor Paperbacks
The University of Michigan Press

*To the memory of*
HARRY A. LEONARD

(1869–1941)

De la famosa México el asiento,
origen y grandeza de edificios,
caballos, calles, trato, cumplimiento,
letras, virtudes, variedad de oficios,
regalos, ocasiones de contento,
primavera inmortal y sus indicios,
gobierno ilustre, religión, estado,
todo en este discurso está cifrado.
—Bernardo de Balbuena.

# PREFACE

WHEN historians of Hispanic America meet, their discussions occasionally turn to the origins of the republics in the southern reaches of the Western Hemisphere. Then the remark is sometimes heard that, in comparison to the Age of Discovery and Conquest and the later period of intellectual ferment foreshadowing the political separation from Spain, the intervening seventeenth century is a "forgotten" or "neglected" era. It seems a sort of night's rest, as it were, between two strenuous days of history, but thoughtful students of things past have an uneasy feeling that history does not really take these respites and that historical processes continue during such quiet moments; indeed, times of quiescence may effect powerful, if subtle, transformations that shape the character of a people and condition subsequent events. The stormy record of Europe in the same age, with its interminable wars, dynastic struggles, commercial rivalries, emerging nationalisms, and developing science, has established the traditional pattern of modern historical writing in which the concept is implicit that the history of the West is the history of the world. Though largely an extension of western culture, colonial Hispanic America, with its isolation, its nearly three centuries of peace, its religious orthodoxy, and its heterogeneous inhabitants, hardly fits into so narrow a scheme. By comparison its evolutionary trend appears scarcely perceptible, uneventful, and quite insignificant. But if for Europe that part of the globe provided little more than its quota of fuel to the current conflagrations of nationalism devastating the Continent, for the peoples who lived out their days in these remote regions of the New World it was a formative period of ethnic and cultural consolidation. It was a quiet era, comparatively speaking, when the processes of hybridization, cultural absorption, and psychological growth shaped the matrix whose imprint on the human elements of present-day Hispanic America is recognizable. Hence, to understand these Western Hemisphere neighbors today it is needful to peer behind the curtain that separates the colonial and national periods and glimpse their social, cultural, and intellectual beginnings. This effort may well be more fruitful for comprehension than the scrutiny of military and political aspects that conventional history so often prefers.

Systematic investigation of this less glamorous nature presents difficulties. Lacking the massive and specific documentation that great issues, battles, and personalities usually provide, sources of a more scattered and disparate nature must be located, and their utilization calls for delicate discrimination. The general absence of striking events shifts attention to more minute and intangible elements of history, and the scholar perforce works more in the climate of feeling of the time than among the flora and fauna of historical evidence. It is not easy to penetrate the inner reality of an era whose anachronistic spirit deliberately strove to conceal substance behind an elaborate façade of intricately ornate design. The comparative success of that decorative effort obliges the investigator to map his course, not so much by the bearings which significant events or the movements of ideas ordinarily supply, as by the prevailing attitudes, principles, and beliefs of the period. These imponderables often reveal themselves in trivial incidents and seemingly unimportant details. This inwardly pulsating and externally inactive stage of historical evolution in New Spain or Old Mexico is conveniently called "the Baroque age."

The broader use of the term "Baroque" is comparatively recent and its definition is controversial. Earlier applied to a style of architecture and plastic arts, it has come to designate a historical epoch and, subsequently, a way of life. For Hispanic America in general and Old Mexico in particular, where its artistic expression was so complex and its spirit so enduring, the semantic extension seems especially logical. The efflorescence of colonial Baroque art is better known through well-conceived studies, but the Baroque as an historical epoch and a way of life is incompletely assessed. The present work does not claim to fill, in any substantial fashion, this gap in historiography, nor does it undertake a profound analysis or interpretation. For such ends the need for more systematic research is still pressing, and a well-founded synthesis awaits fuller information. This account seeks only to give an impression of the cultural, literary, and intellectual aspects of a relatively neglected period of Mexican history. It is, indeed, a kind of mosaic composed of bits of incident and anecdote and of larger pieces of personalistic and customary detail; it is in itself a kind of Baroque design. Like the motifs of a contemporary sculptured retable, the life and culture of Old Mexico present an elaborate pattern of "whorls within whorls," and the whole cannot be fully comprehended in a glance. By focusing on a few "persons, places and practices," and by magnifying a few details of existence a better understanding of the general may emerge.

In a measure the career of the Archbishop-Viceroy, Fray García Guerra, treated in the first chapter, symbolizes the Baroque age in Spanish America, which, in less personal terms, the second chapter seeks to describe. Since profusion of detail, hierarchy, and contrast are among the dominant traits of the Baroque, their human expression appears marked in a description of colonial society offered in the third chapter. An intricate pattern of class, caste, race, and hybridization demonstrates these tendencies. The sections following concern themselves mainly with cultural mores, literary habits, and intellectual concepts of the ruling elements of a neomedieval civilization. The evolution in this last respect is epitomized to a certain extent in two conspicuous figures, the nun-poetess, Sister Juana Inés de la Cruz, and the Creole scholar, Don Carlos de Sigüenza y Góngora, of whom "profiles" are offered in the concluding chapters. In conjunction with the Archbishop-Viceroy Fray García Guerra, they point up, or personalize, the gradual change in thought and attitude discernible in the course of the seventeenth century. Through these and other personalities introduced one dimly perceives the rudimentary shaping of a psychological pattern of a people becoming a nation. Foreshadowed, too, is an ideological revolution destined to undermine the neo-orthodoxy of the Baroque age.

Of even more significance is the fact that these figures reveal that,

over the decades of the century, the Creole was identifying himself
more and more with the land of his birth, and increasingly he was
aware of his separate and unique personality. This dawning nationalism, discreetly obscure at first, asserts itself more boldly in writings
of the late seventeenth century. If the American-born Spaniard
rarely considered the Indian, Negro, and mixed elements of the
proletariat as partners in a new body politic, he did not differ so
greatly in this kind of patriotism from the aristocratic and bourgeois
classes dominant in the more advanced nations of contemporary
Europe with respect to their peasantry. From 1600 to 1700 the
Creole acquired a perceptible consciousness of his individuality and
a faith in his latent, if not actual, parity with his kinsmen in the
old country. His improving economic, social, and political status
gave him increased assurance and it nurtured his ambition to take
the reins of power from the faltering grasp of the Peninsulars.

    In the intellectual sphere the two distinguished Creoles men-
tioned, Sister Juana Inés de la Cruz and Don Carlos de Sigüenza
y Góngora, exemplify the incipient decline of scholasticism and the
beginnings of the critical spirit so much more discernible in the
Europe of their time. If their reflection of seventeenth-century
scientific thought seems hazy and remote, and if their enlightenment appears as only the pallid glow of a false dawn, they heralded,
nonetheless, the coming of the modern age in Mexico and in Hispanic America, and indirectly they prepared the soil for the seedling
of political independence by challenging authority in the intellectual
realm. Because the nun-poetess is so widely known for her literary
distinction, emphasis is here placed on the mental qualities of this
brilliant woman. Her preoccupation with ideas clearly places her at
the side of the Creole scholar as a precursor of eighteenth-century
rationalism in Mexico.

    To point up further the element of contrast, which is an im-
portant component of the Baroque, side glances are occasionally
cast at circumstances and developments to the north of Old Mexico,
particularly in English America. The more recently planted British
colonies, cruder and far less opulent than the Spanish establishments
that were older by a century, presented curious similarities in the
seventeenth century, as well as differences. An interesting instance,
set forth in Chapter XI, concerns the respective reading habits of

the dour Pilgrims of New England and the mercurial Creoles of New Spain.

In several chapters I have drawn extensively on my own studies and previously published articles, but in each case new data are added and, in varying degrees, the text is rewritten.

I am grateful to the University of Michigan for a sabbatical leave that permitted an uninterrupted period for writing a substantial part of this book. For help in assembling illustrations I am indebted to Mr. Christian M. F. Brun of the William L. Clements Library, Ann Arbor, Michigan, to my student, Mr. Edward H. Worthen, and to Dr. Paul Murray, Mexico City.

IRVING A. LEONARD

*Heathbrook*
*South Tamworth (East Sandwich)*
*New Hampshire*

# CONTENTS

Map of New Spain or Old Mexico, *ca.* 1620

(From Ogilby, *America,* London, 1671)

DOMÍNUS. FRATER. GARCÍAS. GUERRA. ARCHIEPÍSCOPUS MEXÍCANUS PROREX ᴱ. DUX 12, GE-
NERALÍS. 1611.

Archbishop-Viceroy Fray García Guerra

(From Rivera Cambas, *Los gobernantes de México,*
Mexico City, 1872)

Mexico City, 1628

(From S. de Educación Pública, Mexico City)

Mid-Seventeenth Century Mexico

(From Ogilby, *America*, London, 1671)

Sor Juana Ines De La Cruz

(From the Museo Nacional, Mexico City)

Don Carlos De Sigüenza Y Góngora
(From *The Mercurio Volante*, Los Angeles, 1932)

# BAROQUE TIMES IN OLD MEXICO

# I

# A BAROQUE
# ARCHBISHOP-VICEROY

TWO heavy cannon shots boomed dully across the murky waters of the roadstead at Vera Cruz, port of entry of Old Mexico, as the first clumsy galleons of the annual fleet from Spain gingerly rounded the island fortress of San Juan de Ulloa, a good musket-shot distance from the shore. Further reports of ordnance hurled echoes landward as more ships limped through the exposed north channel toward the comparatively safe anchorage of the fort's south wall. For the sixty-two vessels that had sailed from Cádiz on June 12, 1608 it had been a good crossing, notably free of the customary threats of storms and pirates. The size of the fleet had shrunk considerably after sighting the islands of the Caribbean as units seceded from the group to deliver cargoes and passengers at Puerto Rico, Santo Domingo, Cartagena, Havana, Honduras, Jamaica, and Yucatan. But the bulk of the flotilla was now putting in at its terminal port, gateway of the spacious realm of New Spain. It was August 19, well over two months since the coast of Spain had faded into the haze, and both crew and passengers were weary of the anxious monotony of cramped and comfortless life on shipboard. These last few days at sea, with the voyage end so near, had tantalized everyone to the point of exasperation. An inopportune calm had delayed arrival and the sun's heat, both by direct rays and reflections on the bright, blue water, had frayed tempers already ragged. Perspiration ran from every pore of unwashed

1

bodies and the pitch fairly oozed from every plank of the small, crowded ships. The tiny, coffinlike cabins below were suffocating and passengers, partly disrobed, sought relief at night among the boxes, crates, and casks littering the decks. Hence a thrill of joy and relief ran through the fretting travelers when suddenly they heard a loud shout "Land! Land! Land!" These glad tidings seemed to stir into action even the offshore breezes, and not a few individuals knelt to give thanks for beholding the continent of the New World and a happy conclusion of the journey.

One by one the tiny vessels, with all but the midsail lowered, awkwardly maneuvered into the shelter of the great wall of the fortress. Its four-hundred foot length presented rows of large, bronze rings which provided mooring and protection from the north winds that so often pounded the open coast. But these installations seldom equaled the number of units composing the fleet and the expedient was frequently necessary of forming parallel chains of two, three, or more ships that tended to sway back and forth with the tide like ponderous streamers. This arrangement was a perilous one, especially when the fierce "northers" raised heavy seas, for the adjacent series of sailing craft sometimes battered each other disastrously or broke loose from their moorings.[1]

Surrounded by a numerous retinue and mountainous luggage, an imposing figure, in the panoply of high ecclesiastical office, stood on the foredeck of one of the ships slowly picking its way toward this precarious haven. Among the swarm of expectant inhabitants lining the shore word had quickly passed that the conspicuous personage was no less than a great Prince of the Church, the Archbishop newly appointed to the See of Mexico, Fray García Guerra by name and renowned for his vast learning and stirring eloquence. Increasingly visible to these eager onlookers, as the vessel hove to, was the commotion on deck caused by the obsequious crew and personal servants who scurried about to initiate the formidable task of lightering ashore the distinguished dignitary and his multitudinous effects.

Even before the laborious process of mooring the many ships began, customs officials of the crown and inspectors of the Holy Office of the Inquisition had put out from the mainland in small boats, and soon they clambered up the sides of the vessels to the cluttered decks. Neither the boatmasters nor the sea-weary passengers greeted these emissaries with enthusiasm, for their presence presaged annoying delays in landing and possibly embarrassing investigations. The commissioners themselves had no illusions regarding their shipboard popularity but this realization did not lessen the mutual jealousy which disposed them to quarrel over matters of jurisdiction. The captains of the arriving ships had learned by experience that, with suitable discretion, both delegations could, therefore, be bribed into a most cursory exercise of their functions. But on this occasion the presence of the highest ecclesiastical authority in the realm moved the inspectors to a more faithful performance of duty and they bustled about their tasks with ostentatious efficiency, exempting from their scrutiny only the possessions of the Archbishop and his attendants. Not even the more distinguished passengers basking in episcopal favor, including a famous Spanish novelist, Mateo Alemán, escaped inconvenience.

The Vera Cruz, at which the travelers were disembarking, had an aspect of raw newness for, indeed, it was not yet a decade old. An earlier site of the port farther south was abandoned at the close of the sixteenth century because the fortified rock of San Juan de Ulloa offered better protection from the heavy gales which descended from the north and from the fierce pirates who might descend from anywhere. Otherwise, there was little to commend the location for human habitation and, important as the settlement was as a trading center and entrance to an opulent viceroyalty, its population barely exceeded two thousand. Situated in a dreary stretch of sand broken by tiny, sluggish streams, swampy bogs, and shallow pools of stagnant water, the moist heat, swarms of mosquitoes, gnats, and other noxious insects made the vicinity singularly unhealthy. The frequent, heavy downpours during the long rainy season, now approaching its end when the fleet put in, left a humid, dank atmosphere that was almost suffocating, and in it every sort of pest and repulsive creature seemed to proliferate. "When it rains, every drop produces a toad, and some are as big as a hat," wrote an early chronicler.[2] The flora and fauna were proportionately lush, while crocodiles and alligators lolled conspicuously on the banks of the marshy estuaries. The rude habitations of rough boards and crude timbers scattered about gave the seaport an unkempt look. The shelters of the rich merchants and of the wretched poor were hardly distinguishable one from the other; the drabness of all the buildings, whether dwellings, churches or convents, was unrelieved by whitewash or other embellishment, and every structure had a rotted, waterlogged appearance in the wet season, while they shook, rattled, and rumbled as the gusty winds beat against them. During the dry months the wood was like tinder and an easy prey to devastating fires that now and then leveled the community.[3]

On that August day of 1608, however, the dismal town strove to offer a more alluring appearance. The coming of the annual fleet was a great event of the year, and on this occasion it was anticipated with more than normal excitement. Preparations, as elaborate as the meager resources of the community permitted, had been arranged, and the whole motley population was on the waterfront to welcome the great prelate. The *cabildo,* or council, of the Cathedral in Mexico City had already sent down two of its eldest and most distinguished canons to greet this illustrious personage, though advanced age compelled one of them to remain in the more salubrious vicinity of Jalapa. The hardier clergyman was already in Vera Cruz, to which he had brought an ample supply of tasty foods and fruits along with forty servants, saddlehorses, mules, and other animals to convey the Archbishop's retinue and the enormous quantity of baggage to the highland capital. For the ease and comfort of this ecclesiastical prince, the Cathedral council had also provided a spacious carriage drawn by well-trained mules.[4]

The prosperous merchants and the clergy of the port town had no wish to be outdone in the homage paid to this powerful minister of God whose esteem they craved, and they spared no effort to insure the comfort and pleasure of the temporary guest. The priests and canons of the local cathedral in their vestments, and the religious orders in their dusty gray, black, and brown habits, had formed a procession, each with an upraised Cross at the head of its column. Chanting a *Te Deum Laudamus,* they picked their way through the muddy streets where scrawny fowls pecked about the refuse, mud-caked pigs rooted in the offal, and spectral *zapilotes,* or vultures, fed on carrion. This solemn parade moved slowly toward the beach, passing raucously braying donkeys protesting under heavy burdens of faggots which almost concealed them, and lumbering, ox-drawn carts, called *chirriones,* whose tortured axles filled the air with shrill squeaks and strident squeals.

Small, naked children, and slightly more clothed adults, mulattoes and Negroes for the most part, ran along the line of friars, or brought up the rear. The ebony skin of these inhabitants glistened with sweat in the humid sunlight, while the marching members of the religious orders perspired profusely beneath their heavy vesture. The dank air seemed oppressive, and its steamy vapor was redolent of the mingled odors of decaying fruit, carrion, excrement, and the sweaty bodies of man and beast.

Now safely on the waterfront Fray García Guerra, in resplendent vestments, stood under an ornate pallium to receive the obeisance of clergy and laymen, while cannon shots resounded sharply from the anchored ships and from the island fortress. Looking slightly harried by the intensity of the obsequious throng, the Archbishop and his servitors who surreptitiously mopped their brows, were slowly conducted through the miry streets amidst further chanting and responses to the rude church and convent of the Dominicans, of which order the honored guest was a member. In due course the friars of other congregations returned to their cloisters while their superiors entertained the prelate in a more private manner.

Fray García Guerra hardly wished to linger in these unhealthy surroundings and, as everything was in readiness for his journey to Mexico City, he began the slow advance inland accompanied by a long caravan of horses, pack mules, coaches, litters, creaking carts, and pedestrians. It was a triumphal march and the progress of his carriage was deliberately slow to permit all his flock along the way to behold the majesty of a Prince of the Church and to pay homage to this intermediary of God. Well over a month elapsed before he made his ceremonious entry into the viceregal capital.

Meanwhile, the bright-hued caravan halted at each Indian village and hamlet where the natives, doubtless prompted by the local *cura,* or parish priest, proffered their most colorful entertainments, often a curious mixture of aboriginal folkloric elements and those acquired from the Spaniards. These festivities were unfailingly accompanied by a noisy salute of fireworks. Between these stops the Archbishop's carriage passed under an endless series of floral arches, erected scarcely a musket-shot distance apart. As the episcopal conveyance approached these Indian communities a small band of villagers came forth to meet it, each individual bedecked in the peculiar attire of the locality and blowing odd strains on trumpets and other wind instruments. Escorted in this manner the Archbishop's coach rolled into the tiny village square invariably adorned with floral chains and varicolored bunting, and there its occupant witnessed the colorful *mitotes*, the most solemn of the ceremonial dances and songs of the natives. Fray García Guerra vastly enjoyed these strange interludes in which these primitive members of his flock, arrayed in picturesque costumes and adornments, performed the most ritualistic of their pagan rites, for he had a special fondness for music in all its forms, and the novelty of these curious strains left him undisturbed by their non-Christian origins. In his train were clergymen from Castile who were gifted instrumentalists, and the Cathedral council, doubtless informed of the new prelate's predilection, had thoughtfully sent down skilled musicians from Mexico City to lighten the tedium of his journey. Thus the Archbishop found delight in the variety of harmonies that charmed his ears along the way.

In this pleasant fashion Fray García Guerra neared his destination. Scarcely a dozen leagues from Mexico City he paused briefly in the small Indian town of Apa where a personal representative of the viceroy, in behalf of that magistrate, welcomed the new head of the Mexican church. Only the fact that his feet hurt, so ran the message, prevented Don Luis de Velasco, viceroy for the second time of this great realm of the Spanish empire, from coming in person to kiss the ring of the chief primate and place himself unreservedly at the Archbishop's disposal. Despite his gouty extremities Don Luis de Velasco assured the prelate that he would not fail to meet him in person before the triumphal entry into the capital.

Mexico City, situated amidst lakes in the lofty valley of Anahuac, suffered periodic inundations that had long called for drastic remedy. Only the year before so destructive a flood had descended upon this administrative center that a transfer of the municipality to another site was seriously contemplated. Commercial and other interests, however, strongly resisted this solution and the viceroy, on the advice of a German cosmographer, Enrico Martínez, and of others, had authored a gigantic engineering project designed to carry off the excess waters in a series of cuts and channels. The most ambitious part of this undertaking was a huge notch in the hills near the village of Huehuetoca. It occurred to Don Luis de

Velasco that a joint inspection of this work would be an admirable occasion for the first meeting of the respective heads of Church and State, and necessary arrangements were, accordingly, made. In due course Fray García Guerra alighted from his carriage at the viceroy's temporary quarters whereupon the king's surrogate in New Spain hobbled out to the front staircase and demonstratively welcomed the new prelate. After dining together the two most powerful dignitaries in the land drove away to inspect the progress made on the large cut. It was on this excursion that the first of an ominous series of mishaps befell the proud Fray García Guerra.

The rise of this Dominican clergyman to the eminence he now claimed in one of the richest archbishoprics in Spain's enormous empire had been foreordained and rapid. Singularly propitious were the auguries of the stars at his birth in 1560 in a village of Old Castile. Of noble ancestry, it was soon apparent that his studious temperament admirably equipped him for the verbalistic intellectualism of the age and culture in which he lived. His native talents splendidly adapted him for a luminous career in the Church, then so powerful in the affairs of man, and at the age of fifteen he sought to don the Dominican habit. In May, 1578, he was duly admitted to the order of his choice at the Convent of St. Paul in Valladolid, and almost immediately he gained distinction in philosophy, metaphysics, and theology. His extraordinary gifts as a dialectician and his consummate skill as an orator quickly brought wide acclaim. His brilliance as an expounder of the doctrines then hardening under the pressures of the Counter Reformation brought recognition from the secular rulers of the land as well as from his Dominican superiors. After filling chairs of theology in monasteries at Ávila, Burgos, Segovia and Valladolid, he became prior of the convent where he had taken his first vows. When the weak monarch, Philip III, was induced to transfer his Court from Madrid to Valladolid in 1600, Fray García Guerra attracted the approving eye of the king's influential favorite, the Duke of Lerma, who soon elevated the talented clergyman to the lofty eminence of the *Patronato* of Castile. After the birth of a royal prince destined, as Philip IV, to preside over the dissolution of the political glory that was Spain, Fray García Guerra officiated at the baptism.

With Madrid once again the capital a few years later, Philip III did not forget the churchman whose eloquence and administrative ability he had admired in Valladolid. When death created a vacancy in the archbishopric of Mexico, it was the royal will that Fray García should accept it. If the clergyman's hesitation was sincere, his Dominican superiors soon convinced him that it was a duty to fulfill his destiny. After papal confirmation Fray García was consecrated on April 5, 1608, and, two months later, he embarked for his New World post. Fate had smiled steadily upon this son of Old Castile and now had placed him in one of the most important offices to which a clergyman might aspire.[5]

The shift of activities from the Old to the New World seemed to mark, however, the turning point in the unbroken good fortune which had attended his career from birth. Almost imperceptibly portents of the future began to gather like clouds on the horizon, and the brightness of the day slowly dimmed until the darkness of death blotted all. The first of these omens, which hardly seemed to have any import, occurred when the new Archbishop and the Viceroy of New Spain rode together to inspect the drainage project at Huehuetoca. The road through the pass, over which they were driving, had been traveled again and again without mishap of any sort, and it appeared free of any hazards to the safety of these heads of the absolute government of the land. Suddenly and without warning their carriage turned completely over, spilling the august occupants by the wayside in a most undignified manner. Attendants hurried to their aid. Though both victims of the accident were badly shaken and slightly injured, they were able to resume the journey the next day. This incident seemed insignificant enough, but Fray García was to remember it as the beginning of his misfortunes.

Again his caravan took up the slow pilgrimage toward Mexico City, stopping in each of the intervening villages for the customary ceremonies of fealty, homage, and entertainment so obsequiously provided by the inhabitants. Meanwhile, the viceroy sped ahead to oversee the final arrangements for the sumptuous reception of the Archbishop in the capital. Even slower than before was Fray García's progress, for he was repeatedly administering the sacrament of confirmation, and the festive journey from Vera Cruz had stretched into a full month. But at last he reached Santa Ana, a suburb of the city, where he alighted from his ornate carriage and mounted a mule to make his entry with the simulated humility of the Founder of Christianity. A group of municipal officials, in brightest livery and astride gaily caparisoned horses, had come out to accompany the Archbishop on this final stage of his travels.

As the small procession entered the outskirts of the capital it stopped at the Dominican monastery. Near a platform, erected by the members of this religious body to do honor to a distinguished brother of their Order, Fray García dismounted from his mule and climbed upon the shaky staging where the Dean, councilors of the Cathedral, and other dignitaries were seated. Scarcely had the Archbishop begun to acknowledge the rejoicing of the assembly when the improvised rostrum trembled ominously and, with a loud crash, the entire structure collapsed, flinging its respected occupants to the ground and crushing a luckless Indian beneath it. Once again, as when he was thrown from the carriage at Huehuetoca, Fray García was badly shaken but received no severe injury, and presently the interrupted ceremonies were resumed. There were those, however, who, having heard of the earlier mishap, shook their heads gravely. These signs did not augur well for the new prelate.

The arrangements for the crowning event went forward—the magnificent spectacle of the entry into the Cathedral under the episcopal pallium. The liveried magistrates, who had met Fray García on the outskirts of the city, now took positions as a guard of honor. Each held an ornate staff supporting the purple and gold pallium with brocade trimmings which sheltered the Archbishop robed in glittering vestments. So massive was this canopy that it required twenty-two of the uniformed *regidores* to hold it aloft in this fashion. This dazzling tableau moved slowly through the streets lined with the awed populace. From the walls, windows, and balconies of the buildings on either side hung rich tapestries and bright-hued bunting. At length the procession halted in front of the Cathedral, still far from completion. Before the ponderous portal stood a gigantic arch with a Baroque profusion of sculptural details, of complex symbols, of ornamental figures, and of erudite quotations.

Leaving the pallium on the Cathedral steps the Archbishop, with attendant priests and acolytes, moved majestically into the gloomy splendor of the interior and advanced toward the gleaming effulgence of the candlelit altar while the great nave resounded with

the swelling paeans of the *Te Deum Laudamus,* sung by an augmented choir. To the edification of all assembled this mighty
Prince of the Church prostrated himself before the Cross with ostentatious humility. After an appropriate pause in this position
Fray García Guerra slowly arose to his feet and the profound
solemnity of the moment yielded to an almost gay burst of melodious song, secular and festive in character. This sudden transition heightened the emotional effect and drama of the scene, filling
the audience with a kind of rapture. The Archbishop, a dazzling
figure in the magnificence of his episcopal robes, then seated himself near the high altar to witness a brief, allegorical play ingeniously staged in the chancel. Elaborately costumed performers,
in witty dialogues of prettily worded phrases, explained and interpreted the fanciful designs and symbols embellishing the enormous
arch at the Cathedral door. At the conclusion of this sprightly
interlude the Dean, prebendaries, and other ecclesiastical dignitaries approached the prelate in single file to offer their obeisance
with impressive humility. The object of this adulation was now
more than ever the cynosure of admiring and reverent eyes.

For Fray García it was a supreme moment. His fortunate career
had brought him to a pinnacle of glory in the neomedieval world
that Spain was expending its blood and treasure to maintain and
that it passionately believed was the fulfillment of God's will on
earth. But like the civilization that he personified, he was already
an anachronism and his own fate epitomized the destiny of that
age. Unforeseen by all that throng was the certainty that, in a few
brief years, his dissected and decomposing body would lie interred
in the very place where he now sat amid so much pomp and circumstance. Long after in the same century a distinguished citizen
of Mexico City, moved by other portents, would exclaim: "O sacred
and most just God, how removed from human reason are Thy
incomprehensible and venerable judgments! And how true are the
Scriptures when they state that laughter is mingled with tears
and that sorrow follows upon the greatest joys!"[6]

The newly inaugurated Archbishop did not fail to display the
piety, benevolence, and oratorical gifts that so clearly justified his
designation to the richest See of the New World. To his flock he
seemed the perfect embodiment of an exemplary minister of the
Gospel and a saintly administrator of the Church of God. In those

first months of his office he appeared to strive for justice for all with an impartiality, a lack of precipitation, and a compassionate rectitude. His varied duties he performed with punctuality, and so zealous was he in distributing alms personally from his vast income that his meals were often delayed. Faithfully he visited all parts of his broad diocese, and in the churches he preached with that moving eloquence and great learning that unmistakably marked him as one set apart to do God's work.

All who came into the presence of this ecclesiastical Prince acquired a conviction that Fray García was, indeed, an inspired person happy in fulfilling a great destiny. Yet a close observer might have perceived that, with all the homage daily bestowed upon him, with all the Croesus-like wealth at his disposal, and with all the assurance of an eternal reward at the end of his earthly existence, a disquieting urge vaguely stirred deep within his consciousness. Omnipotent as he was in the social and economic as well as the spiritual lives of his flock, an unspoken longing, which was growing in intensity, possessed him to dominate the political affairs of the realm as well. Don Luis de Velasco, the reigning viceroy, was a great proconsul of his Majesty who had served with great distinction in both Mexico and Peru. His long experience, proven skill, and sound judgment were indispensable to the weak and vacillating Philip III, sorely needing in Spain such able administrators to manage an empire already betraying symptoms of decay and disintegration. It was but a matter of time before royal summons would compel the return of Don Luis to the homeland. In such an eventuality the viceregal office commonly devolved upon the Archbishop as an interim appointment at least, and Fray García found himself dwelling on this possibility with increasing insistency.

Like most at the summit of human institutions, the prelate's existence was essentially a lonely one. As the accepted instrument of God he was the recipient of obsequious demonstrations of awe, veneration, and fear wherever he went. Nowhere did his basically gregarious nature find the intimate companionship and confidence that it craved. With all his appearance of piety and of a dedicated servant of the Lord, and with all his ascetic ostentation, he longed for the milder sensual delights of his flock. He loved the sweet melody of instrumental music, the singing of ballads and folk songs,

the gustatory pleasures of the table, and the strong tonic of spectacles of the bull ring. To satisfy the first of these tastes Fray
García had fallen into the habit of dropping into the Royal Convent
of Jesus and Mary in the afternoon to visit Sister Mariana de la
Encarnación and Sister Inés de la Cruz, whose company he found
especially congenial. Both nuns were skilled instrumentalists and
singers who infallibly charmed the Archbishop by lively renditions
of popular airs. With perfect mastery they played liturgical music
on the convent organ, and with effortless ease they shifted to the
guitarlike *laúdes* and *rabeles,* strumming accompaniments to worldly
songs that told of sentimental longings, of blighted loves, and of
forsaken hopes. This musical potpourri they interlarded with
sprightly chatter most relaxing to a prelate surfeited by the ceremonious formality of his daily life. The culinary arts of these
talented ladies, manifested in sweetmeats and dainty dishes, added
delight to these restful occasions, and rarely did Fray García miss
these agreeable afternoon visits.

This was a common practice of clergymen noted a few years
after this time by Thomas Gage, the "English American" who reported: "It is ordinary for the Fryers to visit their devoted Nuns,
and to spend whole days with them hearing their musick, feeding
on their sweet-meats. And for this purpose they have many
chambers, which they call Loquitorios, to talk in, with wooden
bars between the Nuns and them, and in these chambers are tables
for Fryers to dine at; and while they dine, the Nuns recreate them
with their voices. Gentlemen and citizens gave their daughters to
be brought up in these Nunneries, where they are taught to make
all sorts of conserves and preserves, all sorts of musick, which is so
exquisite in that City, that I dare be bold to say, that the people
are drawn to their churches more for the delight of their musick,
than for any delight in the service of God."[7]

Even this gentle and harmless association did not exempt Fray
García entirely from the solicitation and importunity that often
beset the powerful and influential, for the hospitable nuns were
not wholly without guile. They, too, had dreams and ambitions.
Long cherished was their hope of founding a new convent under
the rule of the reformed Carmelites, and already a wealthy patron
had willed a sufficient sum for a building and given part of the
endowment. This benefactor had named the Archbishop an execu-

tor, and only the approval and a supplementary grant of funds by Fray García were needed to convert a dream into reality. Hence the devout ladies exerted themselves to charm their opulent guest who remained curiously immune to their overtures. This intimate communion with the nuns, however, had brought forth a confession of his own aspirations of becoming the viceroy of Mexico, and whenever pressed for action on the beloved project of his hostesses he invariably put them off by exclaiming: "Ah, my dear sisters, if God is pleased to bestow upon me the office of viceroy, I shall surely help you to start the convent that you so rightly desire! And what a splendid one I shall make it!"

"Must we wait until then, Sire?" the anxious nuns pleaded.

"Yes, my dears," was his constant answer. "It can only be when I become the viceroy."

Fray García's afternoon visits continued regularly and with equal regularity, as they plied him with appetizing tidbits, melody, and conversation, the nuns repeated their pleas. Invariably the obdurate Archbishop vouchsafed the same reply: "When I am the viceroy . . ." Even when Sister Inés de la Cruz professed to have had a vision in which the viceregal office was bestowed upon the ambitious prelate, Fray García remained unmoved. Until the prophecy was fulfilled he would make no commitment, and the impatient nuns could only pray more fervently for divine intercession.[8]

Another favorite diversion of the Archbishop were the drives in his ornate, mule-drawn carriage to outlying churches and congregations. The upset near Huehuetoca, when he had accompanied the viceroy on a tour of inspection, had in no way diminished his enjoyment of such excursions, which were of frequent occurrence. One day, however, in returning from the Santa Monica monastery it happened that the well-trained mules suddenly took fright and dashed pell-mell through the streets of the city. Frantically the coachman tried to bring the careening carriage under control, and a few bystanders bravely attempted to check the flight of the maddened beasts. Fray García clung desperately to his seat in an effort to ride out the fury of the mules but, as his equipage plunged wildly about the thoroughfare, panic seized him. In a convulsive attempt to save himself he started to leap. Unfortunately, his foot caught in the carriage step, hurling him to the ground where he lay senseless. Though in time he seemed to recover from this mishap, so much more severe than the preceding ones, it had fatal consequences.

Fateful for Fray García was the year 1611 which witnessed his greatest triumph and greatest disaster. It was as if the Fates, having bestowed their bounties so generously on the Spanish clergyman, were growing weary of his claims on their prodigality. His gnawing desire for secular power, after rising so high in the ecclesiastical sphere, appeared to turn his wheel of fortune downward. The series of accidents befalling him were unheeded warnings and now Nature itself was offering disturbing admonitions.

The spring of that year brought the long-expected summons to Don Luis de Velasco to vacate his viceregal office and return to Spain to serve as president of the Royal Council of the Indies. The same decree formally designated Fray García Guerra as his successor in Mexico. The prayerful and seemingly modest acquiescence of the Archbishop did not wholly conceal his inner delight, and his ostentatious humility hardly veiled his keen pleasure in supervising the elaborate plans for a second triumphal entry into the capital, this time with the full panoply of the viceregal office. He gave his closest personal attention to the details of erecting an ornate arch, of selecting the sonorous verses and Latin inscriptions to adorn it, of preparing the magnificent display of fireworks and the illuminations of the façades of public buildings by night, of rehearsing the *Te Deum Laudamus* and the lighter music that so delighted him, and of the construction of the grandstands along the line of march. Absorbed in these pleasurable activities all thought of his promises to the hospitable nuns at the Convent of Jesus and Mary fled from his mind. Indeed, the financial assistance pledged for the new Carmelite establishment was diverted to a pastime close to Fray García's heart—bullfights. To celebrate his elevation to the supreme rank of Archbishop-Viceroy he decreed that these taurine spectacles should take place every Friday for an entire year. And presently he prevailed upon a reluctant city council to construct a private bull ring within the Palace since it hardly seemed fitting for one of his ecclesiastical eminence to attend such functions in public places.

The first of these *corridas* occurred on Good Friday. The choice of the date, curiously symptomatic of the juxtaposition of the sensate and the spiritual in the Baroque age, apparently inspired no adverse comment except from one source. Sister Inés de la Cruz, whose protest possibly arose as much from disappointed hopes as from scandalized disapproval, begged the Archbishop-Viceroy in a note not to encourage such diversions on the day commemorating the Passion of Jesus Christ. But Fray García was too elated to heed this plea and the spectacle took place as scheduled. But a similar event the following Friday brought possible signs of divine displeasure. Just before the appointed hour of the bullfight earth tremors shook the city so severely that the *corrida* was postponed. Undaunted by this warning Fray García comfortably seated himself the following week to witness his favorite sport. Hardly was the first bull charging into the ring when the city experienced another earth spasm so violent that the grandstand and the neighboring houses collapsed. The stone coping of the balcony where the Archbishop was sitting suddenly cracked and a portion of it fell, narrowly missing him and killing several onlookers below. But even so pointed a hint did not deter Fray García, who refused to revoke his decree calling for a weekly exhibition of the popular pastime.

Before assuming his new office Fray García had retired to an outlying village to await formal notification of the departure of his predecessor from Vera Cruz and to make a ceremonial entry into Mexico City as viceroy. When the welcome word arrived that Don Luis de Velasco had sailed the Archbishop's first act was to abase himself publicly before the shrine of the Virgin of Guadalupe. This rite performed, he permitted his attendants to address him by the coveted secular title "Your Excellency."

The inaugural march into the capital on June 19, 1611, duplicated the pomp and splendor of his earlier entry as Archbishop with, however, features of a more secular character. This time he rode a beautiful mare of the most pure blooded stock of the realm, the gift of the city council. Beneath the episcopal pallium supported by the *regidores* on foot, who were dressed in velvet uniforms of brilliant crimson, the Archbishop-Viceroy presented a gallant figure. Next in order came the judges of the Royal Audiencia, the magistrates of other tribunals, and the flower of the viceregal aristocracy, each group vying with the other in theatrical splendor. Slowly the pageantlike procession filed through the streets hung with garlands and past the bordering houses almost concealed by the tapestries and hangings draped from their balconies. But again, as Fray García tasted anew the wine of earthly fame and glory, a tragic note jarred the festive moment.

On the little Santiago square, the Indian community had erected a tall pole called a *volador* from which, as a feature of the celebration, acrobatic members swung high in the air as if from a lofty merry-go-round. This circus-like performance was a death-defying act which thrilled the spectators and added a note of expectancy to the general excitement. Just as the Archbishop-Viceroy drew abreast of this plaza a performer, whirling through the air, lost his grip on the rope and fell, his body horribly shattered, almost at the feet of Fray García. Once again in the midst of rejoicing and at a moment of proud fulfillment tragedy struck, a sinister warning, perhaps, that the Fates were losing patience with the excessive ambition of a favored mortal.

But this macabre incident scarcely interrupted the colorful inauguration. The glittering procession resumed its course toward the triumphal arch which simulated a huge fortress gate decorated by an intricate pattern of symbolic figures painted on its façade. Here the Corregidor administered a ceremonious oath to the new viceroy and handed him a large golden key. The ponderous doors of the imitation stronghold then swung open and the bright column, with Fray García in the lead, wended its way to the Cathedral where the thunderous *Te Deum Laudamus* reverberated through the nave. Presently the Archbishop-Viceroy, accompanied by the city's principal magistrates, departed by another door and entered the viceregal Palace on the east side of the central square. There his accompaniment of judges of the Royal Audiencia and other officials obsequiously took their leave and Fray García retired into the chambers of his secular predecessors to relish the first moments of his ascent to the supreme authority of the State as well as of the Church in the fairest of Spanish realms. Outside, in the plaza, deafening explosions of bombs and artillery-pieces saluted the new viceroy. That night the whole city seemed ablaze with lanterns in doorways and windows and roaring bonfires in the streets and squares.

These noisy demonstrations and the general rejoicing found the Archbishop-Viceroy vaguely troubled. His satisfaction was tinged with disillusionment, a sort of *desengaño*. Realization, somehow, fell short of anticipation. The series of mishaps had engendered haunting forebodings, and already a recurrence of physical pain depressed his spirits. Ever since that dreadful day when he had leaped from the carriage drawn by runaway mules, the pain in his side had become increasingly severe. Also a series of strange phenomena of nature in recent months had filled him and his subjects with uneasiness. Were they harbingers of impending disaster? Oppressed by bodily discomfort and superstitious fears, he confronted with deepening anxiety the heavier obligations which his pride and ambition had thrust upon him.

The disturbing aberrations of nature did not cease as Fray García took up his duties. The very month of his inauguration witnessed a total eclipse of the sun which terrified the masses. An unnatural darkness engulfed the city at noon, and it seemed to deepen as the afternoon advanced. "This phenomenon," wrote a chronicler, "which the astronomers had predicted, produced an effect upon Spaniards and Indians such that both raced frantically to the shelter of the churches to implore God's mercy, and they did not venture out until nightfall."[9] The seismic disturbances coinciding with Fray García's bullfights were followed in August by the severest earthquake in the memory of the oldest inhabitant. With seeming pointedness it wreaked heavy damage on religious establishments where many inmates were crushed beneath the rubble. To everyone this disaster appeared especially terrifying because an inordinate number of tremors had preceded it. More than forty were experienced within thirty hours and all were exceedingly violent.

Weeks and months passed without dissipating the dread and anxiety that pervaded the city. Christmas day brought even more menacing indications of divine displeasure. About half past two in the afternoon the whole sky over the Valley of Mexico turned a dark, reddish black and a shower of ashes fell, sifting a thin layer over the houses and the fields. This strange manifestation lasted until the great, crimson bowl of the sun dipped over the western rim. Just as it disappeared, a frightful downpour of rain deluged the city, transforming its streets into rushing torrents of water.[10] Clearly, these were unmistakable signs of heavenly wrath and inexorable summonses to repentance, most of all, perhaps, for the ailing Archbishop-Viceroy.

Fray García Guerra's symptoms, meanwhile, had worsened, and it was clear that he was gravely ill. Attacks of pain alternated with high fever and confined him to his bed. The best physicians in the land, whose medical knowledge derived almost wholly from the ancients, Galen and Hippocrates, could prescribe no other remedies than repeated purges and bloodletting which further weakened the afflicted prelate. Early in January, 1612, a stormy dispute arose among the doctors in consultation regarding the necessity of an operation. Three of them were promptly dismissed while the others performed some crude surgery which doubtless hastened the patient's demise. In sick despair Fray García had even turned to his good friend, Sister Inés de la Cruz, whose hopes for a new convent he had so long defrauded, and he begged for her prayers. He assured her of his deep repentance and pledged himself to keep his promise to her if he could but be restored to health. The response of the disappointed nun was hardly consoling to the doomed Archbishop-Viceroy, for she merely urged him to prepare for death and to voice thanks to God that his sorrow was only in the temporal realm. Fray García now knew that he must resign himself to the inevitable. Calling his confessor, he received the last Sacrament and thereafter, with the feeble strength left to him, he performed such acts of humility and contrition as he could. Further bloodletting doubtless shortened his period of suffering. With Christian fortitude he endured his afflictions until "he surrendered his spirit to the Lord on February 22, 1612."

The chronicler gives a gruesome account of the autopsy performed upon the noble cadaver hardly had life departed. With morbid satisfaction he describes the advanced decomposition of various organs and the removal of the skull top and the emptying of the brains into a container for separate burial. This writer seemed to share the view of a contemporary Baroque poet Jerónimo de Cáncer that "también en lo horrible hay hermosura" (there is also beauty in the horrible). These repellent details, following almost immediately the recital of the colorful pageantry of the Archbishop-Viceroy's years in Mexico, provide an abrupt transition. Sharpening the contrast still further is the rapid shift from the vital, dynamic scenes of Fray García's existence to the minute description of the veritable orgy of mourning at the public funeral. With morose zest the eulogist tells of streets and public buildings draped in black, of the mournful monotony of endlessly tolling bells, of the almost exuberant frenzy of the chapel decorations, and of the corpse lying in state, of the interminable processions of dignitaries, nobles, officials, monks, and soldiers marching to the rhythm of muffled drums and hoarse fifes, of downcast throngs of the kaleidoscopic society of Mexico, and of the all-pervading solemnity of Death and the futility of things mortal.[11] All of this tremendously heightened the tragic sense of drama infusing the spirit of that age.

The death of the chief of Church and State and the ensuing funeral obsequies increased the mounting tension and anxiety of the inhabitants of the capital. Scarcely were the remains of Fray García deposited beneath the altar by which, a few short years before, he had sat at his episcopal installation flushed with the joy of adulation, when dread rumors and alarms gripped the nervous citizenry. With no successor to wield the absolute power of government to which all were accustomed, the more privileged elements of society especially fell prey to a panic fear. Like a noisome vapor, dark threats against law and order seemed to rise from every quarter. The judges of the Royal Audiencia assumed the executive functions, but their collective rule failed to offer the security that the single figure of the Archbishop-Viceroy, endowed with the legal sanction of the distant Spanish monarchy and, seemingly, of God Himself, embodied in the minds of all. The apprehension of the upper classes spawned vague intimations of plots against the regime, of uprisings in the provinces, particularly of Negroes who had escaped from slavery and had taken refuge in the hills. These *cimarrones* were ever suspected of conspiring with the exploited Indian masses to throw off white supremacy. So great was the terror of Europeans and Creoles that they did not dare to venture out upon the streets and they barricaded themselves within their homes.

This community neurosis became acute one night when a herd of hogs was heard rooting and squealing about the city thoroughfares. These sounds were interpreted as an assault launched by runaway Negroes and they created near panic among the judges of the Royal Audiencia as well as the citizenry. Even the coming of daylight failed to dissipate the general hysteria, and fear-ridden officials rounded up twenty-nine Negro men and four women as alleged conspirators. In a desperate effort to deter subversive elements, the authorities barbarously executed the wretched suspects in the public square before a huge gathering. The severed heads were conspicuously displayed on pikes until the stench of decomposition caused their removal.[12] Similar spasms of uncontrollable fear had shaken Europeans before between the terms of viceroys, but the simultaneous disappearance of both the head of the State and of the Church in one person had let loose a more violent wave of unreasoning fright and terror. Thus, in death as in life, this Spanish Archbishop-Viceroy singularly epitomized an aspect of that strange spirit of the Baroque which subtly dominated the entire seventeenth century and long after.

# ❧ II

# THE BAROQUE AGE

WITH the prescience of hindsight, posterity sees a kind of boundary between two epochs of western history in the quartet of years which witnessed Fray García's rise to supreme ecclesiastical and political office in New Spain. When that illustrious Dominican embarked in 1608 for the New World he could not realize that the Europe he was leaving was turning into a new world of politics, economics, social organization, and science. Already, in parts of the Continent, these changes were so far advanced that they rendered impossible the recovery of the lost unity of Christendom and the medieval tradition that the Archbishop-Viceroy so conspicuously personified. If to him the "kingdom of God" was an empire composed of principalities acknowledging a supreme prince and bolstered by an aristocracy enjoying feudal privileges, with the whole structure cemented by an adherence to the one true Faith, elsewhere in Europe many were beholding the "kingdom of man" emerging from a set of ideas quite different. Among these other peoples the conviction was growing that human will might determine human destiny, and that mankind need not regard itself as a helpless pawn of an all-powerful deity. They glimpsed earthly existence as something more than a painful preparation for eternity, and they were increasingly reluctant to abdicate the mind completely to the dogmatic prescriptions of a medieval Church. The opposing pressures of the Reformation and Counter Reformation had cracked the mortar of orthodoxy and, particularly in the north where new political entities were assuming importance, they had

21

perceptibly loosened a solidarity inherited from the Middle Ages. The great Schism had split the Continent into two Europes, Protestant and Catholic, and the breach was widening. Irreparably sundered already were the bonds of religion and tradition that had promised a unified order, and the process of fragmentation would go on.

In the divided Europe of Fray García's closing years the policies of statesmen were no longer influenced by the *Philosophia Christi*, or the achievement of a perfect universal state, which had conditioned the utopianism of the late Renaissance. While religious affiliations clearly colored the issues of the time, secular concerns were taking precedence over ecclesiastical, though the Catholic South, reacting to the contemporary ferment, was growing more inflexible in its adherence to orthodoxy. But emerging national states in the Protestant North were subordinating spiritual matters to commercial activities, and in public affairs merchant adventurers, trading companies, and the like were outweighing the organized Church in influence. Shifting and multiplying trade routes were expanding mercantilism, revolutionizing society, and facilitating the rise of new kinds of imperialism, capitalism, and colonialism. A class of *nouveaux riches* was slowly usurping the power of the agrarian aristocracy, and an expanding *bourgeoisie* was acquiring a larger measure of political control. Confidence was growing that men could, indeed, shape destiny.

In the very years that Fray García was rising to fame a seed was germinating which would strengthen the conviction that mankind could master its fate. The most portentous discovery of the moment was a new approach to truth destined to transform the western world, and, in time, the entire globe. This was modern science. The Ptolemaic universe, with the earth its center and pivotal point, was yielding, still imperceptibly perhaps and quite precariously as Galileo was experiencing, to the Copernican universe with the earth a mere peripheral planet of an immense solar system. A newer freedom of speculation and experimentalism was undermining the traditional verbalistic methods of scholasticism, and it would lead to discoveries dwarfing the miracles of medieval lore.

If this fundamental divergence of intellectual methodology was hardly discernible at the outset of the seventeenth century, within a few decades it was changing the conceptions of many concerning the world, and it was posing a threat to medieval cosmology and religious orthodoxy. As the methods of analysis and measurement were applied, a new search was underway for the divine plan of the universe; as this endeavor began to create new values, the time-worn monopoly of theology and scholasticism as the avenue to truth was shattered and the infallibility of dogmas was doubted. Already, as the seventeenth century dawned, confirmation of the heliocentric theory of Copernicus (1543) had appeared. Tycho Brahe (1546-1601), intending to reconstitute the Ptolemaic system, had recorded the position of the planets with precision, unaided by the invention of the telescope; Johannes Kepler (1571-1630) was determining the elliptic orbit of these planets by mathematical analysis; and in the very moment that Fray García was symbolizing medieval authoritarianism in Mexico, Galileo Galilei (1564-1642) was making the first use of the telescope, invented in 1608, to demonstrate the validity of the Copernican theory. This positive refutation of age-long assumptions of cosmology was a threat to authority and, in 1616, it moved the Church belatedly to place the Copernican treatise on the Index of Prohibited Works. And even before this Giordano Bruno (1548-1600) was burned at the stake for his belief in the plurality of worlds and populated planets.

As the seventeenth century advanced, startling discoveries in other fields shook orthodox conceptions. William Gilbert (1540-1603) had made systematic observations of the phenomenon of magnetism; William Harvey (1578-1657) demonstrated the circulation of blood; Robert Boyle (1627-1691) would contribute laws of chemistry and gaseous pressures; and Marcello Malpighi (1628-1694) and others would make important findings through the microscopic analysis of living organisms.

Even more direct threats to the older methodology would create tension and harden conservative resistance. In 1605 Francis Bacon (1561-1626), after subjecting medieval science to a close scrutiny, branded it "contentious learning." René Descartes (1596-1650) was still a boy when Fray García was parading his scholastic erudition and watching his bullfights in Mexico City, but this Frenchman, in his *Discourse on the Method of Rightly Conducting the Reason and Seeking for Truth in the Sciences* (1637), would presently deal a body blow to the dialectical verbalism that had carried the Spanish Dominican to such heights of power. And still later the great English mathematician, Isaac Newton (1642-1727), carrying forward Descartes' work, would wreck beyond repair the remaining underpinnings of the medieval world view represented by the Archbishop-Viceroy of Mexico.

As the spiritual, intellectual, and social solidarities of Europe melted in the heat of revolutionary changes, the conservatism of the Catholic South hardened into a reactionary intransigence. Spain, which had become a mighty empire under the sixteenth century Hapsburgs, assumed the role of champion of orthodoxy, and its rulers took an uncompromising stand on the side of traditionalism. This resolute attitude dominated the Council of Trent and set the tone of the Counter Reformation, thus defeating the hope of reconciliation with the Protestant North. The enormous extent of the Spanish empire, scattered over the Old and New Worlds like a sprawling league of nations, seemed to point clearly to a universal hegemony under Hispanic auspices as the divine plan. The large populations threatened by heresy in Europe and awaiting the illumination of Christian doctrine in America were clearly a trust which Providence had bestowed exclusively on the peoples of the Spanish Peninsula. Christianity must be restored to its pristine state on the one hand and, on the other, diffused in its purest form. There could be no temporizing with heterodoxy at home or abroad and hence free inquiry, which had enjoyed relative immunity during the early sixteenth century in Spain, was soon halted. The desperate fear of heretical infection was unhappily withdrawing doctrine after doctrine in both natural and moral philosophy from the possibility of rational proof and relegating them to the sphere of unquestioned dogma. Simple belief and the complete acceptance of authority in every field of thought made for righteousness in the Hispanic view, and they offered the best guarantee of salvation. "In the seventeenth century you do not breathe a 'normal' air of belief," observes a modern Spanish scholar, "but, rather, something like an oxygen of faith."[1]

In this situation ideas, whether secular or religious, were carefully screened in Spain and excluded, as far as possible, from the New World so as to protect the incompletely Christianized natives from contamination. Thus reason fell under the sway of rigid authority and conclusions reached through rational processes were predetermined; the initiative of thinkers was confined to formal details in the treatment of a thesis rather than to any revaluation of the thesis itself. Truth was accessible only through verbalistic methods of scholasticism, and knowledge acquired through the senses was unreliable and potentially dangerous. Under Spanish influence Catholic Europe was becoming stranded in the shallows of authoritarianism and ecclesiastical learning, while other parts of the Continent were slowly moving into the freer currents of experimentalism sweeping onward into modern science and technology.

In the New World realms the preservation of traditional thought was facilitated by a remoteness from Europe's turmoil and by a more solidified feudal pattern of society in which a small white minority dominated large populations of submissive Indians for whom ignorance increasingly appeared to be a blessing. However, for the intelligentsia of the Spanish Indies, the insulation from the changing world and the revolutionary ideas of Europe was much less hermetic than often asserted, and various American-born intellectuals during the course of the seventeenth century displayed a surprising familiarity with contemporary thought. But clearly the climate of opinion in those distant possessions was hardly propitious for overt dissenters from the traditional orthodoxy and scholasticism to which the motherland was passionately committed. Intellectual activity centered almost exclusively in the universities and seminaries of the colonial cities where a decadent neo-scholasticism prevailed and where thinkers of an experimental turn of mind were notably absent. Since this purely verbalistic rationalism dominated Hispanic intellectualism during the so-called Baroque period, and especially in the American realms, a brief description is appropriate.

Scholasticism was, of course, essentially ecclesiastical in origin and, as philosophy grew out of theology, the methods of the latter carried over into secular learning. The basic premise of scholasticism was that God was the source of all truth and that, in His wisdom, this truth, or portions of it, was divinely revealed to chosen individuals as the human agencies of transmission. Their writings were revelation and hence the final authority of all learning. As the product of God's inspiration, the writings of the Church Fathers were the highest court of appeal, and they were held to contain within themselves the refutation of any and every argument advanced by human reason. This concept of knowledge obviously stressed memory rather than rational powers, since the pages of these books afforded an answer to every question. Consequently, intellectual brilliance was manifested by dialectics and by a deftness in quoting authorities. Doctrinal matters were established by disputation and logic, and conclusions were reached by verbal rationalization—not by experimental demonstration perceived through the senses as in modern science. Intellectual activity, then, put stress on arguments based on memorized material from accepted sources. Thus, the supreme equipment for superior knowledge was a photographic memory and a dialectical skill in exploiting it. An impressive example of this kind of mental legerdemain is offered by a record of a prodigious feat performed publicly at the University of Mexico.

Having learned by heart the voluminous writings of St. Thomas Aquinas, a Dominican friar, Father Francisco Naranjo, conducted himself so brilliantly in a contest for a professorship in 1635 that he was induced to give a repeat performance before a "plenary session of learned Doctors, the students of the different faculties, the prebendaries of the Cathedral, and other ecclesiastics and members of different Orders as well as a large number of distinguished laymen, both military and civilian." Selecting at random four out of one hundred and fifty-four difficult questions drawn from a theological work, "He began by addressing a dissertation to the audience on four controversial points of theology which had fallen to him by lot, linking them up one to another with much grace, lucidity, distinction, and learning. He then proceeded to the second part of the test, dictating to four lay brothers, one after the other, four separate theses on the four points of theology, one passage at a time to each clerk, doing so without hesitation or mistake, as if he were dictating a single continuous thesis."[2] His ability to cite readily any appropriate passage from the vast work of St. Thomas Aquinas made possible this extraordinary feat "which seems beyond the powers of the human brain," and to his audience it demonstrated the highest form of cerebration that a mortal mind could achieve.

This neo-scholasticism, of which Father Naranjo gave such a prodigious exhibition, especially re-emphasized certain other peculiarities of the earlier scholasticism. In secular philosophy the writings of Aristotle were almost as infallible as the Holy Writ, and for more than three centuries the works of that ancient Greek reigned supreme in European thought, though the Schoolmen, as the exponents of scholasticism were called, failed to heed, especially in colonial Spanish America, their master's teachings with respect to the need of experimentation in seeking truth. Applying the same procedure to his writings as to theology, the Schoolmen accepted Aristotle as superior to all other pagan masters and the last word in varied fields of knowledge.

Chief among the tools of the scholastics, and virtually regarded as the exclusive method of argumentation, was the syllogism, and the conclusions obtained by this device were regarded as truth. The syllogism consisted of a major premise, a minor premise, and the conclusion deduced from them. An example will illustrate:

Major premise: No finite being is exempt from error.
Minor premise: All men are finite beings.
Conclusion: Therefore, no man is exempt from error.

Such rigid exercises in logic could lead to absurdities and, in time, inspired crude parodies. But scholasticism as a whole was not as sterile as this oversimplified discussion may suggest, though it lent itself to the excessive abuse evident in the striving for cleverness which beset the Baroque intellectualism of colonial Spanish America. It could and did sharpen the wits to the subtleties of expression, it gave rigorous training in logic, and it afforded valuable experience in deductive reasoning, though again in practice the end sought was too often a dazzling verbal dexterity. Its legacy, perhaps, is a predilection for florid rotundity and high-flown rhetoric, still discernible in much public oratory of modern Hispanic America, and in the general disposition, at least until recently, to cultivate philosophy and metaphysics in preference to natural and physical sciences.

In contrast to the more northerly parts of Europe the Hispanic people reacted to humanism by trying to reintegrate a medieval religiosity and science, but the end result was largely a blend of the two intellectual movements. A neo-scholasticism became the methodology of a neo-orthodoxy without diminishing the dilemma of Christendom. Medieval thinkers, for whom science was ancillary to theology, had endeavored to understand how the order of human existence illustrated divine goodness; they sought to determine the objectives, purposes, or final causes toward which things seemed to be striving, but they made little effort to analyze physical conditions of existence, and a quantitative approach to the causes of behavior in matter appeared quite irrelevant. The vain quest of the ultimate undertaken by medieval science yielded to the more mundane and feasible aims of humanism, and the effort to reinstate that intellectual orthodoxy only restored considerable futility. The resulting frustration caused an unconscious substitution of the intellectual devices of scholasticism as ends in themselves and a forsaking of the ultimate objectives.[3] The effect was a tendency to shift from content to form, from ideas to details, to give new sanctions to dogmas, to avoid issues, and to substitute subtlety of language for subtlety of thought; it served to repress rather than liberate the human spirit, and to divert by spectacles, by overstatement, and by excessive ornamentation. Such, in essence, was the spirit of the so-called "Baroque Age" as manifested in the Hispanic world.

There is some mystery about the origin of the term "Baroque," but it is generally agreed that it derives from a nonsense word by which humanists of the Renaissance derided medieval scholasticism. In mockery of that early disputatiousness "Baroco" became a synonym of confused and unclear thinking; later it assumed the meaning of "decadent" and "in bad taste." Not until the nineteenth century did the term acquire a more dignified usage as a historical and technical designation applied successively to the arts and later to a chronological period.[4] Few living in the "Baroque Age" had ever heard the word, and probably no one applied it to his own time. It is, in fact, an unsolicited gift of posterity needing labels to comprehend the stages of evolution through which pass the activities of mankind.

In the long course of western history an alternation of conflicting moods and divergent attitudes toward existence appears, each one extending for varying lengths of time from centuries and generations to decades, or even shorter spans, and to these periods names are subsequently bestowed. In retrospect perceptible oscillations appear in social, moral, and creative life between attitudes of intellectual restraint and emotional freedom, or between conformity or nonconformity to self-imposed restrictions. Greek and Roman antiquity, the Renaissance, and the so-called Neo-Classic eighteenth century were eras noted for a tendency to abide by classic rules; the Middle Ages, the Baroque period, usually associated with the seventeenth century, and the Romanticism of the nineteenth century seem times of more uninhibited feeling.[5] This classification over-simplifies, of course, since opposing tendencies operate at all times to produce tension and conflict. Indeed, some epochs are distinguished more by paradox than consistency, and perhaps none so much as the Baroque Age. Hence arise difficulties of comprehension and definition.

The chronological limits of the Baroque period are roughly set from the mid-sixteenth to the mid-eighteenth centuries, reaching a peak around the middle of the seventeenth. Its intensity was relatively brief in some parts of Europe, and elsewhere it was of much longer duration. Closely linked with the Counter Reformation it proved more durable in the south of the Continent. The Baroque is described as "a continuous polemic on the Catholic way of life with a mixture of the ideals of the Middle Ages and the Renaissance."[6] It is not surprising, therefore, that it lasted longest and its manifestations were most extreme in the Hispanic world. "The Baroque is Spain's true form and fulfillment," it has been said, and indeed the passionate, individualistic genius of the Spaniard, reacting to historical circumstances, points to its truth.

That bizarre age witnessed the mystical exaltation of Santa Teresa de Ávila and of St. John of the Cross expressed in classic prose and verse and a sordid materialism set forth in the abundant picaresque literature of the time. The excessive license in public morals was paralleled by the asceticism of seared consciences, and the intellectual strait jacket of neo-scholasticism accented the un-fettered sway of emotion. Through medieval religiosity chaotic feelings vented themselves in a fierce fanaticism which spawned an arid dogmatism, an uncompromising intolerance, an implacable persecution, and a degrading superstition. Through a degenerate chivalry, a tawdry relic of the Middle Ages, an explosive fervor fathered a morbid punctilio in personal relations and a specious code of honor which prolifically begot vengeful feuds and murderous duels. Baroque passion stimulated an urge to action, an obsession to wield power, and, from the deep recesses of the unconscious, it conjured up an extraordinary vitality and a forward thrust of energy which found no adequate outlet or satisfying release. Unlike the Promethean spark of the Renaissance, it was a vitality which denied life and expended itself in trivia. Having briefly experienced the emancipation of a fecund humanism, the distraught spirit now fell prey to a deep despondency on finding its medieval chains restored. Like Segismund in Calderón's famous play *Life's a Dream*, it pondered on whether the Renaissance vision of life, so fleetingly beheld, was but a dream. Thwarted impulses engendered a restlessness which sought relief from frustration by applying to the accepted verities of orthodox existence an ornamental patina worked in startling combinations of detail, in intricate patterns, in multicolored designs, and in complex arrangements. But these activities failed to ease tensions completely, and they allowed slight sense of fulfillment. Instead, they seemed to induce a vague *desengaño*, a brooding disillusionment which, in turn, provoked moods of pessimism and fatalism and a resurgence of the stoicism so profoundly embedded in the Hispanic psyche. There was a withdrawal within oneself, a closing of the frontiers to newer ideas, much as Spain was closing its geographical frontiers to the rest of Europe and retreating into tradition. And intimately associated with this essential negativism was a morbid concern with death and decay. In "a world of extreme contrasts, of arrogant magnificence and hopeless misery, of carnal indulgence and ecstatic asceticism,"[7] life was not real but a drama, a tragedy enacted upon a stage, a spectacle to be watched.

Yet this strange agitation, this peculiar disquiet, this frustrating dilemma underlying the Baroque attitude released a prodigious creativity in Spain and ignited a pyrotechnic display of artistic genius. A dazzling constellation of stars of the first magnitude emerged. The masterworks of Cervantes, Lope de Vega, Tirso de Molina, Quevedo, Góngora, Gracián, Velázquez, El Greco, and of many more rivaled the finest achievements of the Renaissance itself and made the early seventeenth century an artistic Golden Age. Indeed, the most famous literary work of all, *Don Quixote de la Mancha*, might not have come into being but for the profound preoccupations of the Baroque age in which it appeared. After the Council of Trent the anti-Platonic moralists censured the optimistic belief of humanists in the perfectibility of man. This utopian idea was contrary to the doctrine of original sin. But the genius of Cer-

vantes fused these conflicting concepts into a synthesis formed by
the contrasting figures of the Manchegan hidalgo and Sancho
Panza.

Such triumphs of imagination, however, appear in retrospect like
mountain peaks scattered about a monotonous plain of dense and
tangled verbiage. The clarity of the Humanists surrendered to the
Baroque pursuit of the less clear and the opaque, and the aesthetic
techniques of *culteranismo* and *conceptismo* facilitated the desired
obscurity of expression. The first achieved this result by involved
syntax, words invented from Greek and Latin roots, and strained
figures of speech, while the second, aiming at verbal economy, subordinated meaning to cleverness by ingenious antitheses, paradoxes,
and word-play. These contrary currents fused in the Baroque style
and shifted importance from content to form. Writing, like the
plastic and pictorial arts, tended to become a crowded spectacle
rather than a vehicle of thought, and the repressed vitality of the
age produced a lush foliage which choked out much of the fruit of
true inspiration. Excess energy expended itself chiefly in allegory
of obscure symbolism and in an exaggerated verbalism, relieved
now and then by savage satire. But the Baroque was a time-spirit
with its own aesthetic and ethical canons and only within these,
perhaps, can it be fairly judged.

When Fray García journeyed across the Atlantic to become a
Prince of the State as well as of the Church he dramatically symbolized the transfer of the Baroque to the New World, and the
viceroyalty, over which he presided, offered singularly propitious
soil for the growth of the new spirit as the final grand flourish of
feudalism. The sixteenth century fusion of Romanesque, Gothic,
Renaissance and indigenous elements, particularly in architecture,
had prepared the ground for Baroque innovations. If these were
manifestations of a "time-spirit," it is more accurate to assert, perhaps, that they expressed a "time-spirit-place," for the exotic
Baroque plant soon blossomed in the Spanish Indies into an amazing variety of regional species as the Indian and mestizo shoots
were grafted upon it. "A full blooded Baroque spread to even the
less accessible regions of Latin America," writes an art critic,[8] "and,
with its vast register of variations, developed such regional expressions as the 'Andean Mestizo' and the 'Mexican poblano' style."
This blending process in a relatively immobile society placed so

indelible a stamp on Hispanic America that the Baroque pattern lingered long after the close of the colonial period and traces of it are visible today.

Numerous factors account for the comparative permanence of this culture and its medieval character. Spain's determination to isolate the American realms from European centers of infection, as already suggested, was aided by the immense distance of the seas and by the inland location of the important aggregations of population. All but the few inhabitants of the coastal towns were immune to the increasing attacks of Protestant pirates. Racial, linguistic, and cultural differences divided the elements of a feudal society in which a tiny European minority ruled as an aristocracy over a large primitive mass of aborigines hardly capable of comprehending the theological issues that had torn the Continent asunder. These oppressed natives retained much of the half-barbarous culture which contrasted sharply with the ultrarefinement that wealth and leisure permitted the governing class. The incomplete task of proselyting among the Indian charges of the crown allegedly justified an enormous staff of clergymen who, in turn, required innumerable churches, seminaries, and convents. Much wealth poured into the coffers of the Church, which exercised as pervasive an influence in the secular affairs of these overseas realms as its parent organization had in the Middle Ages of Europe. Besides economic and political power the riches at its disposal enabled this institution to be the patron of the arts, particularly of architecture in which the Baroque fervor was most clearly manifest. Thus a neomedieval regime had emerged, and it survived as an anachronism in which, it seemed, theology could prevail over history. The Indian majority had, in fact, lost its historical past, while the mixed elements resulting from racial fusion had not yet made any history. Only the small European minority could have an active role in the historical process, but even the participation of this group was severely restricted by the reactionary policies of the motherland. Hence, in a community of such social and cultural immobility, the Baroque vitality could only develop deeper tensions and frustration, particularly when bitter jealousies and rivalries divided the dominant white elements. To win favors in this static society the Creole, or the American-born Spaniard, was obliged to cloak his bitter resentment in a hypocritical adulation of the more privileged class, the

European-born Spaniard, and, in an unsatisfying dilettantism, he often frittered away his talents on pageant-like ceremonies, ceremonious functions, and versified panegyrics designed to flatter its vanity. These false and artificial exercises readily carried the Baroque emphasis on form to its most extreme manifestations.[9]

Thus it is that the brief career and varied experience of Fray García in the viceroyalty of New Spain epitomize the Baroque age in the distant realms of Spanish America. Embodying the absolute power of a combined Church and State, this Peninsular Spaniard came in medieval pomp and splendor to rule a kingdom as Archbishop-Viceroy. From the moment of his arrival at Vera Cruz to his entombment in the Cathedral of Mexico City he was the object of the theatrical adulation of his subjects in every form of colorful pageantry and exaggerated ceremony. The passion for drama in public spectacles almost reached a delirium in the macabre magnificence of the funeral obsequies. And the morbid recital of the progressive disintegration of the ailing ecclesiastical potentate, and the meticulous description of the autopsy performed on his cadaver written by a celebrated author of the time, all testify to the pathological concern with death and decay that preoccupied the Baroque mind. Similarly typical of this spirit is the juxtaposition of Fray García's excessive alms-giving and his sensual excitement in the sanguinary spectacle of the bull ring; of his great piety in religious practices and his keen delight in secular music and the pleasures of the palate; of his devotion to his ecclesiastical duties and his insatiable ambition for secular power; and of his position at the pinnacle of his world and his restless *querer más* or vague yearning for still loftier heights. Likewise suggestive of Baroque feeling is the strange coincidence of accidental injury and death and of ominous natural phenomena occurring at proud moments of glory which seemed to confirm its superstition, fatalism, and negativism. In all these aspects of the Archbishop-Viceroy's career the shadow rather than the substance prevails, and form, with its infinite profusion of detail, appears to obliterate the underlying reality. Such were the elements of the spiritual and intellectual climate of the New World centers of Hispanic civilization even long after the seventeenth century had vanished into the mists of the past.

Those years in which Fray García was sealing the triumph of the Counter Reformation in Mexico and setting the tone of its

Baroque age were, as earlier noted, of increasing political complexity in a changing Europe. It was a moment of uneasy lull in the stormy decades of war and disorder that had wracked the Continent in the sixteenth century and would soon resume in the holocaust of the Thirty Years' War and the subsequent clashes of rising nationalism. Hardly comprehending the revolutionary alterations already in movement, the chancellories of Europe were haunted by a sense of impending doom. From Spain the Netherlands had finally wrung a truce in 1609 which recognized the success of Holland's struggle for independence and enabled the Dutch to seize a commanding place in European affairs. This little nation was even beginning to threaten the Caribbean approaches to the Spanish empire in America. In England the wily Queen Elizabeth had recently died, and the first of the Stuart dynasty was pursuing a policy of appeasement with the weakening monarchy of Spain. Across the Channel in France the assassination of the absolutist Henry IV in 1610 frustrated his "Grand Design" for a federal unification of Europe to replace the vanished medieval unity. A feudal reaction weakened centralizing tendencies until Richelieu and Mazarin would organize the "modern state absolute," destined to elevate France to a great continental power. The loose aggregation of principalities composing the Holy Roman Empire of the Hapsburgs had virtually shrunk to the Germanies, and these weak entities were grouped in a series of alliances called the Protestant Union and the Catholic League. The devastation of the Thirty Years' War would soon insure the liquidation of the medieval concept of imperial organization to which Spain obstinately clung. In Italy the Pope, Paul V, stimulated by Cardinal Bellarmine's theory of papal sovereignty, was vigorously asserting the temporal authority of the Papacy against violations of ecclesiastical jurisdiction committed by the Italian republics. Far to the north, in the Baltic region, the ascendancy of Sweden under Gustavus Adolphus was about to get underway, and deep in Eastern Europe, and almost unnoticed, Russia was beginning to emerge from its "time of troubles." In 1613 a grand-nephew of Ivan the Terrible ascended the throne as the first Romanov.[10]

Externally Spain still appeared a powerful and splendid empire despite the successive defeats of the Armada, the deadlocked struggle in France, and the humiliating armistice in the Netherlands. But internally continuous wars, emigration, and withdrawal to monasteries had depleted its manpower and bled the nation white. Materially it was nearly bankrupt. Its weak, vacillating, and bigoted monarch, Philip III, lacked the stern resolution of his father and willingly he delegated his rule to the first of a series of irresponsible favorites who would speed the Spanish people to ruin. The martial qualities of the Spaniards no longer sufficed to maintain an imperial hegemony over a Europe visibly moving from medievalism to a new political and social order. Inflexibly arrayed on the side of religious orthodoxy and tradition, Spain's leaders failed to muster the still tremendous resources of the empire even to bolster the reactionary policies to which they were irrevocably committed. As Brooks Adams later wrote: "[The Spaniards] never emerged from the imaginative period, they never developed the economic type, and in consequence they never centralized as the English centralized. Even as early as the beginning of the seventeenth century this peculiarity had been observed, for the Duke of Sully remarked that with Spain the legs and arms are strong and powerful, but the heart is infinitely weak."[11]

Even as Fray García seemed to personify the unassailable might of the neomedieval Spanish system to the inhabitants of New Spain and to give assurance of the secure isolation of that realm, a great era of European expansion was already threatening Hispanic holdings in the Western Hemisphere. Holland, France and England were openly flaunting the Spanish theory of *mare clausum* which claimed for itself the exclusive possession of all western lands washed by the Atlantic. These rivals were boldly asserting the conflicting right of ownership based on effective occupation. By seizing islands of the West Indies and footholds in Guiana and Brazil the Dutch were threatening to make the Caribbean a Dutch sea. On the north mainland Hollanders settled in the Hudson Valley, and in 1614 founded New Amsterdam, the later day New York. In time they pushed southward to imprint their personality on the countryside of later Pennsylvania. Meanwhile, they were effectively relieving the Portuguese of their richest possessions in the East Indies.

Still farther north on the American mainland Samuel de Champlain, who had allegedly visited Vera Cruz at the turn of the century, was reconnoitering the St. Lawrence Valley region and strengthening the foundations of New France in the following decades. And no less active were the English who, just before Fray García's arrival in Mexico, had planted a feeble colony at Jamestown, and others soon followed in New England. Of more immediate danger to Spanish supremacy were the footholds gained by the English in Bermuda and in the Caribbean area. The neomedieval society of New Spain was but dimly aware of these perils, which, as the seventeenth century advanced, would grow more serious and deepen the vague anxiety and disquiet that haunted the inhabitants of the realm.

Such, briefly, were the circumstances that the pomp and pageantry of Fray García's few years and those following sought to conceal from the subjects of the Spanish crown. Resolutely fixing its gaze on the past, the Hispanic world contrived an illusory stability in a changing universe. For the moment it seemed to succeed, for those were "the sultry years of precarious power"[12] in Europe offering a short interval of equilibrium before accumulating forces precipitated the downward course of peoples dedicated to preserving the old. As inevitable defeat slowly overtook its dream of a neomedieval unity the Court at Madrid blinded itself to reality in the refulgent splendor of the Baroque art and letters created by the amazingly fecund genius of the nation. And even longer, if less brilliantly, Mexico City and other viceregal capitals of the New World would preserve the illusion possessing the motherland, thanks to the latter's protection, to the precariously maintained isolation, and to the rich silver mines that fed their economy. In the intricacy and profusion of a Baroque pattern the frustrated dynamism of Old and New Spain alike found its most enduring expression in life and thought.

# ॐ III

# A BAROQUE SOCIETY

IT WAS the inhabitants of New Spain who offered the most vital expression of the Baroque complexity of their time and place. From the very beginning of Spanish rule a stratified society developed, the ethnic roots of which reached back to Asia through the Indians, to Africa through the Negroes, and to Europe through the Spaniards. The existence of these disparate elements side by side and the inevitable fusion resulting from association soon produced a strange ethnic conglomerate of almost kaleidoscopic diversity. Within this unequal partnership arose a complex system of tensions between men, colors, classes, and races that in ". . . all this inner unsteadiness, seething within a world kept in a thrice secular peace and security from European wars, everything contributed to make the soul of the Indies something strange and rare, almost unique in the annals of the human spirit."[1]

If profusion of detail and hierarchy are among the typical characteristics of the Baroque, they were increasingly present in the ethnic composition of the neomedieval communities of the New World. As the seventeenth century advanced Hispanic civilization sank its roots so deeply in the Spanish American soil that its patterns are discernible three centuries later. Ever more intricate did the constellation of class and caste grow as a prolific miscegenation progressed. And the very fluidity of this ethnic process, which was creating entirely new human species, helped to insure the stability of a neomedieval order. The multiplicity of racial types emerging from a sort of Baroque melting pot gave a sociological expression of

37

the political maxim "divide and rule" to which Spanish policy was securely wedded. By diligently fostering a kind of "pigmentocracy," with caste distinctions based largely on the amount of white blood in an individual's veins, the possibility was slight that sufficient cohesion might develop among the exploited masses to tempt them to challenge the control of the privileged white minority. But a closer scrutiny of the components of this Baroque society is in order.

The basic racial elements, as already indicated, were American, African, and European, together with resulting mixtures. Within each of these groups, however, social and psychological differences tended to compound mutual antagonisms, though prejudice stemmed much less from differences of pigment than in the English and French colonies. Blood played a part in determining position in the Spanish American hierarchy, but antipathies sprang more from the social discrimination maintained by rigid barriers which persons of color occasionally scaled. Though the Indian was the original and numerically the largest element of this New World cosmos, his lowly status in the social organism suggests a more inverted approach to the discussion by considering first the dominant white minority.

All too often the term "Spaniard" implies a collective identity, or a fairly precise national type. It is usually assumed that all individuals so designated have, in general, a common appearance, psychology, and language that give them a recognized national pattern. While such simplification is at all times hazardous, it is peculiarly unsafe when applied to the highly individualistic peoples of the Spanish Peninsula, particularly when nationalism itself was still in swaddling clothes. Shaped into more or less isolated compartments by its irregular topography and moulded by historical circumstances, Spain has long been characterized by a regionalism so pronounced as to endow its inhabitants with striking contrasts of temperament, appearance, and language. The gay Andalusian of the south, the sober Castilian of the central north, the laborious Gallician of the northwest, the enterprising Catalan of the east, the alien, industrious Basque of the northeast, are all "Spaniards" who present traits of character, psychology, and speech so diverse and so dissimilar as to form distinct peoples. This almost Baroque profusion of ethnic detail among the Peninsulars has played a part in retarding national unification in Spain down to the present time.

Owing to the celebrity of Cortés, Alvarado, Pizarro, and many other conquistadors, together with a certain similarity of the Spanish spoken in America to that in Andalucía, a belief was long current that the conquerors and early settlers came almost exclusively from southern Spain. This theory is no longer tenable, particularly when applied to the Baroque seventeenth century. While the men who accompanied Columbus on his first two voyages were probably all from Andalucía, as early as 1506 it was plainly evident that, politically at least, the Aragonese were dominant in Hispaniola, or Santo Domingo. Early chronicles and passenger lists indicate that about forty-two per cent of the emigration was from the southern region of the Peninsula. Nearly an equal percentage came from Castile; the balance originated in other parts of Spain bordering on these central provinces, including Portugal, the Balearic and Canary islands.[2] This early preponderance of Castilians and Andalusians is explained by the monopoly exercised by Castile from the outset in the affairs of the Indies. It is unfortunate, perhaps, that this policy tended to restrict the migration of Basques, Galicians, and Catalans whose thrift and industry admirably equipped them for the task of developing economically the new colonies. But well before the seventeenth century these restrictions were so far relaxed that immigration in the New World represented a cross section of the peoples of Spain.

So strong were linguistic bonds and provincial affinities of these groups, however, that they tended to reproduce in the New World much of the regionalism of the mother country by congregating in certain localities and in *barrios* or districts of the larger towns and cities. In the new environments old world jealousies and antagonisms acquired renewed vitality, occasionally exploding into open feuds and violent clashes attended by loss of life.[3] These enmities were visible even in the military phase of the Conquest. When the troubled Aztec monarch, Montezuma, held captive by Cortés, was informed that other Spaniards under Narváez had come to arrest his captor, he was doubtless puzzled by the explanation offered him. ". . . We came from Castile itself, which is called Old Castile, and we called ourselves Castilians, and the Captain (Narváez), who was now at Cempoala, and the people he had brought with him, came from another province, named Biscaya and they called themselves Biscayans, and spoke like the Otomis of this land of Mexico."[4] This last phrase clearly implied that the Basque language used by Narváez' followers was as outlandish as the Indian language mentioned was to Montezuma. These festering antipathies of Spanish regionalism brought much dissension and disunity among the dominant whites throughout the colonial era, including the religious communities in which the particularism of the old country was occasionally stronger than the vows of Christian brotherhood.

The frequent absence of cordiality among Spaniards of different provincial origin was only one of the discords afflicting the relations of the ruling classes. Even more widespread and vehement was the disaffection traceable to differing official status and social strata. The top administrative and judicial posts were uniformly reserved for Court favorites of the King in Madrid, and many of the lesser offices of a swollen colonial bureaucracy went to Peninsular-born individuals by appointment or, as the financial affairs of the Hapsburgs worsened, by purchase irrespective of merit. Each viceroy usually arrived with a populous retinue of servants, relatives, friends, and hangers-on for whom sinecures were procured or the acquisition of choice property was facilitated. The bait of a title, or the prestige accruing from the mere fact of being European-born, enabled many Spaniards in impecunious circumstances to contract marriages with daughters of wealthy families who willingly bestowed fabulous dowries. Not all new arrivals were so fortunate, and the failure to fulfill similar anticipations left them singularly incapable of admiring the luckier ones. But even more bitter was the resentment of the American-born descendants of the conquistadors and first settlers called Creoles. With envy and anger they saw the fruits of the blood, sweat, and swords of their ancestors consumed by haughty adventurers and newly powerful parvenus. The get-rich-quick philosophy of this parasitic upperclass inevitably poisoned the relations of the dominant whites, and the comparatively small minority of Europeans and American-born burned with passionate feelings of hostility and contempt.

The futile efforts of Hapsburg Spain to check the tide of heterodoxy in Europe by endless wars were destroying its solvency and depopulating its fields. The drain on manpower was not caused by the armies alone, but by the emigration of the more energetic of the humbler classes who, increasingly in the seventeenth century, poured into the Indies. These immigrant peasants and artisans frequently began life in the new environment as itinerant peddlers and small tradesmen. By dint of industry and frugal habits they often amassed a small fortune in a relatively short time. Though many were nearly illiterate and possessed none of the social graces, their thrift and stability, added to a European origin, gave them a certain luster in the eyes of the American-born Spanish women who found their own men much too fickle and irresponsible. Occasionally these *nouveaux riches* of male persuasion presumed on these favors and contracted unions which brought down upon them and their offspring the wrath of relatives with aristocratic pretensions but often of less pure white blood. Where marriages of daughters of genteel families in reduced circumstances to prosperous humble immigrants from Spain took place, the common effect was to produce rancorous antipathies which turned children against parents and cousin against cousin.

If upper-class Spaniards from the Peninsula often gained material and social advantages by favoritism and nepotism, and humbler representatives of the master race prospered through diligence and the better opportunities of the New World, many individuals in both categories were less successful. These self-proclaimed *hidalgos,* who had not found fortune or favor with the powerful, were little disposed to remedy matters by exerting themselves in useful occupations. Their scorn of manual labor and of trades soon reduced them to roving vagabonds on the highways or to loafers, ne'er-do-wells, pickpockets, and the like on the streets and squares of the larger towns and cities—the New World *pícaros* of contemporary literary fame in Spain. These renegade Spaniards wandered about the countryside preying upon the browbeaten Indians and mixed elements, and it was their common practice to note some particularly desirable piece of land for a farm, ranch, or millsite held by an Indian community and report its existence to an influential official or member of the viceroy's retinue. The luckless natives were soon deprived of their property by forced sale at a mere pittance while the knavish Spaniards received an acceptable commission for their dubious services.[5]

In the cities these disreputable whites often became leaders in the dark underworld of half-caste, Indian, and Negro criminals and perverts. Still other unregenerate Spaniards resembled outcasts

later called "beachcombers." Both species were termed *zaramullos*
in the seventeenth century, and a contemporary Mexican writer
describes them as "knaves, rascals, and cape-snatchers [who], in
falling away from their [white] allegiance, are the worst of all in
such a vile rabble."[6] The habitués of local dives and *pulquerías,*
they were ever ready to incite the wretched Indians, Negroes, and
miscegenated masses to riots and tumults, and take advantage of
such upheavals to loot and plunder the shops and homes of countrymen.

The most profound and enduring cleavage among the dominant
white classes was undoubtedly between those born in Spain and
those born of Spanish parentage in America. The latter, called
Creoles, had appeared on the New World scene before the sixteenth century conquistadors had finished their work, and within a
generation they formed a well-defined type acutely sensitive and
continually afflicted by feelings of inferiority. Though it is often asserted that the first conquerors, having left their wives at home in
Spain, quickly consorted with women of the vanquished Indians
and produced a hybrid race, it is clearly evident that white representatives of the feminine sex were by no means absent in the stormy
days of conquest and early settlement. Hence, a generation of
American-born Spaniards promptly emerged upon the scene to receive, in due course, the originally unflattering designation by
which they are known.

The repressed feeling of this class, frequently exacerbated by the
condescension of the Peninsulars, remained one of the most deep-
seated of the Baroque tensions afflicting colonial society, and ultimately it resulted in secession from the Spanish empire. The hated
*gachupines,* as the European Spaniards were dubbed, deliberately
excluded the Creoles from the higher and more remunerative offices
of the viceregal State and Church, and permitted them only subordinate roles in their own government. This discrimination was,
in part, a calculated policy of the Spanish crown which feared
separatist tendencies in the overseas realms, and also, in part, because it needed to appease importunate office-seekers swarming
about the royal Court at Madrid. It rationalized this injustice by
embracing the popular belief that the climate and environment of
the New World had an enervating effect on children born of Europeans there. These offspring, it was assumed, matured early in a

sort of "rotten ripe" fashion, and quickly entered upon a physical and mental decline which, of course, clearly disqualified them for the heavy responsibilities of high office. Few, indeed, were the American-born whites appointed viceroys, archbishops, and judges of the higher tribunals during the three colonial centuries.

This situation was naturally galling to the Creole, in the veins of whom flowed the undiluted blood of the proud hidalgo and often that of the first conquerors and settlers, and this imputed inferiority filled him with a loathing of the *gachupines* that he was compelled to veil. Denied an outlet for his talents and energies in his own government, and endowed with a fierce pride that regarded the countinghouse and factory as beneath the dignity of a gentleman, he too often turned to a life of indolence and outright vice. Frequently a member of the landowning aristocracy, he preferred to live as an absentee proprietor in the cities and larger towns where his vanity was equalled by his lofty ignorance. Other Creoles, who were virtually landless, strove to keep up the appearances and arrogance of the well-to-do. Thomas Gage described one of these types whom he professed to have seen in Chiapas, a southern province of Mexico, but it would seem that his inspiration was the pathetically vain Squire portrayed in the famous Spanish picaresque tale, *Lazarillo de Tormes.*

"And thus, Reader, by this Don Melchor's wit and ability would I have thee judge of the gentlemen Creoles or natives of Chiapa; and yet as presumptuous they are and arrogant as if the noblest blood in the Court of Madrid ran through their veins. It is a common thing amongst them to make a dinner only with a dish of frijoles in black broth, boiled with pepper and garlic, saying it is the most nourishing meat in all Indies; and after this so stately a dinner they will be sure to come out to the street-door of their houses to see and to be seen, and there for half an hour will they stand shaking off the crumbs of bread from their clothes, bands (but especially from their ruffs when they use them) and from their mustachios. And with their toothpickers they will stand picking their teeth, as if some small partridge bone stuck in them; nay if a friend pass by at that time, they will be sure to find out some crumb or other in the mustachio . . . . and they will be sure to vent out some non-truth, as to say: Ah Señor que linda perdiz he comido hoy, 'O Sir, what a dainty partridge have I eat today,' whereas they

pick out nothing from their teeth but a black husk of a dry frijole
or Turkey bean."[7]

Open to this Creole class were the professions of law, medicine
and theology, but the majority was temperamentally unsuited to
sustained intellectual effort and its ample leisure was rarely productive of more than a certain dilettantism and an unrestrained flow
of bombastic verse. The neo-scholasticism of the Baroque age stimulated the shallow erudition and hollow verbalism in which some
members of this group sought a compensatory superiority. But few
escaped a deepening sense of frustration and a festering dislike
of their fellowmen of whatever race or color.

Another sector of this neomedieval society, predominantly white
though including persons of mixed blood and even Indians, was
the clergy. Since the sixteenth century Conquest this ecclesiastical
element had increased rapidly in number and influence as the
Church grew more wealthy and powerful. The continued presence
of a large body of pagan and half-Christianized natives appeared to
justify the ever-enlarging staff of clergymen until, by the seventeenth century, they constituted a considerable fraction of the
population. The Church's forces were divided into the secular
priests entrusted with administering the Sacraments and preventing backsliding among the faithful, and the religious orders such
as the Franciscans, Dominicans, Augustinians, Jesuits, and the like,
upon whom devolved primarily the tasks of education and proselyting among the heathen. As the crusading fervor of the Conquest
died away and as more settled conditions prevailed jurisdictional
disputes and doctrinal differences tended to replace the earlier zeal
of both groups of clergymen. The acquisition of lands and the
existence of a labor supply in the docile neophytes and the Indian
peasantry rapidly increased the Church's wealth, and multiplying
monasteries and convents dotted the land, particularly in the more
populous areas. These institutions in turn drew off a growing number of men and women from more productive pursuits and attracted
a steady stream of clergymen from Spain, usually to the higher
levels of the hierarchy. The number of priests, monks, and nuns
became disproportionate to the needs of the New World society
and a heavy drain upon its resources. Inevitably, the weight of this
burden fell hardest upon the exploited Indian population.

When Fray García Guerra ruled as Archbishop-Viceroy of

Mexico the Franciscans were said to maintain one hundred and seventy-two monasteries and religious houses, the Augustinians ninety, and the Dominicans sixty-nine, to which were added those of the various other orders. In 1611 the excessive number of these establishments moved the Pope, Paul V, to issue a bull suppressing convents not occupied by at least eight friars, but little respect greeted this papal decree. Many of these institutions amassed large properties in lands and goods which enabled them to conduct highly profitable business ventures of a capitalistic character. It was this wealth that made possible the Baroque splendor of so many ecclesiastical edifices and the luxurious manner of living for so many of the expanding membership of the orders. These circumstances inevitably brought in their train a relaxation of monastic ideals, rules, and morals, notorious in the Baroque age and later.

It is, perhaps, a little questionable to summon again the apostate Thomas Gage to give evidence on conditions in seventeenth century Mexico, particularly on matters relating to clergymen, yet undoubtedly his *New Survey of the West Indies* contains much truth. In relating his journey inland from Vera Cruz around 1625 he professes to be shocked by the gambling, drinking, and the profanity of the mendicant friars in the Franciscan monastery at Jalapa where he was a temporary guest. Especially horrifying to him was the hypocrisy of a monk playing cards with his confreres. "Though formerly he had touched money," wrote the scandalized Gage, "and with his fingers had laid it to the stake on the table, yet sometimes to make the company laugh, if he had chanced to win a double vie . . . then would he take the end of one sleeve of his habit and open wide the other broad sleeve, saying: I have vowed not to touch money, nor keep any . . . but my sleeve may touch it, and my sleeve may keep it."[8]

The Baroque age witnessed much constructive missionary activity on the frontiers of New Spain and in the founding of schools; still other endeavors testified to the zeal of the clergy. Unhappily these positive contributions were more than counterbalanced by a moral laxity and a parasitism afflicting many religious establishments. Throughout Spanish America, as in Spain itself, the rules of many monastic orders so far relaxed that numerous members lived outside convent walls and maintained illegal families and dependents in private houses.[9] Nunneries offered commodious refuge for large numbers of unmarriageable daughters who spent their lives in comfortable cells surrounded by conveniences and attended by personal servants and slaves. This idleness was not always conducive to the expected decorum, and permanent confinement sometimes brought antipathies into the open. Friction between inmates hailing from different provinces of Spain, between Peninsulars and Creoles, and between representatives of varied social classes not infrequently produced enough heat to flame into unseemly disturbances, and the quarrels over the election of priors and superiors often assumed such violent proportions that secular authorities of the State found it necessary to intervene. Particularly vexatious for the viceroys and their coadjutors were the rivalries of the religious orders who, with little of the otherworldly piety and concern suggested by their vows, jockeyed for power and preference in the affairs of the universities and even in more political agencies.

Still other human elements entered the white composite, increasing its diversity. Too readily is it assumed that the restrictive policies of the Spanish crown limited emigration to the colonies to approved nationals and excluded other Europeans. Records of licenses and permits issued to passengers embarking for the Indies plainly reveal the presence of Italians, Flemings, Germans, Austrians, Greeks, Irishmen, and even Dutchmen and Englishmen on Atlantic crossings of the merchant ships and galleons. As the Spanish Empire decayed, leaving its overseas possessions more vulnerable to piratical attacks, the king's ministers authorized the sending of skilled artisans, metallurgists, engineers, and other technicians, most of whom were aliens, to modernize fortifications and improve mining and other industries. Similarly, Italians, Flemings, Frenchmen and others, apparently more zealous for martyrdom in the frontier missions than either the Spanish or Creole clergymen, were subsidized for this purpose and sent to America. Spain's restrictive policy with respect to emigration stemmed from a religious rather than an antiforeign bias. Its essential requirement was that non-Spanish Europeans be orthodox Catholics.

If the number of authorized foreigners was fairly considerable, those entering without credentials of any sort were probably more numerous. Seaports such as Vera Cruz invariably harbored subjects of other nations who had deserted their ships, or were left by passing vessels. Though Spanish captains were severely enjoined to carry no unlicensed crewmen or passengers, and port officials were cautioned to prevent illegal entries, many undesirables, like forbidden books, found their way past these barriers and into the interior of the viceroyalties. Though now and then the net of the police-minded Inquisition ensnared them, many more remained inconspicuous in the heterogeneous population. Those who lingered in the seaports sometimes found themselves impressed as sailors in the returning fleets or in maritime expeditions fitted out for explorations.

Such extraneous elements were not always of European origin. Between the West Coast port of Acapulco and Manila in the Philippine Islands a freight and passenger service lasted for nearly two and a half centuries. The annual galleons plowing their tortuous course across the vast Pacific injected a slight admixture of Asiatic blood into the ethnic complexity of the Baroque society of Old Mexico. These clumsy crafts, sometimes the largest ships of the time, carried crews of Filipinos, Malays, and Chinese who, if they survived the arduous voyage of six or more months, settled somewhere along the coast or drifted into the interior to mingle with the varied inhabitants. Some brought technical skills useful to the economy. In commenting on the exquisite workmanship of the goldsmiths, Thomas Gage reports that: "The Indians, and the people of China that have been made Christians and every year come thither, have perfected the Spaniards in that trade."[10]

At the opposite extreme of the ethnic spectrum appeared the Negroes who, from the Conquest itself, had played an active role in the military and economic subjugation of the land. From the outset the Spaniards had displayed an enthusiasm for wealth with a minimum of labor and, as the Indians of the West Indies proved unsatisfactory workers, African slavery was introduced almost at once. Around 1441 the Portuguese had begun this traffic in human beings during their explorations along the Dark Continent, but it scarcely seemed likely to develop into a large-scale operation. The discovery of America and the opportunity offered by its rich soil to satisfy the newly whetted sweet-tooth of Europe by sugar cultivation soon placed a premium on Negro field hands. Even before the death of the discoverer of the New World the Spanish governor of the island of Hispaniola begged that no more Africans be shipped because many were escaping into the hills and joining the Indi-

ans.[11] Thus, almost coincident with the advent of the blackman in
the colonies, arose a menace that endured until final emancipation.
These fugitive slaves, called *cimarrones*, reverted to their tribal
ways, formed wilderness communities, and preyed upon the white
man's commerce.

The high mortality of West Indian workers in the mines and on
the plantations made the governor's protest ineffective and by 1510
the traffic had increased. Eight years later the Spanish crown permitted the shipping of 4,000 Negroes to the Caribbean area, and
by 1540 some 10,000 were imported annually into the mainland;
by the seventeenth century the total each year probably reached
75,000.[12] The year 1522 saw the first recorded Negro insurrection
when twenty blacks owned by Diego Columbus, son of the Discoverer, revolted and killed several of the outnumbered Spaniards
on Hispaniola.[13] But, almost at the same time, Africans were accompanying the conquistadors on their conquests of Mexico and
Peru as burden-bearers. In April, 1533, the Spanish king received
word that, within five months, more than six hundred whites and
four hundred black bondsmen had passed through Panama en
route to the former empire of the Incas, and Cortés' restless lieu-
tenant, Alvarado, also led an army to Quito in present-day Ecuador
which included two hundred Negro servitors.[14] As centers of
wealth and luxury developed in Mexico and elsewhere, Africans
became domestic servants and found their way into crafts and
trades. More enterprising, in general, than the fatalistic Indians,
they practiced ingenious forms of racketeering on the dominant
classes in the cities and large towns where they congregated in such
numbers as to cause profound anxiety among the white overlords.
But their economic contribution was great and their labor provided
the base of many fortunes made by their masters. The Negro's
talent for organization and leadership occasionally brought comparative prominence, while his gifts enriched the arts of music,
dance, folklore, sculpture, and carving.

Like the whites, the Negro also offered variations in the human
spectrum of a Baroque society. Just as the Europeans presented
shades from the alabaster whiteness of some Spanish women to the
dark swarthiness of Peninsular southerners, so the African varied
from jet black to the lighter tints of *café au lait*. Slave-trading activities had extended from the Senegal and Gambia rivers of the

African west coast to Guinea to the eastward and south to Angola, and the traders took captives from the Ashanti, Fanti, Minas, and Dahomean tribes of the Gold Coast and the Yoruba of Nigeria. These Negroes differed as much among themselves in temperament, skills, language, and pigmentation as did the whites, and among them existed vague castes of an undefined pattern.

The third racial group, the Indian, was, of course, of fundamental importance sociologically. Despite recurring plagues and harsh exploitation which, in the early seventeenth century, had severely reduced the aboriginal population, it far outnumbered that of the Europeans. While the social structure of the remarkably advanced civilizations encountered by the Spaniards was largely crushed under the weight of the Conquest, representatives of the Indian nobility did retain some feudal rights and enjoyed a certain eminence. In the more thickly populated districts of the south, members of the conquered race were prosperous merchants. In this region Thomas Gage reports that: ". . . Indians live there who traffic to Mexico [City] and about the country with twenty or thirty mules of their own, chopping and changing, buying and selling commodities, and some of them are thought to be worth ten, or twelve, or fifteen thousand ducats, which is much for an Indian to get among the Spaniards . . ." He also describes a rich Indian in Chiapas with a title of Don, a fine stable of horses, and a mode of living as ostentatious as a Spaniard, who served as governor of a town.[15] But the lot of most Indians was clearly much less fortunate. Their status as a subjugated people tended to compress individual differences into a faceless mass and reduce them to a collective serfdom. Their sedentary nature included a certain passivity and fatalism which facilitated Spanish control and perpetuated a feudal relationship between conquerors and conquered, but these qualities enabled the Indians to preserve many of their characteristics which subtly affected the culture imposed upon them. Their artistic instinct served to enrich the complex patterns of Baroque expression, quietly imbuing them with a character distinct from the contemporary manifestations in Spain and, perhaps, accounting for the longer duration of this intricate style in Mexico and Spanish America generally.

On the outermost fringes of Spanish settlement roamed nomadic, warlike tribes little disposed to abandon a wild, free manner of living. Foiled in the efforts to vanquish these barbarous aborigines by swift, dramatic conquest, the Spaniards were obliged to engage in sporadic guerrilla warfare with these elusive foes. It was particularly aggravating because this resistance excluded the whites from regions which, though uninvitingly arid, might still fulfill their dreams of rich mines and sudden wealth. Courageous friars, with less materialistic motives, penetrated this forbidding hinterland to establish missions and reduce these fierce tribes to a Christian way of life. The seventeenth century witnessed heroic efforts of this sort in the far north and west, in New Mexico, Arizona, Lower California, Sinaloa and Sonora, but success was limited and the effect on the older settlements was negligible.

Where the ethnic pattern of colonial society acquired its most Baroque complexity was among its components of mixed blood. The association of white, red, and black races soon produced a strange conglomerate of humanity which included entirely new species of *homo sapiens*. This miscegenation coincided with the Conquest itself in the basic fusions of European and Indian, European and Negro, and Indian and Negro. By the time that the consolidation of Spanish civilization was giving the populous centers of New Spain a distinct character—and this was clearly visible by the end of the sixteenth century—the progressive mixing of diverse elements had created a veritable kaleidoscope of shades, complexions, and social castes. As time went on the pattern of old and new species became labyrinthine, almost defying analysis and forming a unique composite of human types, pigments, and psychology.

The generally enlightened laws promulgated by the Spanish crown took cognizance of this racial amalgamation by recognizing as prototypes the mestizos, offspring of Indian and white mating, mulattoes, and the *zambaigos* or *zambos*, as the products of Indian and Negro unions were called. But these were, of course, merely rudimentary combinations, and the lawmakers found the ensuing mixtures a bewildering problem of classification. Successive generations of crossbreeding created a confusing maze and a baffling system of nomenclature to identify each variation. Literally scores of designations were invented or applied to the different gradations of color and blood whose varieties taxed the resources of the language. Most of the names were based on shades of complexion, but other anatomical features, such as the shape of the nose, thickness or thinness of lips, body structure and the like, furnished inspiration.[16] Since these appellations were mostly bestowed by the dominant white castes they were intended to be humorous or downright insulting. The progeny of a *mestizo* couple, for example, was commonly called *tente en el aire* (suspended in the air), chiefly because it indicated no advance toward the white ancestry or no retrogression, as it was conceived, toward the Indian blood. If a *mestiza* woman married an Indian, the offspring might be called a *salta atrás* (a throwback) because the trend was toward the less-esteemed indigenous progenitor.

In the more intricate fluctuations of such advances and retreats of a mongrel population, and especially in mixtures in which Indian and Negro blood was dominant, the names bore connotations of scorn, contempt, mockery, and sneers. *No te entiendo* (I don't get you), for example, was the offspring of a *tente en el aire* and a mulatto woman, while an *Ahí te estás* (there you are) was the child of a *mestiza* mother and a *coyote* father, who, in turn, was the product of the union of a *mestizo* and an Indian.[17] Appellations of a zoological origin were deliberately derogatory such as: mule, coyote, wolf, cow, and the like. Each country, and even regions, had names of its own for the multitudinous mixtures, and a given designation might be used for a different combination of genes. The heterogeneous nature of this large segment of society is abundantly clear, a condition accentuated by a confusing array of castes into which it divided. Mutual jealousy and lack of cohesion kept this proletarian mass asunder as similar negative impulses did the more privileged groups, which fact largely explains why the restiveness of these overseas subjects of Spain, occasionally evident, was not translated for centuries into active opposition to the crown's authority.

Social position, based mainly on white blood, determined to a considerable extent the occupation of the individual in the more genteel pursuits, with idleness preferred, particularly in Creole circles. The large hybrid population, with its own complex hierarchy, had callings suited to its varying status. The upper strata with preponderant white blood were scarcely distinguishable from the Creoles or humbler Europeans and might pass as such; the lower approached the lowly condition of the Indians and Negroes and shared much the same destiny. The *mestizo* tended to find a place at the top of the mixed groups; in the sixteenth century the Spaniards accorded him paternal treatment. As his number increased a larger measure of discrimination was his lot—this prejudice often sprang from his "illegitimacy" and was more political and economic than ethical. It was, perhaps, a by-product of the hostile feeling in Spain for the remaining *Moriscos* and the mistrust of the so-called "new Christians" common in the days of the Counter Reformation. The military profession still remained one of the most honored in the contemporary culture, and the *mestizo* could find a place in it. The term "Spaniards," so frequently used in the reports of campaigns against pirates and the Indians on the frontiers, mostly referred to persons of diluted white blood. The trades and crafts were also open to this group, though usually the more menial tasks. The Indians were early taught such practical pursuits and might engage in these activities as well but, in the main, like the Negroes, they found themselves in the *obrajes* or the sweatshops of textile manufacture, in domestic service, or condemned to the hard work of agriculture and the heavy labor of the mines—slaves in fact though not in theory.

The misery and utter ignorance of this variegated and exploited proletariat were extreme. Their neglect and superstition made them a ready prey to a swarm of sorcerers and quacks who practiced magic rites and the black arts inherited from African and Indian barbarism. Faith in witchcraft, illuminati, animism, omens, charms, astrology and the occult flourished in all castes and classes, including the dominant whites. Baroque, indeed, does this profusion of ethnological detail, intricate hierarchy, and superstitious credulity of a New World society appear in retrospect during the "long siesta of the seventeenth century"!

# ❧ IV

# LITERARY MIGRANTS

AS THE Baroque age lengthened, the culture and civilization of Old and New Spain tended to resemble each other more closely. But there were also sharp contrasts. While futile wars, an unbalanced economy, fiscal bankruptcy, and irresponsible monarchs and their favorites were depleting the manpower and irretrievably ruining the Spanish nation, a settled order was developing in the Mexican realm where, comparatively speaking, peace and tranquility flourished despite the coincidence of a part of the "century of depression."[1] Remote from the bloody conflicts devastating Europe and with an economy achieving greater equilibrium between mining, agriculture, and artisan crafts, Old Mexico, despite the ever-increasing taxation to support the follies of the Spanish crown, was enjoying a measure of prosperity that permitted refinement and luxury for many of the white minority, and tolerable conditions for at least some of the masses. It is hardly strange, then, that these trans-Atlantic domains beckoned Peninsular Spaniards, nobles and plebians alike, as a land of opportunity. Already, before the seventeenth century began, Cervantes had written that the New World was a "refuge and haven of all the poor devils of Spain." Though emigration often proved disillusioning, it was also "an incomparable remedy for the few." One of the more pragmatic minds of Mexico City wrote, in 1604: "It happens that the majority of the people coming to these parts are fetched by poverty and necessity. As this realm has been and is," he went on, "by God's mercy rich, fertile and abundant, those who come and wish to apply

53

themselves industriously are able to get an honest living by very modest effort . . ."²

Among the Spaniards hoping to better their lot by emigration were writers, artists, and thinkers of which Spain, in its political and moral decline, produced an astonishing array. An unknown number merely contemplated this solution of their problems, others made brief sojourns, a few wandered widely over the New World in a restless quest, and a smaller number found permanent abode there. Cervantes himself had applied vainly for a variety of posts in the overseas realms, and even the great mystic, Saint John of the Cross, was preparing to depart for the same destination when death barred the way. Other men of letters, including two dramatists, Juan de la Cueva (1550?-1610) and Tirso de Molina (1583?-1648), and a witty writer, Eugenio de Salazar (1530?-1608?), actually spent varying numbers of years in the new lands. Now and then an artist added his permanent presence to the influence his imported works were exerting on the Baroque culture of New World centers. The existence of material wealth, a privileged aristocracy, a strong feudal tradition, and a viceregal court even rivaling that of Madrid in opulence and located in such splendid isolation, all provided a propitious atmosphere for the perpetuation of the neomedieval ideals of the Counter Reformation, and an attractive environment for economically-harassed writers.

For the native-born in these seemingly favorable conditions, however, inhibiting factors hampered the lush growth of genius so notably present in contemporary Spain. If the orthodoxy of the Peninsula was rigid under the threat of heretical doctrines abroad on the Continent, it was scarcely less so in the overseas centers surrounded by pagan, or partially Christianized Indians. Moreover, the ruling whites there grappled with a profound sense of inferiority which reduced artistic expression to a servile imitation of the models of the motherland. Almost nowhere did local works compete in genius with those of Spain, though considerable originality appeared in Baroque architecture, design, and related manifestations. But if no colonial work of art equals the supreme achievements of the Peninsula, now and then one rivaled the products of the secondary creators of the homeland.

From the collapsing economy of Spain the pleasure-loving monarchs rescued sufficient resources to maintain a luxurious court at

Madrid which attracted and held most of the first-rate creative
spirits of the so-called Golden Age. One of the major writers, and
chief rival of Cervantes, however, sought to remedy his fortunes by
a permanent transfer of residence to Old Mexico. This figure was
the dyspeptic author of the celebrated picaresque tale, *Guzmán de
Alfarache* (1599), Mateo Alemán, who arrived on the Mexican
shore in 1608 to pass his few remaining years. The popularity of
his long novel and its sequel probably helped to destroy the age-
long enthusiasm for the adventurous romances of chivalry quite as
much as did *Don Quixote,* and Alemán's narrative of low life long
remained a "best seller" along with Cervantes' masterpiece. If the
Archbishop-Viceroy, Fray García Guerra, in the entourage of whom
Mateo Alemán formed an intimate part, seemed the active incarnation of the Baroque *zeitgeist* in his sensate love of pomp and splendor, his *querer más,* and his morbid preoccupations, the Spanish
writer arriving with him left a more enduring record of the more
passive characteristics of the Baroque attitude—pessimism, frustration, and *desengaño,* or disillusionment.

*Guzmán de Alfarache* is a rambling, humorless tale of the sordid adventures of a runaway lad on the highways of Spain and
Italy and in the underworld of their cities. Each incident enables
the author to expatiate on the evilness of human nature which he
finds singularly corrupt. Hatred and disgust of life exude from its
often dreary pages written, however, in a lean, repressed style that,
somehow, possesses a strangely moving power. Clearly it spoke to
the Baroque generations of the Hispanic world who read it avidly,
to judge by its many editions. Its sixty chapters, amply padded
with tedious moralizing, make it almost seem, as a critic expresses
it, "a dissertation upon original sin"[3] in a wicked and hostile world
from which man's corrupted nature can only be redeemed by conversion and submission to the Church. In fictional form it seemed
to express, with extraordinary fidelity, the prevailing philosophy of
the Counter Reformation Catholic world which explains, perhaps,
the ecclesiastical approval of the novel and its wide circulation.
Though Alemán did not initiate the picaresque genre—the short,
masterly *Lazarillo de Tormes* had done so nearly a half century before—his *Guzmán de Alfarache* most completely assembled all the
characteristics of this type of fiction. It ushered in the seventeenth
century vogue of similar novels which, in varying ways, reaffirmed

the Baroque pessimism regarding human existence. So it was that Old Mexico harbored in his last obscure years one of the most influential writers of Spain's great literary age.

The years 1547 and 1616 may well form a parenthesis of exceptional significance in the history of the Spanish novel, for they represent exactly the life span of the creator of *Don Quixote*. With less certainty, but offering a tempting coincidence, those years may also mark the bounds of Mateo Alemán's existence. The birth date appears to be correct but that of his demise requires a question mark. Neither the time nor place of his death is known, though presumably he died in Mexico. Other similarities in the careers of these foremost novelists include a common struggle against penury despite phenomenal successes in literature, intermittent and poorly compensated government positions, desperate hopes for a better fortune in the New World, spurious second parts of their masterworks, and the consequent stimulation of authentic sequels. Both spent unpleasant but possibly fruitful sojourns in jails. Alemán, upon release from debtors' prison in 1582 sought to migrate, and about this time the same thought occurred to Cervantes. Alemán's journey was long deferred while that of Cervantes, probably fortunately, never took place.

The decision of the author of *Guzmán de Alfarache* to depart to Mexico at the age of sixty arouses curiosity. His application for a permit to sail in 1607 reminded his Majesty of many services rendered on financial commissions, and asserted that he had "spent most of his life studying humane letters and had written several books; now he is unemployed and desires to continue in the royal service in the Indies where the viceroys and other administrative officers need persons of his training (in accountancy)." Then as if an afterthought, he adds: "and also because he has a very wealthy cousin, a mine owner of San Luis, New Spain, who has sent for him."[4]

To reach that "haven of refuge for the poor devils of Spain," as Cervantes had called the New World, was for the aging, poverty haunted novelist, seemingly, a last desperate resort on which he had staked his remaining earthly possessions in the Peninsula. He had signed over his properties in Madrid to a government officer, later granting him a power of attorney and transferring all rights of publication and sale of the second part of *Guzmán de Alfarache* in Castile and Portugal "for the period of ten years left to me by his Majesty's favor." And to the same individual he also made a similar donation of his pious *Life of Saint Anthony of Padua*. The recipient of these assets of the Spanish writer was a Pedro de Ledesma, "secretary of the king, our Lord, in his Royal Council of the Indies . . . which bestowal I make and grant because of the many kind acts which I have received from the said secretary . . ."[5] This assignment of his worldly effects to a functionary of the bureau in charge of imperial affairs overseas invites speculation. It has been suggested that one of these "kind acts" may have enabled Alemán to evade the ban against the emigration to the colonies of individuals with a taint of Jewish blood.[6]

This voluntary stripping of his possessions and the bold decision, for a misanthropic man of his years, to start life anew across the Atlantic hardly seem the result of blind impulse. The explanation lies, perhaps, in the reference to a "wealthy cousin" in his application. Who, then, was the moneyed relative in Mexico who had allegedly sent for him? Since the impecunious novelist fails to mention his name and it has not come to light in any other document, the identity of the would-be benefactor remains obscure. Circumstantial evidence, however, strongly suggests a prominent citizen of Mexico City, Dr. Alonso Alemán. This man of affairs had obtained a law degree in 1567 at Seville (birthplace of the creator of *Guzmán de Alfarache*) and, four years later, had sailed with a brother to New Spain. There, as a *gachupín*, or Peninsular Spaniard, he had married, with the ease that so exasperated the American-born Spaniards, a wealthy Creole heiress, daughter of a conquistador, and thus acquired a fortune, possibly in mines. His legal and business talents were, apparently, exceptional, and he filled various chairs and administrative offices in the University of Mexico. Though retiring as a professor in 1597, he continued to manage the financial affairs of that institution. These and other activities, together with his extensive law practice, undoubtedly increased a substantial fortune and reputation. His distinction seems apparent in existing documents where his name invariably appears as simply "Dr. Alemán," while all other cosigners give theirs in full. In 1604 a viceroy, the Count of Monterrey, referred to this individual "as one of the most learned men and ablest lawyer in Mexico City." He also reported this fiftyish jurist as in excellent health, an observation that hardly prepares one for the fact of Dr. Alemán's death in 1605.[7]

If, as seems likely, this prominent citizen was the *primo hermano* to whom, in his petition, the Spanish writer referred, the latter gives the impression that, in 1607, his relative was still alive. It is possible, of course, that the novelist had received an invitation earlier and was unaware of the death of the sender. Communications between Spain and the Indies were slow by any modern standards, but the news could have reached Mateo Alemán by early 1606, or sooner, on the annual fleet returning from Vera Cruz, or by a dispatch boat. Was it, rather, the possibility of a legacy that prompted the sacrifice of his effects in Spain and emigration so late in life? Obtaining the necessary permit was, apparently, not a simple matter for the famous author, and the knowledge that a well-to-do kinsman awaited his arrival carried more conviction than an expected inheritance that he would not become destitute. Hence the wording of his application. That he did not seek a credential in 1606 for the spring sailing was, possibly, because the word of Dr. Alemán's death arrived too late and, consequently, he had to apply for the fleet of the following year.

Menacing activities of Dutch pirates on the Spanish coast prompted the canceling of the 1607 sailing which obliged the despondent author to wait another twelvemonth for his departure. At last, on June 3, 1608, he embarked at Seville with three alleged children: Francisca de Alemán, a young woman of twenty-four who was, in reality, Doña Francisca Calderón, his mistress; Margarita and Antonio, his illegitimate offspring aged three and eight respectively; a forty-year-old niece, Catalina de Alemán, and two servants, Alonso Martín and María de Gálvez.[8]

At Cádiz the fleet added further units and passengers, including Archbishop Fray García Guerra, and his large retinue. With a total of sixty-two vessels it began the long crossing on June 30. Whether Alemán knew the prelate before, or won his favor on this voyage is unclear, but it is certain that a friendship was established of inestimable advantage to the immigrant writer in the new land. The lugubrious *Sucesos de Fray García Guerra, Arzobispo de México* . . . (Events concerning Friar García Guerra, Archbishop of Mexico . . .) written by the novelist after the death of its subject in 1613 and the last known product of his quill testifies to this intimate

association and the protection received. This short work was a sort
of extended obituary in which, with true Baroque feeling, the brilliant scenes of the Archbishop-Viceroy's triumphs contrasted with
the macabre details of his fatal illness and the excessively somber
spectacle of his funeral.

The record is silent concerning the success of Alemán's quest in
Mexico, but he seems to have acquired the desired economic security that had induced him to abandon Spain. Not long after his
arrival he published in Mexico City a treatise on Castilian orthog-
raphy to which, apparently, he attached greater importance than to
his well-known novel. The satisfactory outcome of his decision
to come to the New World seems confirmed by the grateful tone
of its preface. "Now receive, O generous and illustrious city," he
wrote, "this rejoicing and lucky pilgrim whose good fortune brought
him to your charitable embrace and who, like the worker wearied
by the rigor of the summer sun, desires to rest his tired limbs in the
comfort of your welcome shade . . ." But a prolonged illness during
the first months of his residence and his failing eyesight had diminished, no doubt, these happier feelings and immersed him even
more deeply in his habitual pessimism and despondency.

Only one document on the Spanish author's life in Mexico has
so far come to light to supplement the meager personal data available in his two works printed there. It is a scribal record of a prosaic
transaction, and its uniqueness lends an interest out of proportion
to its importance. It is merely a small docket pertaining to a lease
taken by Alemán on a house which reflects some of the difficulties
confronted by tenants of the time.[9] A few details are illuminating.

Two residents of the viceregal capital, Juan and García Cabezas,
had inherited a run-down dwelling in the district of San Angel, on
the edge of the Pedregal, which they listed for renting with the
business manager of the nearby *colegio* of the Carmelite order. On
December 6, 1609 this agent of the religious community drew up
a lease with "the accountant Mateo Alemán, a citizen of the City
of Mexico" who, it appears, was already lodged in the house. The
agreement stipulated that the Spanish author might occupy the
premises during a three-year period from December 1, 1609 to the
end of November, 1612, for an annual rental of three hundred
pesos, payable in advance in four months' installments. The cost
of repairs needed to make the dwelling habitable was deductible

from the first payment. These improvements included rebuilding the wall separating the yard from the neighbor's property, and the installation of new doors and windows. The ecclesiastical agents shrewdly inserted an "escape clause" permitting them to cancel the lease on two months' notice, a privilege not shared, apparently, by the distinguished tenant. Doubtless harassed by a housing shortage, Alemán accepted these conditions without protest.

It appears likely that the Carmelite real estate dealers were slow in arranging for the needed repairs, or possibly labor was in short supply. At any rate, nothing was done, and the Spanish novelist probably found the windowless and doorless shelter rather too drafty for comfort in the chilly month of December. After waiting for things to happen, he decided to take action. He had been a landlord himself in Madrid and Seville and was handy in such matters. So he offered to attend to these repairs personally. On January 31, 1610, therefore, a clause was attached to the original lease authorizing ". . . the said accountant Mateo Alemán to undertake freely the said repairs . . . necessary for the occupancy of the said dwelling." On completing these improvements the tenant was to render a sworn statement of the expense incurred, which total would be credited to his account. This supplementary agreement, seemingly unnotarized, ends the short docket and no further information is vouchsafed. Presumably, the illustrious tenant remained in this house until his lease expired in late 1612. His account of Fray García Guerra, published the next year, indicates that he was living in the capital at that time, and two years later he was reported at Chalco, a nearby village.[10] Here all trace ends of the writer whose novel still rivaled *Don Quixote* in popular favor.

The symbolic significance of Fray García Guerra's arrival in Mexico in 1608 is heightened by the presence in the same fleet of two of the foremost figures of the Golden Age of Spanish literature. One was, of course, Mateo Alemán, whose misanthropic view of life harmonized so intimately with the prevailing Baroque spirit. The other was a squat and ugly humpback, a Mexican Creole by the name of Juan Ruiz de Alarcón y Mendoza, who was returning to his native land after a somewhat unsatisfactory sojourn in the Peninsula. The contrasts presented by these two men of letters, who traveled on different vessels and probably did not meet, were striking. More prepossessing in appearance and with an established reputation, Alemán had easy access to the circle about the Archbishop and to the special favor that a *gachupín* enjoyed in colonial society. Alarcón, whose physical deformities made him the butt of cruel jeers and whose literary distinction was still to be achieved, was prey to a Creole inferiority complex which moved him to seek compensation in a proud display of aristocratic pretensions. Alemán was already in the enjoyment of his prestige as a leading novelist of the time; Alarcón had yet to achieve a greatness in the Spanish theater that would place him in the front rank of European dramatists, though little recognition would come to him in his own lifetime. If Alemán was the most distinguished creative writer of the Peninsula to migrate to the New World during the colonial centuries, his fellow passenger in the fleet was the most talented author that that New World gave to Spain and to Europe during the same period.

The tone of their writings, the techniques employed, and the attitude toward life reflected in them differed sharply. If in *Guzmán de Alfarache* the succession of incidents is "set down in a casual sequence with little art or invention and with no attempt either to make the characters live or the circumstances revealing,"[11] and if they serve as an excuse for dreary disquisitions on the baseness of human nature, the plays of Alarcón display careful workmanship in plot, characterization, and language, and they exude a more optimistic tone. While the playwright's intention is also didactic, his moralizing is less protracted and reveals less of the cynical distrust of mankind that possessed the Spanish novelist. Perhaps the more tranquil and unruffled atmosphere of New Spain in which Alarcón had begun life had engendered a more wholesome outlook than Alemán could acquire in the disintegrating world of Old Spain, but doubtless it was a matter of temperament. Cervantes, whose experience more nearly paralleled that of Alemán, had developed, as his masterwork clearly shows, a far more charitable understanding of human frailty.

Much less prolific than the fecund geniuses of the Spanish theater of his time—only about twenty of his plays are known—Alarcón nevertheless demonstrated a versatility within this score or so of compositions. Most highly regarded are his comedies of contemporary manners in Madrid in which he gently but firmly ex-

coriates, one by one, the common vices of lying, gossiping, ingrati-
tude, fickleness, selfishness, and the like. This is accomplished by
excellent delineation of character, natural dialogue, usually free of
rhetorical flourishes, and by flowing verse in well woven plots.
The most famous of these comedies is *La verdad sospechosa* (Truth
Suspect) which delightfully depicts the confusions that result
from an imaginative disregard of the truth. The adroit handling of
the theme aroused the admiration of the great French playwright,
Pierre Corneille, who is reported to have declared that he would
give two of his own best works for the privilege of having written
that Spanish masterpiece. Proof of his appreciation is offered in
the flattery of imitation present in his justly famous *Le Menteur*.
Alarcón's ethical intention was an important part of his originality
which won him little popularity in his own time, a fact to which his
own unprepossessing aspect and his quality as a Creole in Spain
probably contributed.

With greater cause than Alemán had for a misanthropic view of
his fellow men, who made his misshapen body the unceasing subject of ridicule, Alarcón's reflection of the *mal de siècle* is chiefly apparent in a slight thread of melancholy and a certain subtlety that
run through his work. Overshadowed by the towering genius of
Lope de Vega (1562-1635) and Tirso de Molina (1583?-1648) in
his own lifetime, the truly Baroque splendor of the drama of Pedro
Calderón de la Barca (1600-1681) entirely eclipsed his plays which
were nearly forgotten for two centuries. Today his realistic portrayal of manners and analysis of character make him seem more
modern than his contemporaries, and his comedies offer more reading pleasure than the pessimistic chapters of the novel written
by his morose fellow passenger in the Mexico-bound fleet of 1608.

Ruiz de Alarcón was born in Mexico City about 1581 into a
family of distinguished connections and his formative years were
spent in that viceroyalty. In 1600 he sailed to Spain and studied
law at the University of Salamanca, later practicing his profession
in Seville. Possibly this experience moved him to conclude that a
Creole might fare better after all in his native heath, for he returned to New Spain in 1608.

Once again in his homeland the hunchback Creole's efforts to
find a rewarding career were unsuccessful. He resumed his studies
at the University of Mexico, acquiring the degree of *licenciado* and

working toward a doctorate which, apparently, he did not receive. He did prepare a dissertation, however, which, in the fond hope, perhaps, of winning the recognition of the Archbishop, Fray García Guerra, he dedicated to that celebrity.[12] There is no evidence that the ambitious prelate took any notice of the implied honor, or ever bestowed attention on this unattractive fellow passenger of his voyage from Spain. Repeatedly Alarcón entered contests to win a university professorship but failed in every attempt. Meanwhile, he practiced law in the viceregal capital without enhancing appreciably either his fame or fortune. As true of Alemán, few documents have come to light to reveal his activities in Mexico City during these years, and none permits any real glimpse of his personality. For both distinguished writers and residents of "the literary metropolis of the New World," this period of their respective careers remains the most obscure.[13]

About the time of Fray García's death the disappointed Creole abandoned his native land once again, for 1614 found him back in Madrid and launching on his calling as a playwright. Whether he had dabbled in this kind of writing before his return to Spain, or began there while trying to find more regular employment, is not at all clear. What is most curious about his plays is the slight indication in any of them of his Mexican origin, and few indeed are the allusions to his homeland. The most clearly discernible appear in a comedy *El Semejante de sí mismo* (So Like Himself), which imitates the models of the contemporary giants of the Spanish theater, Lope de Vega and Tirso de Molina. It contains a brief description of the departure of the fleet from Spain, probably based on personal recollection, a few verses sketching the location of Mexico City, and some laudatory comments on the drainage project that Fray García Guerra and the viceroy, Luis de Velasco, had inspected. Scarcely anything more tangibly Mexican can be distilled from Alarcón's theater, which was written while he held various governmental posts. His death occurred in 1639 at the Spanish capital.

During the years of Alarcón's return to Mexico, a youth from Spain paused briefly in that realm who was also to produce plays for the theaters of Madrid, though they would lack the originality and genius of the American Creole. This Spaniard, Luis Belmonte Bermúdez (1587-1650?), sharing the restlessness of his times,

sought fortune first in New Spain, from which he presently moved
on to Peru and joined the adventurous expeditions of Pedro Fernández de Quirós to the Solomon Islands, the Moluccas, and other
parts of the Far East. There is no evidence that he met Alarcón,
but he did strike up an acquaintance with a fellow townsman and
expatriate, Mateo Alemán. Despite the disparity in age—Belmonte
Bermúdez was a stripling of twenty-two in 1609—a warm friendship budded between the two Spanish-born literary figures. As
the older novelist had testified to his orthodoxy by writing a pietistic *Life of Saint Anthony of Padua,* so the future dramatist and
poet had already composed a *Life of Saint Ignatius of Loyola,* to
which Alemán wrote a laudatory foreword: "It is not the passion
of friendship, and let it not seem that I speak with exaggerated
approval because [its author] is a fellow countryman, and we were
born in the same part of Seville," the ailing author of *Guzmán de
Alfarache* protests in explaining his encomiums.[14] Belmonte Bermúdez later achieved minor distinction in Spain for his epic
poems and some twenty-five plays, the best known of which was
*El Diablo Predicador* (The Devil a Preacher).[15] With themes of
the supernatural and fantastic, mingled with elements of religiosity
and satire, his plays contained the ingredients desired in the
popular theater of the Baroque age.

Another adventurous Spaniard with literary pretensions, whose
errant career brought him to Mexico after extensive travels, was
Mateo Rosas de Oquendo (1559?-1613?). A sort of cultured
*pícaro,* he had been a soldier in Italy and France. Seeking quicker
fortune, like many another Spaniard of his time, he transferred
activities to the New World. His bloodless participation in the conquest of Tucuman, now in Argentina, netted him unimpressive rewards and he drifted on to Lima, the metropolis of South America,
where his engaging personality and talents gained him entry into
the Viceroy of Peru's household. Possibly his sardonic wit displayed
in satiric verses gained him more enemies than friends, making it
expedient to move on. About 1598 his roving disposition brought
Oquendo to Mexico which he favored with his presence apparently for the remainder of his life. Here his nimble quill caricatured in verse various social and ethnic types, notably the mestizo,
but now and then it depicted the Mexican landscape with a sober
charm and lyric melancholy.[16] But the author was too imbued with

a hidalgo distaste for useful work and too disillusioned by his failure to acquire easy wealth to devote himself to sustained effort
of any sort, and he remained a kind of polished *zaramullo,* substi-
tuting versified quips for cape-snatching.

The turn of the seventeenth century saw distinct changes in the
art of literary expression which were promptly reflected in Mexico.
Indeed, this opulent realm gave to the Spanish world of that time
one of the greatest poets in Castilian, Bernardo de Balbuena
(1561?-1627), who, with so much resonant elegance, marks a
transition from the Renaissance to Baroque poetry. The sixteenth
century had produced epic poems and chronicles full of action and
penned with narrative verve, but toward the close of this period
a shift was perceptible from dramatic content to profuse decoration. The color and music of words were claiming attention and
the ornamental qualities of form were becoming more and more
the pretext for literature. The spirited recounting of deeds was
giving way to a detailing of the picturesque and a classic simplicity
was yielding to a mannered style. Baroque patterns were emerging
in literature as in art and, of the new fashion, Mexico would
contrib ite some of the best and many of the worst exhibits.[17]

Somewhat accidentally, it appears, Balbuena was born a Peninsular Spaniard. His father was on a visit to Spain at the time and
soon brought his infant son back to the viceroyalty of Mexico
where he grew up in Guadalajara. Though the poet spent a number of his adult years in the mother country studying in its universities, his career was chiefly in the New World where he
occupied various offices in the Church. In his youth he had attended the University of Mexico, later serving as a *cura* in a
remote village. The quiet leisure of this rural life permitted a
cultivation of his poetic gifts, of which he had already given substantial evidence, and his major works had their beginnings at this
time. Of these the first, though not in the order of publication,
was the *Siglo de Oro en las Selvas de Erífile* (The Golden Age in
the Groves of Eriphyle), a notable collection of eclogues, written
in the highly stylized prose and verse of the current pastoral novels,
though with somewhat more realism than appears in the similar
fictions of Lope de Vega and Cervantes.

The second and most imposing of Balbuena's works, *Bernardo
o Victoria de Roncesvalles* (Bernard, or the Victory at Roncesvalles)

was in the epic tradition inspired by the Italian poets Ariosto, Tasso, and others, and imitated by Spanish and Portuguese bards such as Alonso de Ercilla in *The Araucana* and Camoens in *The Lusiads*. With tedious results uninspired poetasters had made efforts to glorify Cortés and the Spanish Conquest in this manner, but Balbuena, with superb lyric talent, drew upon the rich storehouse of medieval Spain and from its legends produced a Baroque epic of some five thousand octaves. Complex in structure, broad in scope, his *Bernard* possessed an ornate intricacy, lush detail, and the richness of imagery of an immense tapestry. Among its shortcomings are: its enormous length; excessive number of episodes and personages, some poorly developed and often digressive; an abuse of allegory and of the marvellous; and occasional pedantry. Balancing these defects are its remarkable imaginativeness and invention, its musical verses, and extraordinary power of colorful description. The whole glitters with the sparkling splendor of a great diadem, a Baroque extravaganza which moved a beloved Spanish American critic to exclaim that it was "a delight for the eyes, a delight for the ears, and a delight for the mind."[18] Its vast profusion of ornamental details, over which Balbuena labored until near the end of his life, suggests the Baroque façades, altars, and retables of so many Mexican churches.[19]

As literary forms the pastoral narrative and the epic poem are long out of fashion, and the excessive length of most examples makes unlikely any revival. Balbuena's chief compositions, therefore, share with many classics the distinction of being more respected than read. But one of his poems, shorter and more spontaneous, retains an audience. *La Grandeza Mexicana* (Grandeur of Mexico City) is a lyrical description of the viceregal capital, its climate, surroundings, churches and public buildings, gardens, centers of learning, government, diversions, theater, women, horses, intellectuals, clergy, and the like. These altisonant verses, in tercets after the manner of Dante, are strewn with colorful adjectives, intricate metaphors, alliterations, ingenious wordplay, and verbal catalogues which, despite a pyrotechnic effect, convey a sincere admiration for the colonial metropolis. It would be idle, of course, to seek realism in this mellifluous description, yet it does give an impression of what life was like in the Mexican capital which, in its own way, could rival the interest and charm of many cities of Old Spain.

The intellectual activities of the community centered largely in the University of Mexico and the seminaries of the various religious orders scattered about the municipality. The learning was almost wholly neo-scholastic, theological in substance, as already described, in harmony with the ideology of the Catholic Counter Reformation. Its stimulation came mostly from the missionaries and travelers passing through the city on their journeys between Europe and the outposts of empire in other parts of the hemisphere, or in the Far East. Many fine minds with extensive experience and knowledge enlivened discussions often as animated as those in contemporary Spain, but there was little opportunity for the development of more secular philosophies. As in most of Europe, the Ptolemaic concept of the universe remained undisturbed, and the superstitions of astrology, alchemy, and medical lore pervaded the secular mind, though now and then an individual with a more technical type of intellect applied his thought to more practical matters.

The ambitious engineering project to relieve Mexico City from periodic inundation, which the viceroy, Luis de Velasco, had initiated and Fray García Guerra had inspected, brought into prominence a German resident named Heinrich Martin, better known in the castilianized form of Enrico Martínez. His was probably the foremost scientific mind in the viceroyalty during the first decades of the seventeenth century. Born a Protestant in Hamburg some time between 1550 and 1560, his family took him to Spain at the age of eight where he became a Catholic. In his youth he traveled widely in Europe and studied mathematics in France and Germany where he also developed a knowledge of mechanics. Returning to the Spanish peninsula, he lived for varying periods in Madrid, Toledo, and Seville, departing from the latter city in 1589 to become a royal cosmographer in Mexico. This designation implied a scientific capacity for assembling geographical data, compiling maps, measuring longitude and latitude, observing eclipses and movements of the stars, and a knowledge of applied mathematics. Enrico's command of languages also made him useful to the Inquisition as an interpreter, and his wide-ranging interests and technical skills moved him to acquire a printing press in 1599 for general work and the publication of his own writings such as almanacs and occasional treatises.[20]

In 1606 appeared an important item from his press which he had composed. It was his *Repertorio de los tiempos y Historia Natural desta Nueva España* (Almanac and History of New Spain) which was a potpourri of geographical data, astronomical and astrological observations, and historical facts concerning Mexico and Castile from 1520 to 1590. Of interest are its reflections of the scientific ideas of the time. He was a geocentrist, which is hardly surprising when Galileo was being punished about then for the "crime" of espousing the Copernican theory in the comparatively more enlightened Italy. If Enrico's astronomy sounds more like astrology, he was, at least, attempting to draw a line between the two kinds of study. And in the light of the concern with predestination in the Spanish Counter Reformation, the bold assertion of his belief in free will is significant. "Human acts depending on free will are not subject to celestial influences . . ." Even more striking is his declaration that ". . . kings and potentates may reduce realms, provinces, and cities with their thousands of population to their dominion, but the free will of man cannot be coerced"—a rather surprising assertion in an imperial, overseas realm steeped in a neomedieval orthodoxy and a royal absolutism. As an immigrant himself he was convinced that the different food and benign climate of Mexico sharpened the intelligence of the European born and tended to improve the natural gifts that he brought with him. Why this environment did not operate on the native-born Creole with similarly beneficial effect, he does not make clear.

Enrico Martínez' direction of what was a gigantic engineering undertaking for the time—the drainage of the valley of Mexico—brought him only sorrow, failure, and imprisonment. Highly controversial was the plan proposed, and it soon proved exceedingly costly in lives and money. The crown had sent inspectors to appraise the project who added their disapproval to the criticism emanating from local sources concerning the scheme and the work of construction. Some of this opposition stemmed from a provincial dislike of foreigners, especially non-Hispanic foreigners entrusted with conspicuous responsibilities whose technical superiority seemed a reflection on the national character. And this condemnation of the operation seemed justified by its failure to meet the test in subsequent occasions. In 1615, in 1623, and again in 1629 seasons of heavy rain inundated the capital, and these successive demonstrations of the ineffectiveness of the expensive undertakings resulted in the imprisonment of Enrico as its chief promoter. It was too vast an enterprise for the existing facilities, and its final achievement had to await the improved techniques and experience of the nineteenth century. The last days of the German engineer were embittered by a heavy sense of defeat and the harsh denunciations of which he was so long the object. Disillusionment and despondency crushed his spirit, and death followed in December, 1632, thus closing a career which, despite its limitations, had brought to the intellectual atmosphere of Mexico the first feeble intimations of the dawning age of science and technology.

# V

# SCENES, WRITERS, AND READING, 1620

WHEN the new Archbishop, Fray García Guerra, made his triumphal entry into Mexico City in 1608, the isolation of the rich realm of New Spain seemed complete and singularly propitious for the security of orthodoxy and the integrity of the Spanish empire in North America. Yet a heretical nation had already gained a foothold on the mainland of this continent and, in the course of the century, its aggressive intrusions would increase. At the moment it hardly formed a cloud speck on the horizon, but a new instrument of expansion unfamiliar to Spanish authority—the joint stock company—was accelerating a more openly economic imperialism than the messianic crown of Spain had envisaged. The new British dynasty of the Stuarts had bestowed a charter for a New World settlement on the Virginia Company of London which, in 1607, planted the first English colony on a malarial coast north of the Florida outpost at St. Augustine. But, however different this venture might seem, its objectives curiously resembled those of the Spanish conquistadors of the preceding century—discovery of gold and, incidentally, the conversion of Indian inhabitants to Christianity. The English gentlemen-adventurers at Jamestown were displaying as mild an enthusiasm for manual labor as their more vigorous Spanish counterparts had before them, and they were no less ready to exploit the native population in the name of religion. If the disconcerting absence of mines and submissive Indians in

Virginia deprived the English Conquest of the glamor of the Iberian enterprises, it assured the less profitable undertaking a more virtuous renown in history.

While Fray García was viewing the abundance of his bishopric from the Baroque splendor of his episcopal palace, disillusioned neighbors at distant Jamestown were dying by the hundreds in the "starving time," though the surrounding woods teemed with game and the rivers were choked with fish. And it was during those trying times that an Indian maiden, Pocahontas by name, served as intermediary between redskins and white invaders as another, less romanticized daughter of the New World, Doña Marina, had done for the Spaniards nearly a century before.

Another event of portentous significance to the northern region marked 1608. A resolute band of Englishmen departed that year from the homeland to the asylum of Holland. A dozen years later one hundred and two of its members crowded into a small vessel, poetically named "Mayflower," and crossed the Atlantic in sixty-five storm-stressed days to challenge further Spanish monopoly of the New World. These stern-faced immigrants found none of the prodigality of New Spain on landing on a harsh, rock-bound coast late in 1620. The grim, chill harbor of Plymouth, with its Indian-infested backlands, presented an even less hospitable aspect than the hot, vermin-ridden port of Vera Cruz in which Spanish pilgrims debarked only to hurry to the benign hinterland.

No one could foresee that these precarious footholds on the North Atlantic coast were the beginnings of a nation destined to surpass the opulence and power of the Spanish viceroyalty and eventually to seize a great part of its domain. The contrasts presented by that pathetic band, voluntarily marooned on the bleak, gray shore of Massachusetts Bay that dismal winter of 1620-1621, and the teeming population of the sunlit Valley of Mexico put such prophesies far beyond the boldest seers. The dull drabness of the rough settlements on the forbidding northern coast seemed the very antithesis of the polychromatic animation of the southern inland city.

Almost a century before the Massachusetts colony began, the beauty of the Aztec capital had moved to wonder the redoubtable soldier of Cortés, Bernal Díaz del Castillo, and now, when the English footholds were merely dreary scatterings of log cabins, a less valiant traveler in Mexico, Thomas Gage, recorded a similar, if more sophisticated, enthusiasm for the same locality long transformed into a Spanish viceregal city. What stirred both observers as they had approached the municipality was the fair prospect of a broad, green valley, broken by sparkling stretches of water, lying in a pleasing bowl formed by circling mountains. As they descended to the margins of the lake surrounding the great city its details enhanced the impression of beauty and the variety of contrasts. "The situation of this city is much like that of Venice," wrote the seventeenth-century English visitor, "but only differs in this, that Venice is built upon the sea water, and Mexico upon a lake which, seeming one, indeed is two." Even in these waters embracing the capital he noted the element of contrast for ". . . one part is standing water, the other ebbeth and floweth according to the wind that bloweth."[1] The brackish Lake Texcoco was about forty-five miles in circumference, and fringing its shores were thirty or more villages and hamlets which, like the metropolis of Mexico City, now and then experienced the floods that Enrico Martínez so unsuccessfully sought to control. The viceregal capital stood upon an island reclaimed from the lake and, as if to hold the city in position, three causeways reached out to the mainland like mooring ropes over which travelers entered. The one from the west was about a mile and a half long, another from the north was three miles in extent, and the longest projected five miles from the southern mainland.

The insular city appeared spacious within its circumference of two leagues, or about six miles. Its streets were remarkably straight and broad, permitting three carriages to drive abreast in the narrowest ones and six or more in the widest. Low but imposing houses, often enclosed in gardens, lined the main thoroughfares together with neat shops, and ornate structures of stone and brick. Fifteen thousand Spanish families resided in these precincts, while eighty thousand Indians, and possibly fifty thousand Negroes and mulattoes, slaves and freedmen, crowded the barrios, and at almost any hour of the day motley throngs filled its avenues. These avenues varied in character from normal roadways of solid earth and cobbled pavements to mingled land and waterways along which the population moved in vehicles, on mounts, on foot, and afloat.[2]

There were seven of these *acequias* or canals which, after flowing across the city like parallel arteries, emptied into the salty waters of Lake Texcoco. To insure drainage a series of *compuertas* or floodgates were lifted each morning to release water impounded in the canals. In rainy seasons they remained open to carry off the excess precipitation.[3] Over these waterways a thousand canoes and scows brought from the mainland the city's supplies of bread, meat, fish, game, firewood, *zacate* (forage), and the like, while daily over the causeways more than three thousand mules plodded patiently beneath heavy burdens of wheat, corn, sugar and other staples to join the water-borne provisions at the market place and the granaries.

"A thousand lovely canals, teeming with long, narrow boats, veritable mine-hoards of supplies, goods, and singular articles for the shops, twist and turn delightfully like crystalline serpents through its spacious streets" rhapsodized Bernardo de Balbuena in his lyric *Grandeur of Mexico City.* His panegyric suggests that he had no eyes—or nostrils—for the unpoetic reality of these often sluggish, stagnant, and nauseous waterways, whose murky shallows were befouled by corpses of animals—and sometimes of human beings—excrement, and the varied refuse of a congested city. The canals were open sewers as well as a means of floating multitudinous craft. As if to reflect the sharp contrasts of the Baroque age, elongated flatboats, nearly hidden under bowers of sweet-scented flowers or loads of bright-hued fruit and vegetables, glided over these fetid waters and past the foul-smelling banks to the markets. On festive occasions larger barges, gaily decorated with pennants and bunting, conveyed the aristocratic society of the capital, including the viceroy and his family, along these odoriferous passages to places of recreation.

Widely scattered about the city were splendid public buildings and ecclesiastical establishments built of neatly quarried stone of brilliant hues and presenting façades of sculptured design, each rivaling the other in intricate patterns of carvings, niches, statues, and pillars. Impressive exhibits of ornate architecture were the palaces of the viceroy, the archbishop, the Royal Audiencia, the Town Council, the structures that housed the busy mint, daily melting the silver bars from the Zacatecas mines, and the University, its lecture halls buzzing with the dull drone of neo-scholastic verbalism. Most elaborately decorated of all were the fifty or more churches, temples, convents, monasteries, and hospitals distributed broadly within the confines of the capital. Dominicans, Franciscans, Augustinians, Carmelites, and Jesuits all vied with each other in the number and magnificence of these buildings and the luxury of their furnishings. The Convent of St. Dominic was counted one of the richest in all the Spanish Indies, while six similar institutions of the Franciscans competed in brilliant ornamentation which seemed strangely at variance with the simplicity and poverty preached by the saintly founder of the Order. Almost as many monasteries with ornate cloisters, dormitories, and refectories housed monks of other communities. And the altars, marble pillars, and interiors of the adjoining chapels glittered with wrought gold and the jewels of images garbed in richest fabrics.

At least sixteen nunneries provided refuge for unmarried daughters of families able to supply dowries, and these cloistered females learned such skills as cooking, needlework, and playing musical instruments as well as routine obligations. If constricted, life for these "brides of Christ" could be pleasantly social. Not all such inmates, however, led quiet, inactive lives, nor were all religious establishments devoted solely to worship and comfortable living. Numerous were the charitable institutions which included some nine hospitals for the care of the sick, the poor, the aged, and the orphans of the community. One of these infirmaries, founded by a viceroy, the Count of Monterrey, was for the Indians. It derived its support partly from the proceeds of the local *corral de comedias*, or theater, where the public attended daily performances of plays by contemporary Spanish dramatists. Cortés, the conqueror, had endowed the Hospital de la Concepción for indigent sufferers, while the Hospital of Saint Hippolytus, one of the wealthiest in the Indies, was an insane asylum. In these institutions many nuns and clergymen spent their lives in noble service, their piety and sacrifice contrasting sharply with the moral laxity and luxury of other ecclesiastics.

The center of the city was the Plaza Mayor, now the Zócalo, a spacious though littered square which served as an important market place. Lining the south and western sides were buildings with arcades through which, sheltered from sun and rain, pedestrians idly sauntered to inspect the silks and fine wares of the bazaars. Often they stopped to haggle with Indian, Negro, or mulatto women squatting by mats covered with fruits, vegetables, and trinkets, offered as wares. Across the square on the east side was the viceroy's palace which, with its gardens and the stout stone prison adjacent, occupied almost the entire length. Its two stories had the appearance of a fort with small towers at the corners, regularly spaced loopholes in the walls, and two great gateways with massive doors. On the north side of the plaza was rising the great mass of the Cathedral, begun in the late sixteenth century. The viceroy preceding Fray García reported that the walls of this rectangular structure, with interior dimensions of 387 by 177 feet, were half of the planned height and that the vaulting of four of the chapels was complete.[4] The long, slow progress of construction was subjecting the original design to changes which marred its architectural unity. Begun when the severely classic spirit exemplified in Philip II's El Escorial prevailed, the lush manner of the Baroque had now modified the plan. Presently the architects reverted to classic influences and the massive pile, though majestic and splendid, would acquire a labored grandeur as it dominated the Plaza Mayor.

If this central square was the focal point of the worship of God and Mammon, several blocks west lay the favorite place of recreation of the aristocratic classes. Called the Alameda, it was a pleasant park of shady trees and walks which lured fine ladies in decorated carriages and sedan chairs, accompanied by slave attendants, and young gallants, mounted on mettlesome steeds, about four o'clock in the afternoon for the much cherished *paseo*. The Viceroy, attended by a stately retinue outshowing all others, frequently honored these occasions by his presence. Everyone came to see and be seen, to consume endless quantities of sweetmeats and drinks, and to promote flirtations and amorous intrigues. These gay and airy moments occasionally experienced violent transitions as jealous swains, contending for a lady's favor, drew swords or daggers and wounded a rival sometimes fatally. The Alameda was often the breeding place of bitter feuds and bloody skirmishes growing out of trivial causes exaggerated out of all proportion by hot-blooded individuals. Yet this park long remained a favorite place for the ostentatious display of luxury in dress, carriages, horses, and servants in which the wealthy indulged their excessive vanity.

The streets leading away from the Plaza Mayor were lined by

shops where goods were manufactured and sold. Certain crafts like, for example, silversmithing monopolized whole blocks which often bore the name of the predominant occupation. Thus there were sections which produced objects of gold as well as silver, precious stones, and feather work, all of exquisite workmanship, while others provided more practical wares such as saddles, ironwork, candles, pastry, furniture, and the like. As a halfway station between Europe and the Far East, and a point of convergence of the trade with outlying provinces of New Spain, including Guatemala, Yucatan, Tabasco, Nueva Galicia, Nueva Vizcaya, and others, Mexico City was an emporium of the most assorted goods, from the fine laces and textiles of Europe to the silks and chinaware of Asia, and from the exotic fruits and herbs of the provinces to the expertly wrought handicrafts of its own artisans.

The transplanted Spaniard, like his kinsmen at home, lived much of his life in the streets, enjoying the continuous jostle and animation of bustling activity and of endless throngs. At almost any hour of the day gilded coaches of the gentry, attended by brocaded lackeys, passed by. Thomas Gage alleged that in 1625 there were some fifteen thousand of these vehicles whose trimmings of gold, silver, and Chinese silk outshone anything that the Court of Madrid had to offer. In this busy traffic mingled sedan chairs, whose bejeweled occupants swung rhythmically to the trotting pace of the uniformed bearers, squeaking carts with ponderous, solid wheels, haughty riders on horseback with silverstudded saddles on gay yellow blankets, and raucously braying donkeys laden with faggots, charcoal, chicken coops, and strings of red-clay pottery. Weaving about these vehicles, mounts, and beasts of burden moved a throng of pedestrians representing the whole spectrum of a society of class, caste, and race. Clergymen and friars in black, brown, and grey habits of plain cloth strode among the crowd as ladies in bright *basquiñas* or petticoats, their faces plastered with powder, lipstick, and artificial beauty spots, picked their way over the cobblestones or rutted surface in satin high-heeled *chapines* or slippers, followed by pages holding parasols over their mistresses. Lordly gentlemen strutted under large plumed hats, displaying silver or pearl-hilted swords as insignia of their rank. With an easy disdain they ignored the submissive, ragged Indians in rough sandals and dirty *sarapes;* the garrulous *léperos,* or beggars, even more ragged and bare, who wandered aimlessly about reciting incoherent ballads, whining out their ills, or muttering prayers; the old hags with wrinkled faces hardly visible under their *rebozos*, or shawls, counting the beads of a rosary, or patting *tortillas* with rhythmic precision, or mutely vending pitiful wares spread out on straw mats; and the cursing muleteers guiding their docile but occasionally obdurate animals through this maze. Now and then these haughty gentlemen dropped the mask of disdain to turn and leer at a buxom mulatto wench passing by, her black and shiny breasts bare under strings of beads, a small bodice revealing her midriff, and a tight, flaming petticoat emphasizing the enticing movement of her hips. Lascivious Spaniards and Creoles preferred these blackamoor Jezebels to their white wives, and many a dusky Thais thus won her freedom and wore finery and jewels rivaling those of the *grandes dames* of the viceregal court. Indeed, in this strange Baroque society, where moral looseness jostled with ascetic practices, it was not rare to observe a dark-skinned strumpet prancing along the public way in a fetching array of silk, lace and ribbon, while a patched *zaramullo*, or ragged Creole, slunk miserably by, ignored and despised.

An almost continuous counterpoint of the street noises was the sound of bells. Life seemed ruled by an infinite tintinnabulation which filled the air day and night, usually loud and clamorous, sometimes lugubrious and mournful. From churches and chapels came melancholy tones of *Ave Marías* and the solemn notes of the Angelus, but more clangorous bells seemed to pick up these slow strains and accelerate them with rapid, resonant strokes maintained interminably. At times the din rose to a hammered crescendo calculated to deafen the ears and shatter the nerves of the most impassive. In the vicinity of the convents the tinkling of smaller bells regulating the routine of inmates day and night might be heard against the clanging cacophony of the belfries. Even after the ten o'clock curfew, which emptied the streets of all save an occasional furtive figure and the *ronda*, or police, making the rounds with lighted lanterns, the comparative silence was broken by the low pealing of bells summoning friars and nuns to nocturnal devotions. In days of public mourning the racket of pounding yielded to a slow, measured, and lugubrious tolling whose melancholy monotony worked its own tensions on distraught hearers by inspiring morbid reflections on the inexorable destiny of mortals and the need for repentance.[5]

Cultural life in this animated community, at least for the privileged few, was rich. The abundance of the realm permitted ample leisure for the arts and letters, a fact, as already evident, which attracted writers from abroad and stimulated local talent. Indeed, seventeenth century Mexico City was "the Athens of America" and, as a distinguished Spanish critic wrote, it ". . . continued being the literary metropolis of the New World, famed for the learning of its schools, the cultivation of its citizens, and for the care and distinction with which our Spanish was spoken."[6] The Mexican Court, as in contemporary Madrid and Lima, teemed with poets of minor stature whose lyric and satiric effusions, much of which proved ephemeral and have, perhaps happily, disappeared, constituted the bulk of the literature produced.

If lacking in genius a few local writers, some of whom were mestizos or even Indians, produced enduring works. Conspicuous as a chronicler and collector of the Aztec lore of the Lake Texcoco region was Don Fernando de Alva Ixtlilxochitl (1568-1648), whom William H. Prescott in his *Conquest of Mexico* called "the Livy of Anahuac." He was a descendant of the only Texcocan chieftain who remained loyal to Cortés during the siege of Mexico City, and for this fidelity his heirs had enjoyed aristocratic privileges in the viceregal community. When Fray García Guerra, for whom he served as interpreter, arrived in 1608, De Alva was compiling his *Chichimecan History,* a record of the achievements of his native forebears. His assiduous collection of the data, legends, and lore of the pre-Hispanic peoples of the Valley of Mexico inspired Lew Wallace, author of the popular nineteenth century novel, *The Fair God,* to attribute his tale to a chronicle allegedly found among De Alva Ixtlilxochitl's papers, thus employing a timeworn device of storytellers. This Indian nobleman also left much verse called "mestizo elegies" because they incorporated into Castilian themes elements of Nahuatl poems coming down from the Texcocan emperor, Netzahualcoyotl. A nostalgic and melancholy charm infuses much of this poetry whose hybrid nature was genuinely Mexican.

More widely esteemed is a famous sonnet attributed to an obscure Augustinian clergyman living at Tiripitío in Michoacán about 1620, by name Miguel de Guevara (1585?-1646?). Celebrated as a perfect example of Christian poetry, it reads:

### TO CHRIST CRUCIFIED

I am not moved to love Thee, O my Lord,
By any longing for Thy Promised Land;
Nor by the fear of hell am I unmanned
To cease from my transgressing deed or word.
'Tis Thou Thyself dost move me,—Thy blood poured
Upon the cross from nailed foot and hand;
And all the wounds that did Thy body brand;
And all Thy shame and bitter death's award.
    Yea, to Thy heart am I so deeply stirred
That I would love Thee were no heaven on high,—
That I would fear, were hell a tale absurd!
    Such my desire, all questioning grows vain;
Though hope deny me hope I still would sigh,
And as my love is now, it should remain.[7]

Closer to the Court of Mexico and enjoying a sort of poet laureateship was a native of Spanish Extremadura, Árias de Villalobos (1568- ? ), whose life passed almost entirely in Mexico. His precocious way with words won him a contract to compose the annual morality play, and the Royal Audiencia of the capital commissioned him to write a versified *jura*, or oath, of submission to Philip IV on his accession in 1621. Árias de Villalobos, in a similar manner, signalized the centennial of the Spanish Conquest, and was a conspicuous participant in many poetic contests of the time. These literary activities temporarily brought him a distinction which exceeded that of his contemporary, Bernardo de Balbuena, whose latter years were spent in Jamaica and Puerto Rico. Though Árias de Villalobos' subject matter was usually Mexican, his art reflected too faithfully the artificiality of Baroque fashion.

Four printing presses functioned in 1620, but few of their products were more than utilitarian "job-printing." One of the more literary publications of that year was a curious work entitled *Los Sirgueros de la Virgen,* quite possibly inspired by Cervantes' pastoral novel, *Galatea.* Written by Francisco Bramón, a counselor of the Royal University of Mexico, it vaguely resembled its model, though preoccupied by the theme of the Immaculate Conception

which, in New Spain, had the force of dogma, rather than by the
customary mournful amours of rustics. Combining musical prose
and lyric verse, this short narrative is sometimes considered a rudimentary novel.

As a center of varied cultural life Mexico City did not lack
books, nor was the available printed literature limited to the professional requirements of the clergy who were important book
buyers of the community. In an age when religion was the dominant thought of men, works of this nature, whether from the local
presses or imported from Spain, overshadowed all others and constituted the chief stock in trade of the local booksellers. Yet the latter
sold surprising quantities of purely secular writings, fiction, poetry,
plays, history, and other nonfiction, not only to the substantial lay
public of the viceregal capital and outlying regions, but also to the
many churchmen who found relaxation in popular works. Many
of the convents and monasteries possessed rich libraries which
steadily grew in size and variety, while the lordly officials of the
state, merchants, wealthy Creoles, and even individuals in humbler
categories, owned book collections of impressive proportions. Much
evidence of their existence emerges from notarial records of the
period, such as inventories, wills, promissory notes, and the like,
and even from the surviving archives of the overly maligned
Inquisition.

The efforts of the Holy Office to combat the spread of heresy
have left an impression that it severely censored, or excluded, all
literature save that of orthodox theology. This institution did, of
course, adopt precautionary measures against the admission and
circulation of heretical writings in the viceroyalty, and for its files
it did demand from time to time lists of books in private and commercial hands. Most often, however, this requirement was a mere
checking and not a confiscation, and the resulting records provide
valuable, if incomplete, indications of the literature being read.
In 1620, for example, a certain Simón García Becerril of Mexico
City submitted to the Inquisition an inventory of his small personal library, supplying abbreviated titles.[8] Nothing in this document suggests that he was the object of criminal proceedings, or
that his book collection was confiscated. Rather, it appears a merely
routine check-up on the part of the policing agency. The identity
of García Becerril is obscure, for the list bears only his signature,

rubric, and the succinct statement: "These are the books which I possess and declare." Other sources mention a schoolmaster named Juan García Becerril at the time, possibly a relative. Of more significance, however, are his books.

A recent Spanish scholar has remarked: "If a personal library reveals the spirit of its owner, how much more true this is in periods when the scarcity of accessible book collections, the rarity of books themselves, and their excessive cost, oblige the collector to make his purchases with greater care and at larger sacrifice than is the case nowadays."[9] Hence, even so small a group of volumes may be representative of the reading preferences of ordinary citizens in Old Mexico during the first decades of the seventeenth century.

Omitting from consideration the religious writings which, in this layman's library, were unusually few, it will suffice to notice an occasional item of nonfiction while commenting on the purely creative literature that probably entertained the owner. Of special interest among belles-lettres is the variety of Italian works present, several in the original language, which testifies to the close cultural and political ties of the Spanish and Italian peninsulars since the fifteenth century and earlier. The importance of these works of Italianate origin in García Becerril's collection lies in the fidelity with which it reflects the current tastes of the mother country in a remote center of the New World.

Besides a *Dictionary of the Tuscan Language,* the *De Claris Mulieribus,* and *The Labyrinth of Love,* a prose satire against the widows of Florence—the last two being works of Boccaccio—there appear *La Cortegiana* (1524), a comedy by the sardonic and sometimes pornographic Pietro Aretino;[10] the *Tragedy of Phedra,* by the less known Francesco Boza Candioto; and the *Arcadia* of Sannazaro, a pastoral novel and the inspiration of so much falsification of rural life in European literature. All these García Becerril possessed in Italian, with a Spanish version accompanying the last named work.

Even more celebrated representatives of Italian letters are present in Castilian garb. Aside from the Latin poet Vergil, the most prominent is the often reprinted rendition of Ariosto's *Orlando Furioso,* an epic poem which fascinated readers everywhere and influenced writers of Spain's Golden Age. Of scarcely less renown is the *Jerusalem Liberated* of Torquato Tasso, who helped to mould the expression of many Spanish poets. Perhaps the most robust exemplar of Italian influences was Alonso de Ercilla (1533-1594), whose vigorous *La Araucana* drew inspiration from the author's participation in the campaigns against the Araucanian Indians of Chile. Considered the best historical poem in Castilian, it was certainly a popular success. Its three parts are present in the Mexican collection along with the Portuguese epic of Luis de Camoëns (1525-1580), *The Lusiads,* which recounts the exploits of his nation in another part of the globe during the great Age of Discovery. Local pride as well as a taste for lyric verse probably account for the copy of *The Grandeur of Mexico City,* which Bernardo de Balbuena had written in the tercets of Dante.

García Becerril was evidently partial to such devout verse as the *Vergel de Flores Divinas* (1582), (Garland of Divine Flowers) by a sixteenth century native of Toledo, Juan López de Úbeda, and the more interesting *Flores de Poetas Ilustres de España* (1605), (Garland of Illustrious Poets of Spain) which, in some respects, opened the era of Baroque verse. It was compiled by Pedro Espinosa (1578-1650), one of the minor poets of his time who, crossed in love, gave evidence of the enduring influence of romances of chivalry by becoming a hermit after the manner of Amadis of Gaul on the Peña Pobre, and so suggests that Cervantes had contemporary objects for his satire in *Don Quixote.* Espinosa's poetry had the sensuous, decorative, and ornate character, and the relative absence of content, that characterized much Baroque expression.

Miscellaneous works in the less esteemed medium of prose formed about two-thirds of García Becerril's collection. The most notable title was *The Tragi-comedy of Calixto and Melibea,* the first genuinely European novel which appeared in 1499. Written in dialogue form by a converted Jew, Fernando de Rojas, this Romeo and Juliet-like tale is eclipsed by the lifelike portrayal of minor characters, particularly the old procuress, Celestina, who so far overshadows the other protagonists that the novel is best known by her name. Its realistic depiction of low life and the contrast of idealistic and erotic love captured a permanent audience at home and abroad. Translated in 1631 by James Mabbe as *The Spanish Bawd,* it exerted an influence on English literature. Though its subject matter and frank language might have incurred the displeasure of the Inquisition as a work contrary to good morals—

rules laid down by the Council of Trent were fairly explicit on this head—it is significant that specific expurgation was first required in the *Index of Prohibited Books* issued in 1632, a dozen years after García Becerril reported his copy to the Holy Office.

Only one other novel appeared in the collection, the greatly inferior *Desengaño de Celos* (Jealousy Undeceived) by Bartolomé López de Enciso. It reflects the current taste for the unreality of pastoral fiction, mingling artistic prose and verse. Cervantes had sardonically consigned this narrative to the bonfire in the courtyard consuming so many of Don Quixote's bibliographical treasures with little immediate effect, apparently, on the reading public. That same year of 1620 it was still read from one end of the Spanish empire in America to the other, judging by a notarized sale of one hundred and forty books on the public square of Lima which were destined for the still more remote outpost at Concepción in Chile. On September 19, 1620—only three days after the Pilgrims embarked for the rock-bound coast of New England—the transaction was completed and the volumes started for the scarcely less inhospitable settlement in South America, still beset by attacks of savage Indians, and where leisure for reading seemed unlikely. The shipment contained volumes of pious verses as well, four copies of Mateo Alemán's *Guzmán de Alfarache,* and a copy of *Jealousy Undeceived,* whose artificiality must have contrasted sharply with the harsh reality of pioneer life in Chile.[11]

If prose fiction was rare in this Mexican library, essays were numerous. These varied from *El Estudioso Cortesano* (The Learned Courtier), a collection of proverbs by the Erasmist scholar, Lorenzo Palmireno, to the translated *Epistles* of Cicero, noted for their fluid style, and the *Familiar Epistles* of one of the most influential sixteenth century writers, Antonio de Guevara (1480?-1545). His mannered style and lavish imagery foreshadowed the Baroque fashions clearly evident in 1620.

García Becerril's inventory clearly suggests that music as well as reading was a hobby. There he listed four different manuals on guitar-playing, the *Músicas de Vihuela* of four leading authorities, Luis Milán, Enríquez de Valderrávano, Fuenllana, and Narváez. Classic as well as popular music was an art universally cultivated in colonial Mexico, and perhaps never more devotedly than during the seventeenth century. Both the conquered Indians and the

Spanish masters had musical aptitudes of high order, and between 1530 and 1680 at least three major composers flourished in New Spain. The most notable was Juan Gutiérrez de Padilla (d. 1664), originally a singer in the Puebla Cathedral whose great talent was developing in 1620. He was soon to prove the equal of any Peninsular composer in manipulating the sonorities and in investing his music with the somber magnificence of famous masses and magnificats. Every musical form of the Baroque he essayed, arranging impressive works for double choirs, and composing masses, motets, Marian antiphons, and carols that have been preserved.[12] But, while the naves of cathedrals and chapels resounded with the exalted strains of liturgical music by the best composers at home and abroad, outside these majestic walls the strumming of melodic and rhythmic improvisations, more plaintive than gay, on guitars was heard on every street corner and square. Somewhere in the city the obscure García Becerril apparently added his notes and flourishes with a skill which he strove to improve by the help of the best manuals available.

The inventory of this seemingly intelligent layman of a rudimentary middle class of the viceregal capital presents some curious omissions. The classics of antiquity, for example, have merely a token representation in translated versions of Vergil and Cicero. Is this symptomatic of declining interest in a Renaissance humanism? The complete absence of plays is surprising when the Spanish theater was in the full flush of Baroque splendor, and the drama in printed form was popular reading. And one looks in vain for any appreciation of the supreme genius of Cervantes, so recently deceased. On the other hand, the abundance of poetry, lyric and epic, much of it written under Italian influence, appears a more authentic index of prevailing tastes which clearly leaned toward the mannered expression of the late Renaissance and the early Baroque. But whatever other deductions may be drawn from this book list it is clear that, in the year of 1620, the inhabitants of the century-old realm of New Spain could indulge a fancy for polite letters of far wider range than could the struggling settlers of contemporary Jamestown, or the new arrivals at Plymouth who had little to solace their hardships besides their Bibles and Captain John Smith's inadequate *Description of New England*.[13]

# THE STRANGE CASE
# OF THE CURIOUS
# BOOK COLLECTOR

FRAY GARCÍA GUERRA, arrayed in his episcopal robes, stood by an altar in the partially constructed Cathedral of Mexico. He was fulfilling a routine obligation as primate of the viceregal Church—administering the sacrament of Confirmation to members of his flock deemed fit to enter upon the privileges of the Faith. Those presented at this solemn rite were mostly small children dressed in white and accompanied by proud parents and *padrinos*, or godfathers. There is no reason to suppose that, among these eager young aspirants, Fray García took particular notice of an awed little boy, baptized Melchor Pérez de Soto, nor is it likely that the thought passed through the Archbishop's mind that presently this tiny lad, as an architect and builder, would help to further the construction of the unfinished Cathedral in which he was officiating. And much less could any one present at this ceremony have foretold that this child of such touching innocence would die tragically in the dungeons of the Inquisition accused of being remiss to the Faith into which he was being formally ushered.[1]

Melchor Pérez de Soto was born in 1606 under the shadow of the great Indian pyramid at Cholula near the city of Puebla. His father, a mason by trade, had come from Galicia in Spain, the son of humble peasants, and had married the daughter of a Creole family of aristocratic pretensions. Her father, Sebastián de Espinosa, was the alleged descendant of a hidalgo and conquistador of Cholula, while her mother hailed from Guatemala. Shortly after Melchor's birth the family moved to Mexico City where, presumably, his father could profitably work at his craft. The child early learned to read and write in the private schools of Francisco Clavijo and Juan García Becerril, the latter possibly related to Simón García Becerril, owner in 1620 of a small book collection. Later young Melchor began to study Latin but soon abandoned this effort and apprenticed himself to his father's trade. This failure to master the current language of learning had unforeseen consequences which cost him dearly. But if this Creole builder never acquired the formal education of a scholar and gentleman of his time, he did develop a passion for books. In due course his house was cluttered with the boxes and trunks in which he stored his many volumes on almost every subject. These purchases must have absorbed no small part of his modest income judging by the comment of a later colonial figure who stated: "There is another matter worthy of mention which . . . clearly testifies to the love and affection of Mexicans for literature. I refer to the high cost of books, so excessive indeed that they cost us (imported) three and four times as much, and even more, as they do in Europe . . ."[2] Pérez de Soto probably did not read all of his collection—many volumes were in the Latin that he never mastered—and it is likely that, with the true ardor of a bibliophile, he bought many for the sheer delight of possession.

At what stage in his career he began to acquire his library, which now appears one of the finest of seventeenth century Mexico in private hands, is unknown, but the recorded total of 1,663 volumes must have been the result of many years of assembling, given his meager means and busy life as a workman. In 1628 he married Leonor de Montoya, a native of Florida. Illiterate like the majority of the women of her time, her husband's mania must have seemed incomprehensible. She bore him eight or nine children, all of whom died in infancy or childhood. Perhaps it was his extravagant devotion to his hobby that obliged her to supplement his wages by opening their home to roomers, an economic measure which inadvertently contributed to her spouse's undoing. The household also included two young girls, admittedly products of extramarital pursuits of the bookish Melchor.

In the years following his marriage his life appears uneventful. While his wife's energies must have been wholly absorbed by domesticity, the architect-builder immersed himself more deeply in his bibliographical interests. Seemingly, however, the year 1643 provided a break in this quiet routine. Lively rumors of pearl fisheries along the coasts of Lower California caused considerable excitement in the capital, and a maritime expedition under Admiral Pedro Porter de Casanate was organized to reconnoiter the region. This distinguished officer, a Knight of the Spanish Order of Saint James, possessed an intellectual curiosity that moved him to peep into odd corners of knowledge, some quite unorthodox. Perhaps it was a mutual concern for curious bits of learning that drew this gentleman and Pérez de Soto together, for he appointed the latter a captain of one of the ships with a crew of thirty men. Among other things the Admiral liked to cast horoscopes, in which prohibited exercise he had developed considerable skill. The three months together on what proved a fruitless undertaking apparently stirred in Pérez de Soto a desire to venture into the dangerous shallows of Astrology into which his influential companion had piloted him.

Upon his return from Lower California the architect-builder had little opportunity to pursue this fascinating subject, for his well established professional reputation caused the viceroy to send him on a mission of inspection to the damaged fort at San Juan de Ulloa. Scarcely back in Mexico City from this assignment he departed on a trip to some mines at Tetela with his brother-in-law. These interruptions possibly diverted his mind temporarily from his new interest but a seed was planted that would grow and presently involve him in fatal consequences.

After these various excursions in 1643, Pérez de Soto resumed the quiet tenor of his way, spending much time with his books and acquiring many more in varied fields. His extensive knowledge and studious habits doubtless impressed those about him, perhaps arousing suspicions among his uncultivated fellow craftsmen, jealous of the reputation which had won him the coveted appointment of chief mason on the uncompleted Cathedral and other important buildings. There was something queer, it seemed, about a person who spent his spare time poring over strange tomes and perhaps dabbling in occult matters.

And it was true, as the inventory of his book collection later revealed, that this capable artisan was allowing his curiosity to carry his mind over a wide range of secular subjects, most of them well removed from the "divine science" of theology and religion. Of special significance was a group of a hundred or more volumes pertaining to astrology, astronomy, and related subjects. It seemed as if the inquisitive, exploring mind of Pérez de Soto, after wandering about the intellectual map, had found astrology, palmistry, and similar black arts a congenial resting place for his curiosity and enthusiasm.

These pseudo sciences, with their associations of sorcery, necromancy, and magic, possessed a morbid fascination for the superstitious classes of a neomedieval society, and many dark practices found adherents even among the literate and more cultivated elements.[3] Some stealthily cast horoscopes, read palms, and made predictions by unhallowed means of divination despite the efforts of the Holy Office to stamp out all such forbidden practices. Even clergymen were known to dabble in these matters, and the Chair of Mathematics at the University of Mexico included formal instruction in astrology as an aid to the compilation of almanacs. Particularly seductive was "judiciary" astrology which sought to read the future in the stars. This activity the Church vigorously assailed through its secular arm, the Inquisition, which institution, as recently as 1616, had issued an edict forbidding, on pain of total excommunication, illicit practices, including the casting of horoscopes. "There is no human art or science capable of manifesting the things which are to come," the Holy Office had declared, "when they are dependent on the will of man, for this has been reserved by God our Lord for Himself, with His eternal wisdom."[4] Even so stern a stricture did not discourage clandestine interest and the book-loving Pérez de Soto found its fascination irresistible.

About 1650 it appears that he aroused the suspicions of the Inquisitors who began to form a dossier on him. That year they had arrested a freed mulatto named Gaspar Rivero Vasconcelos, whom they charged with possible heresy, defamation of the Holy Office, and practicing astrology. As usual in such matters these judicial authorities urged the accused to do his "Christian" duty both by confessing his misdeeds and by informing on persons known to him to have committed sins of any sort. Doubtless hoping that compliance would soften the severity of the judges, Rivero gave testimony against several individuals, among them Pérez de Soto. This person, he alleged, on more than one occasion had loaned him treatises on astrology; moreover, he had even employed the mulatto to translate some of them from Latin to Spanish. And earlier, before starting on a journey to Yucatan, Rivero had left all his papers with the architect; subsequently, when he returned to Mexico City and demanded their return, Pérez de Soto coolly reported that he had lost them.

Whatever importance the Inquisitors attached to these statements it evidently was not enough for them to take action, and two years elapsed without adding anything to the dossier. Then it was that a former roomer in Pérez de Soto's house made damaging disclosures. He was a scribe, named Nicolás de Robles, who had also made translations from Latin for the architect. Halfway through one of the volumes he came across a discussion of free will and the prediction of the future. Fearing that the book was heretical, Robles had confided his misgivings to a clergyman who urged him to report the matter to the Inquisition. He decided, however, to finish the translation first as otherwise his quick-witted employer might divine his intention to denounce him to the Holy Office. But Robles added he had not actually seen Pérez de Soto practicing astrology. Nor did this testimony move the Inquisitors to press charges against a man whose services were so useful in the construction of the Cathedral. Instead, they continued to maintain a posture of watchful waiting.

As the months passed further bits of evidence accumulated. A garrulous student, José de la Cruz Benites, one of various translators hired by the bibliophile, decided that he must unbosom himself to the Inquisition officials. He rattled off a series of allegations concerning his former employer, including his possession of banned books, his formulation of remarkably accurate predictions, his casting of horoscopes, and related activities. A number of women also came to unburden consciences to the vigilant Inquisitors, asserting that Pérez de Soto had read their palms and made prognostications. By late 1654 the dossier was bulky with testimony indicating that the injudicious architect was not only guilty of horoscopy and of owning forbidden books, but also of using sorcery to discover stolen property. The moment for action had arrived, the judges decided. On January 12, 1655 they dispatched the familiars of the Holy Office to seize the person of Melchor Pérez de Soto, whether or not he had sought sanctuary in a "church, monastery, or other sacred or privileged place," and to sequestrate all his books and manuscripts.

Well before his arrest the Creole bibliophile must have had intimations of the difficulties into which his ill-advised hobby was leading him for, when the officers came in the evening with summonses to his house, he temporarily evaded detention by entering through a side entrance and locking the front door. But this stratagem merely delayed the event until the following morning when, bringing his own bed and fifty-eight *reales* to pay for his food, he was confined in the jail of the Inquisition.

For many weeks he remained incommunicado and in solitary confinement, interrupted now and then by brief hearings before the judges. Though uninformed of the charges against him he readily guessed their nature and stoutly declared his innocence of any evil intent. He denied being remiss to his Christian obligations, he asserted that, because of his ignorance of Latin, he had hired the translation of his books merely to ascertain their contents—among them were geometrical treatises that, in his profession as architect, he needed to know about—and he alleged that his predictions in no way refuted the doctrine of free will. The judges listened impassively and returned him to his cell with an injunction to make a total recall of his transgressions. This was customary judicial procedure designed to wear down the resistance of the prisoner who was presumed guilty until innocence was established. Justice was slow and the Court's patience was long. In desperation the accused frequently demanded hearings to confess even more than happened in the hope that the judges would relent and close his case. Meanwhile, witness after witness appeared before the Inquisitors, unbeknown to the hapless prisoner, to give testimony against him. One of those who thus added to the record declared that he had been acquainted with Pérez de Soto for thirty years and that he knew him to be dabbling in astrology during the last fifteen of them.

As the weeks of solitary confinement passed into months the accused architect grew profoundly despondent. The separation from his beloved library rendered his lot far more cruel than that of his illiterate fellow captives, and he implored the jail attendant to bring him just one book to divert him from the somber thoughts that oppressed him. Moved by the abject misery of his charge the sympathetic jailor cautiously slipped into his hands a treatise on the duties of a good monarch and his subjects, and later stealthily supplied him with writing materials. For these acts of charity the compassionate turnkey was later tried by the unpitying Inquisition and sentenced to four years of labor in the Hospital de Nuestra Señora de la Concepción.

Sinking ever more deeply into dark depression, Pérez de Soto read and reread this dull guide in his tiny cell until he almost knew it by heart. His ink and paper he used to pen a pathetic epistle to his wife, blaming his enemies for his plight. His mind often reverted to his work on the Cathedral—he had been working out a scheme for transferring the huge bells of the old Cathedral to the lofty belfries of the new when misfortune overtook him—and he wrote a barely decipherable missive instructing a workman on the execution of a constructional detail. Neither communication reached its destination, for the Inquisition authorities intercepted them to add to the bulky proceedings.

Anxiety, frustration, and isolation were rapidly unhinging the prisoner's mind. The only sound of the outside world penetrating into the dark recesses of his cell was the melancholy tolling of the Cathedral bells, and he strove to interpret the meaning of their slow strokes. More and more this distant ringing obsessed him, haunting his distraught spirit, filling him with foreboding as if it were the dread warning so poignantly expressed in the words of Macbeth: "Hear it not, Duncan, for it is a knell that summons thee to heaven, or to hell."

The mental deterioration of Pérez de Soto did not escape the notice of the Inquisitors who relaxed their severity enough to counsel him not to abandon hope but to bow to the Divine Will. This gentle admonition was hardly adequate to the need of their afflicted victim, and his utterances became almost incoherent. The stern judges doubtless believed that considerations of genuine charity decided them to lessen his solitude and relieve his melancholy by allowing him a cellmate. They selected a mestizo fellow prisoner, Diego Cedillo by name, who accordingly moved into the narrow quarters of the now unbalanced book collector.

When the jailer made his rounds the next morning at seven o'clock a sickening sight met his gaze on looking into the cell. Sprawled at the foot of his prison cot lay the battered body of the demented Pérez de Soto, while cowering in a corner was the half-caste, his hands and face spattered with blood and his clothes in tatters. The hastily summoned Inquisitors immediately questioned the trembling cellmate who, in broken phrases, gave his version of the tragedy. After extinguishing the candle the night before, the insane architect had crawled over to the sleeping form of Cedillo and seized him by the throat with the manifest intention of choking him to death. The mestizo awoke and grappled with his assailant in the blackness of the tiny cell. During the fierce scuffle Cedillo's hand encountered a loose stone with which he struck down the maddened Pérez de Soto, killing him with repeated blows. The investigators discovered some discrepancies in Cedillo's account and an autopsy performed upon the dead man did not entirely corroborate his story. Further efforts to determine the exact circumstances of the killing came to an abrupt end, however, when, a few days later, the body of Cedillo was found hanging from a beam of his cell by a rope made of a twisted bedsheet.

Meanwhile, the remains of the ill-fated bibliophile, wrapped in a Carmelite habit, were buried in the Saint Dominic monastery. Only when her husband's effects were brought home did the distracted wife fully sense what had happened. Screaming hysterically, she flung herself upon a bed where a merciful unconsciousness presently enveloped her.

After taking Pérez de Soto into custody the agents of the Holy Office promptly carried off his library for minute inspection by the *correctores,* or censors, of that institution. Confiscation of an accused person's property was a normal formality of judicial procedure and the owner's rights were deemed adequately protected by a written inventory preserved in the legal proceedings. The inquisitional representatives, accordingly, made a hasty list of the books, seemingly in the order that they were found in boxes and trunks, without apparent classification and with abbreviated titles. The exact number remains in doubt owing in part to the carelessness of the compilers, and in part to an unsuccessful effort of Doña Leonor to protect her husband by withholding volumes that she thought incriminating. Her indiscreet remarks in this connection quite nullified her laudable intention, for the Inquisition thus learned of her action and soon placed the missing works with the others in its possession, making a probable total, as already suggested, of 1,663 volumes.

This remarkable collection is much too large and varied for detailed analysis. It included not only an amazing diversity of religious literature, secular nonfiction, and belles-lettres in such different languages as Latin, Italian, French, Flemish, Dutch, and even English, but much in the owner's native Spanish. The prevalence of Italian and Italianate writers and works noted earlier in García Becerril's personal library is here more amply confirmed by the presence of such names as: Dante, Petrarch, Guicciardini, Guarini, Sannazaro, Ariosto, Tasso, and Castiglione in pure literature, and of many others in more technical fields. It is an astonishing miscellany of books assembled by a man of little formal education and modest means, and its existence testifies both to the wide circulation of printed volumes in Old Mexico and to a high level of culture achieved in this outpost of western civilization in the seventeenth century.

Religious literature, currently the most esteemed, claims about one-third of the total, chiefly homiletic writings by Santa Teresa of Ávila, Saint John of the Cross, Luis de Leon, and Luis de Granada, and many others. Perhaps the most unexpected items were those advocating silent prayer for they seem to anticipate the Quietist heresy about to agitate the Catholic world.

A much larger portion of the works falls into the category of secular nonfiction, with many items relating to history, philosophy, architecture, sculpture, music, medicine, mathematics, military science, navigation, astrology, and astronomy, along with numerous treatises on practical arts such as agriculture, mining, horsemanship, carpentry, cookery, and the like. Of history alone there were over one hundred and fifty titles which traced the story of the world from its beginnings to Pérez de Soto's own time. Conspicuous among the works on astronomy were the names of Copernicus and Kepler who were still suspect in the Orthodox Catholic world of which Old Mexico was a part. Indeed, at the mid-point of the seventeenth century when the Baroque age was in full flower, when the neomedieval culture of theology and scholasticism seemed all pervasive, particularly in the overseas possessions of Spain, such an abundance of scientific, mathematical, and technical literature

in the library of an artisan with no apparent connection to the
intellectual circles of viceregal society is surprising. Almost no field
of knowledge evaded his curiosity, and his aggregation of writings
provides an impressive sampling of the scientific as well as the
esthetic thought of the sixteenth and seventeenth centuries. It
makes evident the fact that, beneath the surface of the excessively
verbalistic learning of the time, there was a hard substratum of
knowledge based on observation and measurement that now and
then had outcroppings in New Spain in figures of solid capacity
and pragmatic erudition.

Although the third category embracing fiction, poetry, fables,
essays, and proverbs claimed only about one-fifth of the collection,
it represented the writings that enjoyed most popularity and were
most widely read throughout the Hispanic world. They were the
books that more frequently passed from hand to hand, particularly
in the New World realms of Spain, and hence a few representative
titles deserve mention.

If García Becerril in 1620 had been content with only two
novels, the famous *Tragi-comedy of Calixto and Melibea* or *La
Celestina,* and an inferior pastoral tale, Pérez de Soto owned two
*dozen* of these prose narratives, not counting numerous novelettes
and short story collections. And some of them hold a surprise for
literary historians accustomed to a long-standing article of faith.
Cervantes' great masterpiece—which is also absent in this inventory—had allegedly given the *coup de grâce* in 1605 to the protracted vogue of the romances of chivalry. This assumption,
enjoying something of the sanctity of dogma, receives a disconcerting jar as the eye roves over this book list of a half century later.
Names of fictional heroes, whose exploits had enraptured sixteenth-
century readers, bob up unexpectedly. *Amadis of Gaul, Lisuarte
of Greece, Amadis of Greece, Don Florisel of Niceae,* in two parts,
recount the familiar adventures of legendary knights, curiously
impervious to the satire of *Don Quixote.* Present also is the rival
dynasty of Palmerin in *Palmerin of Oliva* (in Italian and Castilian), and *Palmerin of England,* and still other tales of this sort
have a place in this mid-seventeenth-century library: *Don Belianis
of Greece, Knight of the Cross,* and the *History and Military Service of Knight Pilgrim,* the last a pious romance designed to lure
readers from the delights of the more mundane species. It is un-

likely that Pérez de Soto's taste in this matter was unique, for these old-fashioned entertainments had some of the durability of modern Westerns. The inventory of the Creole architect's books, therefore, supplies an interesting sidelight on the story of chivalric literature after *Don Quixote*.

Still another shopworn form of reading pleasure—and one of even greater longevity—had charmed this Mexican bibliophile. It was the pastoral novel which told about lovesick shepherds and lassies. Of these saccharine tales he had a goodly number, including Sannazaro's epoch-making *Arcadia* (both in Italian and Castilian), Guarini's *Pastor Fido*, and *Diana*, the first and most famous of these falsifications of peasant life in Spain, written by the Portuguese-Spaniard, Jorge Montemayor (1520?-1561). This bestseller helped to inspire Sir Philip Sydney's *Arcadia* and the *Astrée* of Honoré d'Urfé, and it also influenced Cervantes' *Galatea*, and Old Mexico's own Bernardo de Balbuena's *Golden Age in the Groves of Eriphyle*, the latter two works being among Pérez de Soto's treasures.

For the other extreme of the novelistic spectrum—the crassly realistic and satiric tales of roguery—the architect of Mexico City also indulged a taste. The second part of *Guzmán de Alfarache*, whose famous author he had seen, conceivably, on the streets of the capital in his own childhood, stands beside the brutally cynical *History of the Life of the Buscon* by the great Spanish satirist, Francisco de Quevedo. *The Varied Fortunes of Pindaro, the Soldier,* by Gonzalo de Céspedes (1585?-1638), had the added spice of Gothic eeriness in the picaresque adventures related.

Novelettes and short story collections constitute a large miscellany among which is conspicuous the fourteenth century group of fifty moral tales, *Conde Lucanor,* recounted with subtle humor and irony by the grandson of Ferdinand IV of Castile, Juan Manuel, who thus presented a rich vein later tapped by such geniuses as Shakespeare and Cervantes. And similarly plentiful is the didactic literature of fables, proverbs, and aphorisms, often in dialogue form, beginning with Aesop's *Fables* (in Latin, Flemish, and Spanish). Of special interest is the *Book of Live and Witty, Clever and Sententious Sayings* of the great Dutch humanist Erasmus who, by his own admission, owed much to Spain where, however, various of his writings now adorned the *Index of Pro-*

*hibited Books.* Since García Becerril had submitted his book list to the Inquisition in 1620, the 1623 and 1640 editions of this Index had appeared, each more inclusive and more severe to suspected writers such as "magnus Erasmus."

Poetry had a generous representation in Pérez de Soto's library. The epic is noted in Homer's *Iliad,* Vergil's *Aeneid* (in Latin and Spanish), Dante's *Divine Comedy,* Camoen's *The Lusiads* (in Portuguese and Spanish), Ariosto's *Orlando Furioso,* Tasso's *Jerusalem Liberated,* Ercilla's historical *La Araucana,* and finally Balbuena's enormous *El Bernardo,* much of it written in Mexico. Of lyric verse the Creole architect's inventory almost provides an index from the fifteenth to the seventeenth centuries, including the *Works* of Luis de Góngora (1561-1627), the tutelary deity of Baroque poets and poetasters, particularly in Spanish America.

Among the many historical works present one author deserves a brief comment since his writings are acclaimed for their literary distinction and have a peculiar interest to colonial letters. The Inca Garcilaso de la Vega (1539-1616)—the "first American writer" as he is sometimes called, American in the special sense that he represented a new human species in the New World as the offspring of European and indigenous parents, and dealt particularly with American themes—was the product of a union of a Conquistador and an Incan princess. Born in Cuzco, high in the Andes, he departed for Spain after a childhood spent amidst the alarms of civil strife among the conquering masters. In the Peninsula he passed the rest of his life nostalgically recalling the scenes of his youth and the glories of his imperial ancestors. His *Royal Commentaries of the Incas,* now a classic of colonial literature though written in the mother country, idealized the vanishing civilization of his maternal progenitors. The eloquent simplicity of his style resulted from severe self-discipline in the language of his father gained through rigorous exercise in translation and through the composition of a novelesque account of De Soto's four years wandering in the lower Mississippi valley entitled *The Florida of the Inca.* Both of these artistically written narratives found a place in the admirably selected library of the Mexican Creole.

As a final comment on specific items which appear in Pérez de Soto's inventory, it is of interest to point out a curious coincidence of omission noted in García Becerril's list of 1620. Both collections lack copies of *Don Quixote,* though it is certain that many copies came to Mexico from 1605 on and circulated there. Even more notable is the complete absence in either report of indications of Spanish drama which, in the first half of the seventeenth century and later, was favorite reading fare as well as a popular spectacle throughout the Hispanic world. Odd indeed are these omissions in the personal libraries of two "average" readers of the time.

The existence of this remarkably rounded library in the hands of a relatively humble layman in a region remote from the cultural centers of Europe invites several queries. Where did this Creole of modest means acquire so many volumes? Was he unique in the possession of a collection of books so predominantly secular and nonreligious in nature? What significance is to be deduced from this mid-seventeenth century inventory? Only brief and tentative answers suggest themselves.

It seems reasonably certain that Pérez do Soto purchased his library little by little in local bookshops. Individuals in his circumstances rarely imported, it appears, directly from Peninsular booksellers who, in general, preferred to deal wholesale with colonial merchants. Itinerant peddlers and enterprising persons coming from Spain frequently brought salable volumes in their baggage to help defray the expenses of the voyage, and possibly the Creole bibliophile had acquired items in this manner. The trial proceedings tend to support this theory of local purchase, since one of the witnesses against him, Antonio Calderón, son of the proprietor of the best-established printing and bookshop in the capital, testified that the architect often came to his parent's store where he chatted about his astrological interests. While smuggling of prohibited books was certainly not unknown, it is likely that the Mexican booklover could acquire most of his, including those on his hobby, through legitimate channels.

It is too much to suppose that the arrest of this amateur astrologer revealed the only personal library of such varied works in the entire seventeenth century of Mexico. The earlier, less impressive collection of García Becerril disproves this belief. If one of such modest resources assembled so large and varied an aggregation of books, it is almost certain that wealthier members of the community, laymen as well as clergymen, brought together even richer

assortments. Notarial records, published and unpublished, testify
to the validity of this assertion, and it is hardly necessary to provide
further proof of the inefficacy of earlier legislation against the free
circulation of books, the application of which has been greatly mis-
understood. The presence of so much creative literature and secular nonfiction on colonial book lists, of which Pérez de Soto's
inventory is only one of the more interesting, indicates how little
the Inquisition interfered with acquiring and reading works other
than those of religious heresy. With the exception of astrological
treatises the Holy Office returned in due course the entire collection of Pérez de Soto to his widow. It is clear, therefore, that only a
little short of complete freedom of circulation was permitted in the
Spanish overseas realms and that the variety and richness of the
literary fare enjoyed there far exceeded what was then available to
contemporary New Englanders who had to largely content themselves with the Bible and the locally printed *Bay Psalm Book*
(1640).[5]

It remains, then, to inquire what became of this particular book
collection of mid-century Mexico? Three days after the fateful end
of Pérez de Soto in the dungeons of the Inquisition, a careful ex-
amination of his library was decreed. Prohibited works and those
requiring expurgation, a very small minority, were put aside, and
the much larger number of harmless volumes were divided into
lots and returned to the widow. Less than two months after her
husband's death she received a batch of 524 books, a few days later
416 more, and a third lot of 356 on June 5, 1655. Some 385 titles
were withheld for close scrutiny by the Correctors, but six months
later 304 of them came back to the deceased architect's domicile.
On February 20, 1656, a final group of sixty-three expurgated
volumes was delivered to Doña Leonor—actually the total now
exceeded the number originally listed in the hasty inventory made
by the familiars.

And what became of this remarkable book collection? On December 4, 1655, the impoverished widow begged the Inquisitors to
return all permitted works, and especially "a book whose author is
Argote de Molina, and the *Efemérides modernas,* because I have a
purchaser. And the rest," she added, "I wish to sell as old paper
because they seem such a lot and I am in very needy circumstances."

# ❧ VII

# THE INQUISITION
# AND A PLAY

THE melancholy fate of Pérez de Soto is, unquestionably, a tragic indictment of the Inquisition. Clearly a flagrant miscarriage of justice had precipitated the bookloving architect into an acute manic depression ending in violence and death. The torturing slowness of a due process of law, built on the assumption of guilt until proof of innocence, seems a deliberately malicious procedure calculated to produce outrage and injustice. The methods were undeniably crude and cruel, if not primitive and barbarous, and they fully merit the opprobrium that posterity has so unsparingly heaped upon the tribunal that sanctioned them. Yet critics are unjust who make a sweeping condemnation without allowing the institution a hearing. To be entirely fair the Inquisition must be viewed in its time even more than its place. In that age the presumed guilt of the defendant, the snail-like movement of judicial machinery, its intent to provoke the victim into damaging admissions, the confiscation of property before adjudication, and the resort to physical torture, were legal practices all too common throughout Christendom. In many parts they operated without the restraint that the Holy Office usually exercised, and without the voluminous records that it kept. The surviving documentation is remarkably full and, by a curious irony of historiography, the meticulous detail thus preserved has enabled later generations to single out this particular tribunal for special invective. To the popular mind the Inquisition remains a uniquely sinister and despotic agency which diffused a miasmic pall over the community, darkening individual lives with corroding fear, and shriveling thought to a grisly skeleton of dogma.

This mental image, though with occasional validity, overlooks certain limiting factors. As in most human institutions the degree of severity varied with the character of the administrators and with the existing climate of feeling. Moreover, its power was diminished by jurisdictional and other conflicts with state officials, with business elements fretting at interference with profitable pursuits, and even with the hierarchy of the Church. Quarrels with religious communities on moot matters of doctrine often hampered the undivided sway of the Holy Office and the absolute authority of the Inquisitors. Since viceregal agencies, lay and religious alike, tended to exercise unseparated legislative, executive and judicial powers in performing their functions, each organization was inordinately sensitive about its prerogatives. Paralyzing disputes arising from overlapping jurisdictions were, consequently, almost continuous, and this friction frequently reduced the Spanish system to a vexatious equilibrium. Hence, the Inquisition, representing both Pope and King, often encountered resistance in both lay and ecclesiastical elements of society, and its effectiveness was less complete than commonly believed.

To defend, protect, and maintain "the purity of the Holy Faith and Good Morals" were the repeatedly announced aims of the Holy Office, branches of which Philip II had introduced into Peru and Mexico in 1570 and 1571. Prior to these dates bishops had exercised similar authority in their dioceses much as their predecessors had done in medieval Europe. The religious schisms sundering the Continent, and the determination of Spanish Catholicism to preserve orthodoxy at all costs from the contamination of heresy led to the installation of the Inquisition in outlying parts of the empire. This institution was not a Spanish invention, for it had existed in the Middle Ages and had functioned in Italy since the thirteenth century with little adverse effect on the Renaissance. It was later introduced into Aragon and, when the marriage of Prince Ferdinand of that region and Isabel of Castile established a diarchy in the Spanish Peninsula, it was the one institution common to both kingdoms. With its severity greatly tempered, it passed to the overseas realms of America where the Indian population, clearly recognized as children in the Faith, was specifically excluded from its jurisdiction.

The New World tribunals were staffed by two Inquisitors, or judges, a prosecuting attorney, and varying numbers of *consultores, calificadores,* and *familiares.* The first of these three functionaries were experts who gave advice on technical matters of law and procedure and who often included distinguished members of the viceregal society such as the judges of the Royal Audiencia. The *calificadores* or "qualifiers" were versed in the fine points of theology and their duty was to assay books and ideas for heretical content; hence they acted as censors. The *familiares* performed the pragmatic functions of plainclothesmen, detectives, jail wardens, and informers operating at large in the community. Other employees were constables, accountants, secretaries, lawyers for defense, a physician, jailers, and the like. The court archives were stuffed with wordy records of arrests, confiscations, inventories, transcripts, judicial opinions, and general correspondence. These endless sheaves of repetitive evidence and registers of court decisions that survive offer rich insights into the procedures of a notorious institution, and even more revealing glimpses of Baroque life in Old Mexico.

The emphasis so often placed on the persecution of religious heresy is misleading, for the Inquisition's energies went chiefly into adjudicating crimes and misdemeanors nowadays handled by municipal courts. Offenses of every variety against "good morals" far outnumbered those against "the purity of the Faith." The commonest cases were: bigamy, apparently as usual among women as men; solicitation in the confessional; sexual perversion; blasphemy; perjury; witchcraft; quackery, and superstition in multiple forms; and, finally, the practice of astrology. Prosecution was vigorous and stern edicts carried the authority of laws. Exceptional cases sometimes required instructions from the Supreme Council in Spain, which occasionally was a court of appeal, but generally the local tribunals acted independently, for they commonly confronted problems peculiar to their region. A curious instance appears in an edict of 1620, the year that García Becerril presented his list of books for scrutiny.

Vague reports for a long time had reached the Inquisition concerning the widespread use of a tiny, gray-green, spineless cactus called "peyote" (*Lophophora Williamsii*), possessing remarkable narcotic properties. Back in the middle of the sixteenth century a famous Franciscan missionary and pioneer anthropologist, Friar Bernardino de Sahagún, had noted the intoxicating effect of this plant, and Juan Cárdenas, in his *Primera parte de los secretos maravillosos de las Indias* (First Part of the Marvellous Secrets of the Indies), published in 1591 at Mexico City, had written about hallucinations caused by eating peyote.[1] Knowledge of its use by the Indians was not limited, however, to scientific minds, and the Inquisitors were increasingly aware that other elements of the population were experiencing its peculiar effects. By 1620 the decision to ban it was reached. "Inasmuch as the use of the weed or root called Peyote has been introduced into these Provinces," ran the edict, "for the purpose of detecting thefts, of divining other happenings, and foretelling events, it is an act of superstition and is condemned as opposed to the purity and integrity of our Holy Catholic Faith." The omniscient officers of the Inquisition went on to deny this "weed" some of its demonstrated properties. "This is certain because neither the said weed, nor any other, can possess the virtue, or inherent quality, of producing the effects claimed, nor can any cause the mental images, fantasies, and hallucinations on which the above-stated divinations are based. In these latter are plainly perceived the suggestion and intervention of the Devil, the real author of this vice, who first avails himself of the natural credulity of the Indians and their tendency to idolatry, and later strikes down other persons too little disposed to fear God and of too little faith." Because this abuse was spreading rapidly, the Inquisitors declared that "after consultation and conference with learned and right-minded persons, we order that henceforth no persons of whatever rank or social condition can or may make use of the said weed Peyote, nor of any other kind under any name or appearance for the same or similar purposes, nor shall he make the Indians or any other person take them, with the further warning that disobedience to these decrees shall cause us, in addition to the penalties and condemnations stated, to take action against such disobedient and recalcitrant persons as we would against those suspected of heresy to our Holy Catholic Faith."[2]

Matters of moral turpitude, then, largely preoccupied the Holy Office, while those of purely doctrinal heresy and censorship engaged it more rarely. Though the *calificadores* kept fairly busy checking over newly arrived books and pamphlets, the literature that concerned them was almost exclusively ecclesiastical in character and, as already noted, they seldom hindered the free circulation of secular and fictional works.

The awesome *autos de fe* are usually depicted as occasions when the victims of the Inquisition writhed in the tortures of public incineration while sadistic executioners and cowed masses looked on. Again the common tendency to regard the extreme and the spectacular as typical or, in modern parlance, as newsworthy, has created a distorted impression of reality. The proportion of death sentences was, perhaps, not more than one in a hundred, a ratio far exceeded in contemporary Europe, notably in the days of witchcraft prosecution. The penalties in Mexico were harsh, of course, for everywhere in the seventeenth century brutal punishments publicly administered were the accepted expression of justice, yet a review of the *votos*, or judicial opinions, of the Mexican Inquisitors often reveals unexpected moderation. The judges frequently differed among themselves as to the guilt of the accused, or regarding the proper retribution, and the prosecuting attorney usually abstained from injecting his biased recommendations.[3] Hence it appears, as in every court, justice varied according to personalities and prejudices.

Penalties for the many crimes against "good morals" ranged from penance rendered by marching in public processions, candle in hand and a rope about the neck, or other symbolic indications of guilt, to heavy fines, property confiscations, public whipping, varying periods of banishment from the vicinity or from the realm, and uncompensated service on royal galleys or sailing ships. Death was reserved for the most obstinate heretics, and in especially flagrant cases penalties were compounded. Not long after the establishment of the Holy Office at Mexico City in the late sixteenth century a certain Pedro de Trejo, who included being a poet among his crimes, was condemned not only to public penance and forced service on his Majesty's galleys, but to perpetual renunciation of composing couplets![4] Occasionally the dead received posthumous sentences for offenses subsequently discovered, and punishment was visited upon their effigies or disinterred bones.

After the middle of the seventeenth century, burning at the stake was rare, possibly because the cause of orthodoxy was largely won. The *auto de fe* of 1649, in which 109 persons received sentences of one sort or another, thirteen of whom were put to death, was, apparently, the culminating spectacle of this kind in the viceroyalty of Mexico, though a decade later a smaller one occurred.[5] Among its victims was a mysterious adventurer with illusions of grandeur, an alleged Irishman named Guillén de Lampart, who claimed to be an illegitimate offspring of the king of Spain and aspired to be the Emperor of an independent Mexico. He had, indeed, implicated the Inquisitors, who had imprisoned him, in a fancied conspiracy to detach the viceroyalty from its allegiance, which circumstance may have moved the judges to impose the extreme penalty upon him. During his long years of incarceration— the unhappy Pérez de Soto was briefly a fellow prisoner—Guillén de Lampart had diverted himself by composing in various languages remarkable treatises and literary pieces which survive.[6]

As the century passed its mid-point the routine of the inquisitional tribunal more and more resembled that of a modern police court with petty crimes and misdemeanors filling its docket. Sporadically its censorious activities intensified, and books, pamphlets, and especially plays, continued to receive careful scrutiny, though expurgation and emendation rather than outright prohibition usually resulted from this inspection. It was always expedient to keep a watchful eye on the local theater, which was frequented by the clergy as well as the lay public, for all too often a licentious note crept into the acting of the players, or offensive lines and dubious situations were discovered. But normally the Holy Office limited its interference to the deletion of disapproved passages, after which the play returned to the boards.

The early seventeenth century witnessed the Baroque effulgence of Spain's literary Golden Age, and the most dazzling manifestation of its prolific genius was a popular theater rivaled only by that of England. In the Peninsula a cluster of inspired playwrights burst like rockets in a scintillating display of brilliance and color that drew enthusiastic throngs to the rude playhouses to see and hear the latest comedies from their inexhaustible quills. "In the Castilian drama the stress is on action, on destinies rich in vicissitudes and, at the same time, on the lyrical embellishment of ornate verse," wrote Ortega y Gasset, who likened the prodigious output of the reigning dramatist, Lope de Vega, to painting rather than to sculpture. He declared it "a vast canvas, now luminous, now murky, on which all the figures shine with life and color, noblemen and commoners, archbishops and sea captains, queens and country lasses, a restless, garrulous, extravagant lot, madly swirling about like infusoria in a drop of water . . . ." And the twentieth-century philosopher continues: "Over the varied and intricate pattern of intrigue the poet poured his elaborate volubility, a profusion of glittering metaphors expressed in a vocabulary of darkest shadows alternating with brilliant light, a vocabulary reminiscent of the altar pieces of the same century."[7]

No less enthusiastic were the audiences of the New World capitals and cities who thronged the local *corrales* at the performances of the latest "hit" from Spain. The time lag was slight and, by the turn of the seventeenth century, troupes of Spanish actors entertained the colonial public with recent products of Peninsular dramatists. As early as 1604 Balbuena could metrically declare in his *Grandeur of Mexico City* that:

> entertainments and new comedies every day,
> each with several entr'acts and attractions,
> (give) pleasure, diversion and gaiety.

In the viceregal palace, imitating the luxury of the pleasure-loving court of Philip IV at Madrid, private performances of plays with elaborate costumes and scenery were common features of aristocratic life, while the popular theater offered aspiring Creole writers an opportunity to supply short skits for performance between the acts of the imported comedies. As in Spain these slight pieces served to keep the turbulent audience in check during such interludes.

As the successive decades of the century rolled by the popularity of the theatre remained despite a decline in the quality of plays and actors. Though little is known of the theatrical companies who graced the boards of the Mexican *corrales,* nor are many of the titles of the plays recorded, it appears that, toward the end of the century, the histrionic art in Mexico City had fallen to low estate. In the last ten-year period an Italian traveler, Gemelli Careri, spent a few months there during a remarkable tour of the world. He attended the local playhouse with some regularity and, with equal regularity, he complained to his diary about the inept acting and wretched performances. Under date of April 7, 1698, he wrote: "I went to the theater in the afternoon to see a comedy entitled

*La dicha y desdicha del nombre* (The Good and Bad Fortune of a Name). It was so badly played that I would more gladly have given the two *reales* it cost me to go in and take a seat not to have seen it. The actors performed badly; there were sixteen of them, American born, for Europeans consider it discreditable to play to the general public." The most charitable of his entries was on July 14, 1698: "Sunday I heard something rare in the theater, that is, a comedy decently played."⁸

Among the literate the Spanish drama evoked enthusiasm in print as well as on the stage, and this public avidly snapped up the collections of plays published in dozen lots called *Partes* and the single plays in pamphlet form known as *sueltas*. Imported from Spain, these publications poured into the bookstores from about 1605 and remained a stock in trade until the end of the colonial period. Whether heard in public or read in private this dramatic literature, like the cinematographic art in the twentieth century, exerted a profound influence on contemporary manners and morals. From the pulpits of the time came ringing denunciations in sermons and exhortations. A pious biography of a saint published in 1633 at Madrid loudly protests that ". . . the reading of books of plays was so general in ladies' drawing rooms and in maidens' chambers that women could only feel sophisticated when they talked about a love affair, an amorous difficulty, the vanquishing of male indifference, or the humble devotion of a swain."⁹ Manners, dress, and ways of speaking were subtly modified on both sides of the Atlantic as the three-act plays, in inexpensive editions, attained a universality even greater than that of the romances of chivalry during the previous century. Readers were as absorbed by the shallow intrigues spun by nimble playwrights as their forebears had been by the fantastic adventures of the knights-errant. In Guatemala a chronicler related in shocked tones an incident in which a lady of easy virtue, an actress who had involved two suitors in a murder, impassively read a volume of plays while the men were being executed on the public square. "What I wish to relate so that the readers of these lines may be astonished and learn what women of easy virtue are like is the case of *la Catalina*. They took her to jail and, while they were hanging the two men, she unconcernedly took a seat in a small window facing the square. There she was reading a book of comedies and, when they dropped the body of the first man off the scaffold, she merely glanced up and then resumed reading. When the second man was hung, again she merely looked up and then went on reading her play. Those are the prayers she offered for the men whom she had brought to the gallows!"[10]

Though moralists assailed this diversion with unrelenting vigor this theatrical fare, whether in the form of cold type or live performance, like the earlier fiction of chivalry, never achieved the distinction of a collective ban. Now and then the self-styled custodians of "good morals" forced the withdrawal of a play from the boards and from printed circulation on the grounds of irreverence, disrespect, or downright blasphemy, and these allegations sometimes cloaked other reasons. One such instance occurred in 1682 when the manager of the Mexico City *Coliseo,* a name which had supplanted the plebian *corral de comedias,* was required to omit from the repertory a comedy by the popular Spanish playwright, Juan Pérez de Montalbán entitled *El valor perseguido y traición vengada* (Courage Persecuted, and Treachery Avenged).

Until his death in 1632 the three-act plays of the prolific Lope de Vega, true father of the Spanish theater, dominated the offerings of the stock companies on both sides of the Atlantic. In due course the works of his disciples, together with those of his great successor, Calderón de la Barca (1600-1681), whose theater most perfectly, perhaps, reflected the Baroque spirit, crowded his stage-pieces off the boards during much of the remaining colonial period.[11] An uncritical public grew more indiscriminate and, after the first quarter of the seventeenth century, it bestowed a more lasting favor upon the short-lived, spiritual son of the great Lope, Pérez de Montalbán (1602-1638), storyteller and dramatist of a sort.[12] Despite or, perhaps, because of his mediocre talent, his plays still attracted a colonial audience as late as 1805.

This continued popularity is possibly attributable in part to the enduring success of his short stories and miscellaneous essays, notably a collection, *Para Todos* (For Everyone) inspired by the *Decameron* of Boccaccio. It had the good fortune to draw the fire of the remarkably talented satirist, Francisco de Quevedo (1580-1645), who parodied it in his *Perinola* and thus increased its sales in Spain and abroad.[13] An admiring merchant and bookseller in

Lima, Peru, Tomas Gutiérrez de Cisneros by name, purchased a chaplaincy for the young writer, thus delivering him from the grip of economic insecurity.[14]

Montalbán's playwriting began with a comedy *Morir y disimular* (To Die and Dissemble), written when he was seventeen, and during his remaining nineteen years, which were truncated by insanity, he managed to crowd in some fifty-eight plays in a futile effort to equal the prodigious output of his friend and mentor, that "marvel of nature," Lope de Vega. Like the latter he drew his themes from religious, legendary, historical, and adventure literature, and clothed them in ornate and fluent verse. His characterizations were less competent, and his style betrays more clearly a Baroque artificiality, but like his master, he pleased the masses by exploiting familiar ballads and, occasionally, topics of contemporary notoriety. One such work was his play *La monja-alférez* (Nun-Ensign) which utilizes the experience of a strange woman whose last years passed in Old Mexico.[15]

Catalina de Erauso presents a remarkable phenomenon of a masculinized female whose career became legendary. As a young girl she escaped from a nunnery in Spain and, in the garb of a man, fled to the New World in 1603. During the next twenty-one years her adventurous wanderings took her over the west coast of South America, where she gallantly battled Indians and won a commission as *alférez* or ensign. Her sex undetected, she transferred her activities from Chile to the sprawling realm of Peru, and in the mining camps of the Andes and in the underworld of the cities, she became involved in innumerable escapades, which included gambling, courting unsuspecting maidens, street brawls, and duelling. In an affair of honor she allegedly killed her own brother, her identity unbeknown to him. Only when severely wounded on another occasion was her gender revealed and, under the protection of a bishop, she temporarily resumed feminine apparel. Returning to Europe in 1624, she traveled widely and in Italy her celebrity gained her an audience with the Pope and the lavish entertainment of princes, bishops and cardinals. After some years she returned to the New World, in masculine attire and with an incipient mustachio, to spend her last years as a mule driver in packtrains transporting goods between Vera Cruz and Mexico City. On one of these journeys in 1650 a fatal illness reportedly overtook her and, with as much pomp as the circumstances permitted, she was buried on a hillside near the village of Cuitlaxtla.[16] With the theme of the heroine disguised as a man an indispensable part of the stock in trade of the Spanish theater, Montalbán's use of so newsworthy a personage as the "Nun-Ensign" for a play causes no surprise.[17]

His *Courage Persecuted and Treachery Avenged,* whose improprieties merited the unusual distinction of banishment from the Mexican stage in 1682 by the Inquisition, was certainly not his best comedy nor was it even a good play. Indeed, its esthetic defects might justly have entitled it to proscription, but these were not the reasons that moved the Holy Office to so stern a measure. There exists, to be sure, some doubt regarding the authorship of the play, but the evidence points an accusing finger at Pérez de Montalbán as the true begetter. The following summary may suggest its mediocrity.

## Act I.

Ramón de Moncada, second son of the Count of Barcelona, returns to Naples flushed with a sea victory over the Turks and eager for the Princess Matilde's love. This daughter of the King of Naples invites the hero to her garden after midnight. Durón, who supplies the comic relief, reminds Ramón of his erstwhile interest in Octavia, daughter of the Duke of Ferrara, and warns of a possible mischance in his rendezvous with the Princess. Count Arnesto, the rejected suitor of Matilde, plots to keep the appointment in place of Ramón and induces the King to detain his rival that night. With Ramón thus held in a game of chess Count Arnesto, mistaken by Matilde in the darkness for Ramón, is admitted and enjoys her favors. The servant Durón, sent by Ramón to watch at Matilde's balcony, falls asleep but awakens to see Arnesto leaving the house. Ramón, arriving later, learns that he has been tricked and, though the Princess from her balcony asks why he fled her arms so abruptly and invites him to return, he believes himself ill-fated and resolves to return to Spain. Durón urges him to go by way of Ferrara and seek Octavia whom he formerly loved.

## Act II.

Princess Matilde confesses her dishonor to her father, the King, and demands that her disgrace be avenged. This apparent betrayal and Ramón's subsequent marriage to Octavia angers the King, who seeks Arnesto's aid in bringing Ramón back by guile. Arnesto, fearing discovery of his own guilt, urges that Ramón be compelled to kill Octavia and marry the Princess. Reluctantly the King acquiesces. In an abrupt change of scene Octavia, with forebodings of disaster to her husband, tells Durón of the King's summons to Ramón. Octavia's fears are confirmed by her husband's confession of his projected rendezvous with the Princess and the King's reported command to repair the damaged honor of Matilde by killing Octavia. The latter's devotion to Ramón moves her to sacrifice herself and, as he embraces her, Arnesto arrests him, leaving Octavia fainting in Durón's arms. Arnesto reappears, asking Octavia's favors in return for sparing her life. Her refusal causes the angered Arnesto to tie her to a tree, telling her to die in the knowledge that it was he who dishonored the Princess and that Ramón, though innocent, will be imprisoned. Octavia, about to give birth, is rescued by a farmer, Alberto, who takes her to his cottage.

## Act III.

The King of Naples learns that Ramón's insanity has frustrated his scheme to vindicate the Princess' honor. In a mad scene Ramón declares that the truth will out. In another abrupt shift of place Carlos, a farmer lad, pondering over his unknown parentage, comes upon the King lost in the woods on a hunt. Unaware of the King's identity, Carlos recounts the low esteem in which this monarch is held by his subjects and enumerates the qualities that royalty should possess. Octavia, who is the mother of Carlos and is dressed in the garb of a peasant woman, informs the King, likewise ignorant of his identity, of his ill repute and the anger of his people at Arnesto because of the murder of Octavia. Greatly perturbed, the King departs and Carlos learns from Octavia who was his father. Carlos vows to avenge Ramón. From Durón, now a soldier foraging supplies, Octavia learns that her father and the Count of Barcelona are sending troops to liberate Ramón. The King repents accepting Arnesto's advice to kill Octavia and, acquiescing to the demand of Carlos, who has just freed Ramón, his father, he reveals the identity of Arnesto. The latter confesses his crime, whereupon the King orders him to marry the Princess, after which he will be flung to wild beasts. Carlos demands a duel instead, and slays

Arnesto. As the armies close in, all is happily resolved. The Princess becomes a nun, Carlos marries the King's younger daughter, Ramón and Octavia will rule Ferrara with her peasant companions exalted to household servants, and the King will pay the costs of war.[18]

This crude play with its silly plot and unnatural situations exemplifies the Baroque decadence which soon overtook Spanish dramatic genius. Structurally, it is poorly knit, and there is little logic in the ordering of the scenes. Incidents known to the audience are needlessly recapitulated in tiresome monologues of hollow rhetoric, while the unities of time and place receive more than ordinary cavalier treatment. Bad taste obtrudes in the scarcely witty coarseness of Durón, yet the play somehow manages to present a few interesting moments. The tragic dilemma of Ramón when ordered to kill his wife at the King's command and marry the Princess probably recalled the ballad of the Count of Alarcos and the Princess Solisa familiar to the theatergoers of the time. This theme a sixteenth century dramatist, Torres Naharro, had utilized, and it was impressively exploited as late as 1917 by Jacinto Grau, another Spanish playwright, in his *Count Alarcos*.

But what circumstances caused the exceptional penalty of banning in toto *Courage Persecuted and Treachery Avenged* in Mexico City? What were the reasons of the Holy Office for so drastic an action? The answer to these queries is, perhaps, a fruitful means of observing the criteria by which that dreaded institution reached its decisions.

Since this episode occurred in 1682 it is possibly connected with the elevation of Fray Aguiar y Seijas to the archbishopric of Mexico that year. This prelate was of an excessively puritanical cast of mind and, in many respects, the direct antithesis of his famous predecessor earlier in the century, Fray García Guerra. In contrast to the latter, Archbishop Aguiar y Seijas was inclined to attribute the universal state of sinfulness to the general indulgence in the pleasures of the bull ring and the theater. One of his first measures upon assuming his exalted office was to limit, if not eliminate, such public spectacles. His antipathy for the drama extended to the reading of plays as well as to their performance, and he tried to dissuade, somewhat vainly it appears, the local booksellers from keeping in stock the exceedingly popular collections of comedies. His limited knowledge of human nature seems further demonstrated by a naive plan he adopted to induce readers to part with their treasures of dramatic literature in exchange for copies of *Consuelos de pobres* (Consolation of the Poor), a pious tract lauding the virtues of almsgiving, of which he had apparently imported 1,500 copies from Spain. A few devout possessors of printed plays, perhaps fearing the righteousness of the Archbishop, turned over their well-thumbed volumes to the prelate who carefully burned them.[19] But the success of this stratagem was hardly encouraging for no appreciable decline in play-reading or attendance at the local playhouse is recorded.

One Sunday of April in 1682 the Reverend Friar Bartolomé de San Antonio, a Dominican, dropped into the Coliseo of Mexico City and witnessed the first act of a comedy and the *entremés,* or short skit, which followed. Shocked by what he heard he hastily departed from that profane precinct without pausing to ascertain the titles of the plays. Whatever had drawn him to that unholy place of amusement—gentlemen of the cloth frequently found diversion there—he felt obligated to pen a complaint which he promptly presented to the Holy Office the next morning. Specifically, he declared in his *denuncia* that he had heard distorted and profane allusions to the story of Jacob and Esau contained in Genesis 27, and also to Psalms 23 and 31. Obviously, it was his duty to report such sacrilege to the Inquisition.

The Chief Inquisitor lost no time in dispatching a messenger to the manager of the theater to fetch scripts of the offensive comedy and entr'acte. The inquisitional emissary soon brought back the required text which proved to be that of *Courage Persecuted and Treachery Avenged,* authorship attributed to Montalbán, and of *El sacristán* (The Sexton), a skit by Pedro Bezerra. The tribunal promptly passed the manuscripts to the *calificadores,* Fathers Augustín Dorantes and Antonio Núñez de Miranda, the latter a Jesuit.

Three days later the first-named censor, a Dominican, reported his findings. These dramatic pieces, he stated categorically, must not and could not be allowed on the stage or in circulation. He cited examples of the reprehensible material in them, especially the comedy. Blasphemous verses indeed were those of Ramón's overenthusiastic acceptance of Princess Matilde's invitation to visit her after midnight.

> I shall count the minutes of the sun,
> and pray God that, as I desire, it will hasten
> its course, and that night, the cloak of lovers,
> may soon cast its sable shadows.
> And I pray God, as a favor, not to bring out
> the panoply of His bright stars.*

Such a prayer was sacrilegious since it requests God's connivance in the satisfaction of an illicit desire and seeks to make Him an accomplice in a sinful and immoral act.

Similarly condemned was the repeated use of symbolic language and allusions to sacred writings as, for example, Arnesto's aside as he accepted the ardent, if unintentional, invitation of the Princess to enjoy her favors.

> Coming in the disguise of Esau
> I would deceive an Isaac,
> and steal the blessing,
> like Jacob in falling heir.†

The use of the word "blessing" for the intended sin was utter impiety, and especially since it is repeated in the same act. When Ramón finds out that someone else has kept his assignation, he mutters:

> If a man left by the door,
> he doubtless arrived on time,
> and stole the blessing . . . ‡

---

* Ramón:  Contarele los minutos
                del sol, que en su paralelo
                ruego a Dios (como yo quiero)
                passe, y que tienda sus lutos
                la noche capa de amantes,
                y le pido por favor
                no saque el aparador
                de sus estrellas brillantes.
† Arnesto:  Entró con piel de Esau,
                enganaría a un Isaac
                y hurtando la bendición
                qual Jacob al heredar.
‡ Ramón:  Si hombre salió por la puerta
                sin duda a tiempo llegó
                que la *bendición* me hurtó. . . .

The Inquisition's unceasing efforts to eradicate the common evils of sorcery, fortunetelling, faith in omens, astrology, predictions and any disposition to anticipate individual destiny often brought harsh punishment to the guilty, as Pérez de Soto had learned so grievously. Hence, a foreboding speech of the hapless Octavia in Act II was deemed ample justification for a complete ban on *Courage Persecuted and Treachery Avenged.* The offending passage reads:

> The soul never betrays
> and alas! tonight, if I heed
> the melancholy signs and auguries
> in crossing the stream
> that flows through the gorge,
> the horse on which Ramón was riding,
> stumbled on wading through the chill waters,
> and threw him to the ground.
> The nocturnal birds were singing
> amidst the ash trees and beeches
> and, quoth the echo: Don't go!
> for they foretold some great ill.
> The somber crow cawed continuously,
> and its melancholy plaint
> seemed more like weeping than a song.
> Under these and other tidings of evil
> he had hardly reached the Palace
> when almost immediately,
> the King summoned him . . .*

And Ramón's gloomy speech on leaving Octavia to obey the

---

* Octa-
via:

El alma nunca es traydora
Y esta noche, ay tristes señas,
si los agüeros apoyo
al pasar aquel arroyo
que corre entre aquellas peñas.
El cavallo tropeçó
adonde Ramón venía,
al cortar el agua fría,
y en la arena le arrojó.
Aves nocturnas cantavan
entre los fresnos y hayas,
diziendo el eco: no vayas,
que algún gran mal anunciavan.
La lamentable corneja
no cessava de cantar

que más parece llorar
que canto su triste quexa.
Con estos y otros agüeros
apenas llegó a Palacio,
quando dentro en breve espacio
le llamó el Rey . . . .

royal summons to repair the damaged virtue of the Princess involved theological definitions. In it he declared:

> I had great good fortune in possessing thee,
> and great misfortune in losing thee.
> If it was grace to win thee,
> it is eternal penance to leave thee.*

"Eternal penance," it is explained, could only be appropriate in
case of deprivation of, or separation from, that which is infinite,
that is, from God Himself.

As for another speech of Ramón uttered when he fondly em-
braced Octavia:

> Hug me again and again,
> so that love may order
> that you be indelibly
> printed on my soul
> like a sacred symbol,†

that sentiment simply did not sound well! In conclusion Father
Dorante asserted that the author displayed too little delicacy in
handling "immoral matters" in the play; in fact, he treated them so
persuasively that they could not fail to be detrimental to modesty
and good morals.

The second examiner, Father Antonio Núñez de Miranda, con-
tented himself a week later with echoing the objections of his
colleague and confirming his judgment. It would be well, indeed,
he agreed, to put a stop to such unnatural and pernicious mingling
of the reverent and the blasphemous, the sacred and the profane,
to which so many, many playwrights were addicted!

Some three weeks later the prosecuting attorney advised the
Chief Inquisitor of his acceptance of the findings of the *calificadores,* and he heartily recommended that the play and accompanying skit be prohibited *in toto.* In a marginal note the judge ordered
the gathering up of all copies of the offending plays and the pub-

---

\* Ramón: Tuve gran suerte en gozarte
           y gran desdicha en perderte,
           si fué gloria el merecerte
           es pena eterna dexarte . . . .
† Ramón: Abráçame muchas vezes
           en fee que en el alma asida
           como caracter sagrado
           me manda amor que te imprima

lication of a corresponding edict forbidding entirely their performance in public or reading in private.[20]

These proceedings required about three months from the date when Father Navarro made his hasty exit from the local theater, but the resulting edict was not immediately posted. Following the customary practice, it was withheld until a sufficient list of books, pamphlets, and other papers meriting expurgation or banning had accumulated. Thus almost a year elapsed after Father Navarro's shocked visit to the Coliseo, it was April 12, 1683, to be exact, before the formal decree against *Courage Persecuted and Treachery Avenged* by the currently popular dramatist, Pérez de Montalbán, was tacked upon the doors of the Cathedral and churches in the cities, towns, and villages of the realm. Meanwhile, the *empresario* of the local theater had dropped the offensive pieces from the extensive repertory of his company of actors.

# ⁑ VIII

# A MASCARADA

"TO MAKE of life a drama, and of drama, life" was, in a sense, a fundamental principle of the Baroque age. If this was true in Old Spain, where the tragedy of bloody strife and imperial disintegration was unfolding, it was even more so in New Spain to which the alarms of incessant war in Europe came as distant, muted echoes, and where emotional excitement required the more artificial stimulation of colorful spectacles and histrionic devices. If the mother country was fatally engaged in making of life a tragic drama, its remote and sheltered possessions, dwelling in relative peace and settled order, felt impelled to make of diverting drama a more pulsating way of life.

This isolation of the overseas realms from the turmoil of the Old World presents a contrast which has moved many to picture existence in the former colonies of Spain as tediously dull, monotonous, and drab. There, it is sometimes imagined, the cowed populace passed its days in almost monastic austerity, breathing an atmosphere of fear under the heavy shadow of the Church and the Inquisition, its vitality inhibited save in the devout practices of an intolerant religion. This depressing vision, however, overlooks the inventive resources of an imaginative people and is a false impression of reality. To those whose destiny it was to live divorced from the fratricidal contentions of rising nationalism and sectarian partisanship tormenting Europe, this freedom did not seem so gray nor life so empty as posterity is prone to believe. Indeed, for many, especially in the cities and large towns where much of the

117

populace resided, existence was far from colorless and dreary. If for the majority hard labor, long hours of toil, social indifference, and harsh neglect seemed the law of nature, its severity was mitigated and the heavy routine was broken by feast days and public celebrations so numerous as to make serious inroads on the calendar year. Religious and civic festivals, organized with the pomp, ceremony, and lavish display that the Baroque mind so easily contrived, multiplied in a vain effort to overtake the increasing demand for public spectacles as the seventeenth century progressed. Appropriate occasions for colorful observance seemed to proliferate, and the Mexico of the viceroys experienced no lack of amusements, both public and private.

The temperaments of the Spanish overlords and their wards of whatever racial composition were not so far apart as their social differences. The natural gaiety and love of show were common characteristics of conqueror and conquered, and this similarity made mutual participation in diversions a frequent feature of community life. It was an association, half democratic in spirit, which went far to lessen the tensions of ethnic diversity and caste distinction. The Church, whose influence so clearly permeated every phase of social and cultural existence, did not fail to recognize this general passion for pageantry which it shrewdly utilized to its own advantage by sponsoring processions displaying the richly clothed images and ornate symbols of the Faith with all the pomp, splendor, and wealth at its command. To the many holy days for this kind of observance were added special occasions, such as the canonization of a saint, the arrival of sacred relics, the investiture of bishops, convent festivals for patron saints, and the like. The revered treasures and trophies were then brought forth to dazzle the eyes of the faithful and to convey to their simple minds the great Glory of God and of His Church. Now and then friars and monks of the religious orders solemnly paraded about the streets and public squares to voice their thanks to the Virgin for her favors and to solicit her intercession in times of stress. Especially impressive was the celebration of Corpus Christi, which invariably featured a specially written and lavishly staged morality play. And, much more rarely, occurred an awe-inspiring *auto de fe,* a grave and universal "act of faith."

If these functions appear to confirm the oppressiveness of colonial life, other spectacles, probably outnumbering them, brought joyous excitement and childish delight to the onlookers. Public reaffirmation of allegiance to the crown, births, baptisms, marriages in the royal and viceregal families, oaths of fidelity to the royal standard, news of victories in Europe, the safe arrival of the annual fleets, and many other secular events were occasions for celebration lasting days and weeks. Then gay processions of decorated floats and uniformed figures, with a flourish of trumpets and strains of martial music, wound through the streets festooned with banners and bunting, damask, velvet, and lace hangings, and rugs and tapestries suspended from balconies. All other community activities ceased as every caste and class lined the thoroughfares to enjoy the multicolored spectacle. Similarly, for the emotion and frenzy of war-stricken Europe, they substituted the less sanguinary contests of the bull ring and the cockpit, and found emotional release in romantic and liturgical plays performed at public theaters and temple courtyards. The magnificence and pleasing agitation of these diversions, which appealed to their instinctive *gaieté de coeur,* served to distract the masses from a preoccupation with their ills and thus helped to keep unrest from exploding into violence greater than an occasional riot.

The commonest public spectacle was the *máscara* or *mascarada.* It was, essentially, a parade of persons dressed in varied costumes and wearing peculiar masks, who promenaded about the streets by day or night, on foot, or mounted on horses or other animals; if after dark, they carried lighted torches, giving the city an unaccustomed illumination. They represented historical, mythological, and Biblical personages, gods of primitive religions, astrological planets, allegorical figures of Virtues, Vices, and other abstractions, and almost any bizarre creature, real or imaginary, was a welcome novelty. Impersonations reflected themes which varied from the sublime to the ridiculous, from the refined to the grotesque, and from the exalted to the most satirized. To an illiterate public the *mascarada* was like an animated magazine bringing before their avid eyes a semblance of things real and imagined; it instructed, it diverted, it entertained, and it often expressed their moods, their reverence, and their resentment. Not infrequently these spectacles indulged in satire of such crudeness and vulgarity that they would seem offensive to authorities, but the usual lack of interference from that source reveals a freedom of expression and an absence of censorship hardly suspected in that Baroque society.

The *máscaras* sometimes brought to the vast, unlettered population visual conceptions of characters in well-known novels and books currently enjoyed by the literate minority of the community. On January 24, 1621, at Mexico City, a spectacle of this sort featured a special attraction. Almost entirely composing the masquerade were the familiar figures of heroes of the still-popular romances of chivalry: Amadis of Gaul, Don Belianis of Greece, Palmerin of Oliva, and the Knight of Phoebus. As evident by the presence of these novels in the library of the ill-fated Pérez de Soto, Cervantes' recent burlesquing of the fantastic adventures of these fictional supermen had not yet destroyed their vogue. Perhaps the youthful Pérez de Soto was among the spectators lining the streets when this particular parade was passing and possibly this incarnation of the mythical heroes whetted his appetite to read and acquire copies of these exciting stories. And, likewise, the older García Becerril may have witnessed the same event, though his modest collection of books fails to reflect any influence of this sort.

Immediately following the revue of fictional exemplars of derring-do indicated came the latest and most amusing, the Knight of the Sorrowful Countenance, Don Quixote de la Mancha, whose misadventures for fifteen years now were common knowledge. But only the comic eccentricities of this chivalrous idealist were displayed before the crowds thronging the streets. Behind this most recent paladin of chivalric fiction appeared two odd-looking figures mounted on camels easily recognized as Melia, the Enchantress, and Urganda, the Protectress of medieval knights, here irreverently depicted as a tattered hag. Next in order rode two renowned eunuchs, Ardian and Bucendo, each astride an ungainly ostrich which strutted in awkward fashion before the appreciative onlookers. The climactic feature of this diverting spectacle was a caricature of the rotund Sancho Panza and of Don Quixote's light-of-love, Doña Dulcinea de Toboso, both mounted in comic dignity on patient, decrepit donkeys, whose arrival was the signal for a final, spontaneous burst of laughter from the delighted spectators.[1] The presence of these figures inspired by the novel *Don Quixote* on the streets of Mexico City that historic year of 1621 offers curious testimony to the acceptance of Cervantes' great work in a distant realm so soon after its publication in Spain and indicates the place it already occupied in popular lore.

These *mascaradas* featured the garbs of many nations, and a partiality for that of the Turks still threatening in Europe, was second only to the costumes of Indian tribes nearer home. The impersonation of familiar and exotic types did not, however, exhaust possibilities, for the participants frequently marched in the simulated forms of birds, animals, and imaginary creatures. Variations on these themes were devised by merely inverting these figures, that is, by depicting them upside down, with feet in the air. Rarely missing from these processions were *carros*, or floats, of allegorical or grotesque nature, often with intricate decorative detail.

Spectacles of this sort fell into two more or less distinct categories: a *máscara a lo serio*, in dignified character and *máscara a lo faceto*, composed of ridiculous figures. The two were often combined, but a love of robust humor and crude satire made the second more common. It is hardly surprising that students of the Royal University liked to relieve their ebullience by noisy and sometimes ingenious participation in these activities. Gleefully they flaunted their disrespect of authority by coarse caricatures of persons and by crude buffoonery. Indeed, the *máscaras* provided a convenient outlet for the strong satirical strain in Spanish genius, and in this visible form it was effective in a society predominantly illiterate. The *máscara a lo faceto* was frequently a useful medium of criticism, and it provided opportunities to pillory prominent officials and unpopular dignitaries. A diarist of the time relates that, in the important town of Puebla, a very disrespectful *mascarada* had a float which represented the ruling viceroy and his wife being soundly chastised. As this blatant display of *lèse majesté* rolled through the streets, raucous shouts of approval and foul epithets greeted it from every side. The chronicler piously voices his horror at this scandalous procedure, but he leaves the impression that such overt demonstrations of popular displeasure were not uncommon.[2] Freedom of expression, in the former Spanish possessions, as already stated, was greater than traditionally believed.

The *máscara* was, to a certain extent, a democratic institution in which all castes and classes participated, though usually in separate units. Noble gentlemen delighted to exhibit their equestrian skill and sallied forth, arrayed in polychromatic livery and mounted on magnificent steeds almost concealed in luxurious trappings. Rich merchants and shopkeepers appeared in ornate costumes, and the influential guilds of craftsmen often organized special features. In general these commercial and industrial elements bore the heavy expense of these exhibitions, and they could usually be depended upon to compete with each other in the ingenuity and costliness of their floats. The celebration of the nuptials of the pathetic Charles II lasted for weeks, during which the silversmiths, saddlers, bakers, candlestick-makers and many other guilds vied with each other in the magnificence of successive processions.[3]

The humbler elements of society were also conspicuous in these diversions, and quite often organized elaborate pageants with varied features. The Indians readily shared the enthusiasm of their overlords, drawing inspiration both from European and their own lore. Thomas Gage once again provides curious evidence. "This town (Chiapas)," he reports, "lieth upon a great river, whereunto belong many boats and canoes, wherein those Indians have been taught to act sea fights with great dexterity, and to represent the nymphs of Parnassus, Neptune, Aeolus, and the rest of the heathenish gods and goddesses, so that they are a wonder of their whole nation. They will arm with their boats a siege against the town, fighting against it with such courage till they make it yield, as if they had been trained up all their life to sea fights. . . . They will erect towers and castles made of wood and painted cloth, and from them fight either with boats or one against another with squibs, darts, and many strange fireworks, so manfully that, if in earnest they would perform as well as they do in sport and pastime, the Spaniards and friars might soon repent to have taught them what they have . . ."[4]

Negroes, mulattoes, and other mixed elements paraded in their own máscaras, while children occasionally marched in similar manner. Even women took part in these festivities. It is recorded in 1700 that the gentler sex masqueraded in masculine attire, while their mates provided unfailing humor by donning feminine apparel. These functions required little talent and large numbers participated. In February, 1672, over four hundred people, together with many floats, passed through the streets of Mexico City in gala array to celebrate the Fiesta of St. Francis Borgia.[5]

As the century advanced this form of public entertainment occurred more frequently, with ever-increasing lavishness. The expense became a heavy burden as costumes and decorations grew more bizarre and costly, and occasionally the business community resorted to evasive procedures. When the viceroy wished to signalize an event by a customary spectacle of this sort, he rarely evinced a disposition to defray or share the cost. Private individuals, consequently, betrayed a noticeable lack of enthusiasm for such invitations. The news that the Queen had given birth to a Prince reached Mexico City in April, 1658, and the viceroy dutifully summoned one hundred and fifty citizens to remind them tactfully that so auspicious an event called for suitable recognition by her Majesty's subjects. The rich realm of Old Mexico must, of course, celebrate with a splendor proportionate to its wealth, and it was no accident that the viceroy had called in men of acknowledged substance. Many offered rather transparent pleas of poor health, an inability to ride a horse, and similar pretexts, but the king's vicar was adamant, stating firmly that only the payment of a fine, and one proportionate to the deficit incurred, could procure exemption.[6]

This form of public entertainment was not restricted to the celebration of secular events, as already noted, and the impropriety of mingling the ridiculous and the grave in religious festivals troubled no one. Hilarity and reverence were easily reconciled, with little implication of sacrilege. On the whole the *máscaras,* whether *a lo serio* or *a lo faceto,* were a salutory release of emotions and a comparatively innocent diversion. Now and then, they might be the occasion of disorders, particularly when feelings concerning some local or political matter ran high, but this rarely happened. And seldom did accidents or mishaps mar these spectacles. A contemporary diary, however, gravely reports an exception: "a man in Santa Cruz died of a kick which he received from one of the horses in a máscara."[7]

The history of this picturesque custom in the New World goes back to the earliest days of Spanish domination. In 1539, less than two decades after Cortes' conquest, the *máscaras* were so common that licenses for these spectacles were required, presumably because of disturbances associated with them in that unsettled period. But they continued to flourish and enliven the life of a still raw and frontier society. In 1565 the son of the conqueror of Mexico took

part in a *máscara* which, with impressive fidelity of detail, simulated the famous entry of his father into the Aztec capital less than
a half century before.[8] In the seventeenth century, as already perceived, these spectacles were intimately woven into the pattern of
life. It was, indeed, a custom so general and stereotyped that
chroniclers seldom bothered to give detailed descriptions despite
a common tendency to dwell on the ornamental minutiae of contemporary existence. Of particular interest, therefore, is a lengthy
account of a *mascarada* of 1680, contained in a slim volume entitled *Glories of Querétaro*, published that year. The author was
a Creole, Carlos de Sigüenza y Góngora, foremost authority of his
time on the Indian antiquities of Mexico.[9]

The *Glories of Querétaro* is, in many respects, a typical product
of the colonial press. Without newspapers and periodicals to chron-
icle the happenings of daily life, it was the practice to record in
print events deemed important in suitably edifying *relaciones*. Institutions or private individuals usually commissioned these de-
scriptive narratives as a form of self-glorification, hence they were
a sort of "vanity literature" whose writers dutifully flattered the
paying patron. The style employed was pompous and ornate, the
syntax involved, the metaphors strained, and the hyperbole extravagant—a heavy-footed prose that moved ponderously amid a
mass of trivia. Now and then glints of pure metal shine amidst the
verbal slag, and in this respect the *Glories of Querétaro* assays
higher than the average work of its kind. What lifts it above the
usual level and gives it a certain documentary importance is the
description, among other features, of a *máscara*, peculiarly Baroque
in character, in which the Indians were conspicuous.

Querétaro, about thirty leagues northwest of Mexico City, was a
pleasant community tucked away in the enclosing hills. From its
fertile soil the plow, "with its effective tongue of iron," in the
genial phrase of the writer, "coaxed abundant harvests," greatly to
the advantage of the white landholders. These favorable circumstances stimulated local pride and even stirred ambition, notably
among the clergy, to rival the viceregal capital in the splendor of
its public buildings. The fervent cult of the Virgin of Guadalupe,
for whom a magnificent structure had been reared near Mexico
City, suggested emulation by the construction of a suitable temple
in Querétaro to promote this veneration. A successful campaign of

soliciting funds brought about the erection of an ornate church formally dedicated in 1680. The varied program of solemn ceremonies and festive events was then duly chronicled in the *Glories of Querétaro*.

The account begins with some curious facts of pre-Cortesian history, moves on to a tactful appreciation of the natural beauty of Querétaro, and then dwells on the singular means by which the devotion of the Virgin of Guadalupe was introduced. With scrupulous care the architectural and sculptural details of the new church are catalogued after which, with barely concealed satisfaction, the author passes on to the more mundane features of the dedication. Such solemn ceremonies as the installation of the Holy Sacrament, the singing of Masses, and the preaching of sermons soon give way to gayer festivities. "Adorned with showy canopies and tapestries," wrote the author, stood a platform at the church entry where, with brilliant costumes and stage settings, a company of actors performed a comedy of Calderón before a large and appreciative audience. "Nothing of all things that are respectable in the comic style was missing" in the performance, the reader is assured, while bullfights, poetic contests, parades, and *máscaras* enlivened successive days, each terminating in noisy and spectacular displays of fireworks. All of this appears, however, a preliminary warming up for the description of the *mascarada*, which affords the writer an opportunity to intercalate data on the Aztec civilization drawn from his formidable erudition. His pages are crowded with a heavy, Latinized diction intermingled with polysyllabic and unpronounceable Nahuatl terms, that hang like shiny baubles on a Christmas tree of Castilian prose. This characteristic Baroque style, turgid, involved, ornate, and ponderous, lends itself better to paraphrase than translation.[10]

His chronicle begins with a grandiose peroration. "If I could present this *máscara* to the ears as it delighted the eyes, I doubt not that I could achieve with my words what the Indians accomplished in it with their adornments. I shall do all that I can, though I know that I shall expose myself to the censure of incredulity," whereupon he launches into his recital.

"At three o'clock in the afternoon the masquerade in four sections started to make its appearance on the city streets. The first part was not especially noteworthy as it consisted of a disorganized band of wild Chichimeca Indians who swarmed about the thoroughfares garbed in the very minimum that decency allows. They had daubed their bodies with clay paints of many hues, and their disheveled hair was made even more unsightly by filthy feathers thrust into it in no particular pattern. Like imaginary satyrs and demoniacal furies they whooped, yelled, and howled, waved clubs, and flourished bows and arrows in such a realistic imitation of their warlike practices, that spectators were quite startled and terrified.

"More enthusiastic applause greeted the second section, a company of infantrymen formed by one hundred and eight youths marching six abreast, each one bedecked in finest Spanish regalia, with bright-colored plumes fluttering from the crest of helmets and multihued ribbons streaming in the breeze from their shoulders. They presented a noble and inspiring appearance, but nothing amazed me quite as much as the superb precision and perfect rhythm with which they marched, with no other practice or training than that acquired in festive parades and on like occasions. Veterans could not have kept their ranks more evenly, or shown greater dexterity in firing and reloading, or manoeuvered their squads more expertly." The Creole author here gives evidence of a growing Mexicanism that would, in time, evolve into nationalism. "This indicates very clearly," he went on, "that these American-born youths are not incapable of discipline should it be necessary to make professional soldiers of them. The rapidity and skill with which the company leader flourished his pike astonished everyone.

"Next came four buglers, mounted on well-trained horses barely visible under scarlet trappings and silver trimmings. The clear, shrill notes of their instruments heralded the approach of the most important section of this brilliant *máscara*. This was the part representing the nobility and lords of the aboriginal aristocracy which, even though it was pagan and heathenish, must be reckoned as majestic and august inasmuch as it held sway over a vast northern empire in the New World. In taking part in these festivities it is quite unthinkable that these Indians should put on tableaux borrowed from an alien culture when they have such an abundance of themes and subjects for pageantry in the lives of their kings and emperors and in the annals of their history. So it was that, on this occasion, they appeared in the ancient garbs of their people as portrayed in their hieroglyphic paintings and as still preserved in tribal memory. All were dressed alike with an amazing array of adornments.

"Leading off was a figure representing the great Conquistador, Don Diego de Tapia, who headed a troop of native monarchs. Behind came the aged Xolotl, first emperor of the Chichimecas in these provinces after the destruction of the Toltecs. Following him were: Nopalton, Tlotzintecuhtli, Quinatzin, otherwise known as Tlaltecatzin, Techotlala, and Ixtlilxochitl, all six of the Chichimeca lineage. Then came two Tepenacs, Tezozomoc and Maxtla who, though tyrants, enjoyed universal rule. The death of the second mentioned and the defeat of his armies brought in the fourth king of the Aztecs, Itzcoatl, and then in succession, Moctecuhzuma Ilhuicamina, Axayacatzin, Tizozic Chalchiuhtonac, Ahiutzotl, Metecuhzuma, Xocoyotzin, Cuitlahuatzin, and the ill-fated, most unfortunate Cuauhtemoc. But the three first Aztec kings were not missing from the *máscara,* that is, Acamapich, Huitzilihuitl, and Chimalpopoca, though they did not achieve the same degree of majesty; nor did the last six kings of Texcoco, namely Netzahualcoyotl, Nezahualpilli, Cacamatzin, Cuicuitzcatl, Coanacotzin, and Ixtlilixochitl, the second of that name who did not win back the control of the empire after the death of Ixtlilxochitl.

"Each monarch bore a crown of turquoises (Xiuhtzolli), the characteristic symbol of authority. Each headpiece presented a complicated arrangement of scintillating jewels of Oriental perfection, tasseled ribbons to hold the hair in place, and shimmering, golden green plumes of the Quetzal bird (Quetzaltlalpilloni). This native royalty was further adorned by featherwork from the same bird (Malacaquetzalli), or the Tlauhquechol (Tlauhuecholtontec), and heron plumes (Aztatzoontli), all alike in exquisite arrangement and beauty. Legbands (Icxipepetlachtli) and bracelets (Icxitecuecuextli, Matzopetzli) decorated ankles and wrists; and exceeding in loveliness all their other garments were the elaborate and costly tilmas, or small cloaks, fastened at the shoulder by a knot and with embroidered hieroglyphic designs (Xiuhtlalpiltilmantli). These the ancient monarchs wore only when seated on a throne . . . But why weary myself cataloguing all these decorative details when it is very likely, since these objects can be properly named only in the elegant tongue of the Aztecs, that those who are unacquainted with the language must inevitably be bored?

"Bringing up the rear of this colorful section was a figure representing the august person of the most valiant Emperor Charles V of Spain and the Holy Roman Empire, whose dominions extended from Germany in the north to the western hemisphere of America. He was arrayed in full armor, burnished black and engraved in gold. Like the Indian monarchs preceding him in the procession, he rode behind airy steeds that pranced with grace and stately rhythm as if fully aware of the sublime majesty of the ruler who held the reins. Indeed, these gallant horses, with the rhythmic swaying of plumes and the even gait of their hooves and the carriage gliding like Apollo's chariot across the heavens, made them seem so like Pegasus that onlookers burst into enthusiastic applause. In short, the elegance and splendor of the trappings harmonized completely with the august majesty of the figure represented.

"Then came the triumphal float, lovelier than the starry firmament and its twinkling constellations. The base, supported by wheels, was six yards long, about half that width, and from the ground it was raised about a yard and a half. On this ample space rested the form of a large ship plowing through imitation waves of silver and bluish white gauze. The sides covering the underparts of the float bore complex designs of involuted spirals, ornate capitals, and decorative emblems, imbuing the whole with an aura of brilliance and splendor. From a large figurehead at the bow of the ship ribbons of scarlet taffeta fell away, intertwined so intricately with the harness traces that they actually seemed to be drawing the conveyance. Above the stern of the simulated vessel rose two exceedingly graceful arches, forming a throne, in the middle of which reposed a large, curved shell, supported from behind by a pair of Persian caryatids. Within it was an image of the Virgin of Guadalupe, and from her canopied throne descended a staircase with silken mats. Further embellishing this lovely ensemble were varicolored taffeta streamers, and a plethora of bouquets of many hues. Like an ambulant springtime, it appeared, dedicated to the immortal Queen of the heavenly paradise, and far exceeding in beauty the Hanging Gardens of Babylon which, in their time, were dedicated to Semiramis. At appropriate intervals stood six graceful angels, symbolizing some of the attributes of the most Holy Virgin. Kneeling on the first step of the throne was a lovely child garbed in the native raiment of the Indians, who thus represented the whole of America, particularly this northern part which, in pagan days, was known as Anahuac. One hand held a heart while the other supported an incensor diffusing perfumes and delicate aromas. All about this triumphal float the Indians were dancing one of the famous, royal *toncontines* of the ancient Mexicans. If their costumes in such ceremonial festivities were lavishly colorful in the days of their monarchs, how much more they would be on so auspicious an occasion as this one!

"This was the fourth and concluding part of the *mascarada* which included several venerable old men who, in chants of marked devotion, intoned praises of the Most Holy Virgin. These were beautifully rendered to the accompaniment of native drums (Tlalpan-Huehuetl) and others beaten by rubber drumsticks (Teponaztli), long, flutelike instruments (Omichicahuztli), timbrels (Ayacaztli), wooden fifes (Cuauhtlapitzalli), and various other instruments typical of the Indians. For hours this magnificent procession wound through the main streets of Querétaro and past the various convents where it paused to recite the versified *loas* which set forth in majestic language the motive of this splendid celebration . . . Night fell at last and once again the brilliant fireworks lit up the skies. . . ."

# IX

# TOURNAMENTS
# OF POETASTERS

THE Baroque passion to make a drama of life exploited art in every form to provide the theatrical spectacles that its spirit craved. Its intensity, exuberance, and extravagance of feeling sought release in bizarre and exaggerated decoration of every aspect of existence: in architecture, in plastic arts, in elegance of dress, in manners, and in public ceremony. All these kinds of expression, however, were, in a sense, scarcely more than scenic effects, even the half-animate pageants and *mascaradas*. Besides settings, drama also demanded articulation in oral and written form. Clearly then, language had an important part to play in externalizing the repressed emotions of the age. Since its use was the privilege of literate and illiterate alike, it was the medium most universally subject to the decorative impulse. Poetry, of course, was its most exalted mode, and the natural music and consonance of Castilian seemed to put this outlet well within the reach of everyone. With form elevated above content, ingenuity, a cheaper commodity, replaced inspiration, and an old institution grew in popularity. This was the *certamen poético,* or poetic tournament which, in the Baroque age, permitted the self-styled elite of Old Mexico to demonstrate an alleged devotion to Euterpe, the muse of lyric verse, by exhibitions of metrical manipulation and verbal gymnastics.

The Renaissance ideal of a gentleman, which required distinction achieved by sword and pen, survived in the seventeenth century, and its difficult fulfillment in the New World was among the major frustrations of transplanted Spaniards. Many of the great writers of Spain, during their career, had served their king as a soldier and had thus helped to form the accepted success pattern. The aspiring Creole, more fortunate than he appreciated, was too remote from the battlefields of Europe to acquire military eminence. Nearer home, to be sure, were opportunities to distinguish himself by repelling hit-and-run attacks of pirates on seaport towns or by suppressing sporadic Indian uprisings on viceregal frontiers. Now and then riots and social upheavals broke out in more settled areas, even within the capital. But to the American-born Spaniard, these disturbances failed to offer occasions for the kind of military valor that brought genuine prestige or fame. Neither buccaneers, rebellious natives, nor riotous masses were foes worthy of a gentleman's steel, and triumphs over them lacked glamor. To the Creole these unpropitious circumstances seemed to close the door of martial renown, leaving open only that of literary distinction.

But even the doorway of letters seemed more than half blocked. Even if the American Spaniard possessed rare talent, as the Mexican dramatist, Ruiz de Alarcón certainly did, he was sure to escape notice unless he transferred his efforts to Spain where, at best, he might expect grudging attention. Until the seventeenth century was well past its mid-point the artistic genius of the Spanish Peninsula was flowering with pyrotechnic brilliance. The names of Cervantes, Góngora, Lope de Vega, Tirso de Molina, and Quevedo, and a host of others echoed so loudly in Europe that quill wielders of the New World could hardly hope to be heard. Plays, novels, and verse poured from the mother country in torrents of printed books, inundating local bookshops and private libraries, even reaching remote mining camps, and this competition could only discourage their endeavors. With the Baroque spirit reaching its culmination in the drama of Calderón (1600-1681), which cast its seductive spell over the remaining colonial period, the would-be writers of the overseas realms felt reduced to abject imitation and artistic inanition. Even when they persisted in creative endeavors, the excessive cost of publication, the chronic scarcity of paper, the requirement of licenses from Spain, and the monopolistic practices of Peninsular printers virtually doomed their works to remain in manuscript.

These obstacles seemed so insuperable as to make literary distinction quite as much out of reach as distinction in arms, yet such were the prestige of letters and the passion to versify in the Hispanic world that few could resist the temptation to sharpen their quills. The tutelary gods of the age were Quevedo, somber and dark in his concettism, and Luis de Góngora, musical, pictorial, and polychromatic in his floridity, called gongorism. These artistic techniques were toys with which to play in an era when the tyranny of kings and the domination of the Church prevented a concern with the great issues of life, and Creole poetasters turned to them eagerly. Such canons of esthetic excellence invited any literate person, with a modest command of the vernacular and a smattering of Latin with which to invent neologisms, to essay his skill in verbal legerdemain, and few failed to accept the opportunity tendered. Industry of this sort required occasions for display, of course, and, since the day of periodicals and "little reviews" had not arrived, public poetic contests provided gratifying showcases. They offered the powerful incentives of a visible audience and, in important tournaments, the possibility of publication in homage volumes.[1]

The origins of these competitions go back to the ancient Greeks, and the revival in later times was a part of the recovery of the classic tradition in Renaissance Europe. Literary academies and societies quickly crossed to the New World to become a familiar feature of cultural life, notably in the seventeenth century. Whether first introduced by the Jesuits or not, these *concursos* were no novelty in Mexico during the closing decades of the sixteenth century. Bernardo de Balbuena could proudly recall that, in a poetic contest held at Mexico City in 1585, he had won a prize against three hundred other contestants. The occasion was the celebration of Corpus Christi, and the laurel was bestowed upon the youth "in the presence of seven bishops assembled there at the time for an ecclesiastical Council." And later that same year he was equally successful in a *certamen* honoring the arrival of a new viceroy.

The lush efflorescence of this custom coincided with the remaining colonial centuries during which it produced the most exuberant growth of Baroque verse. Surviving *relaciones* that record these affairs preserve, probably fortunately, only a fraction of these lyric effusions. Vacuous bombast and extreme artificiality are the prevailing characteristics, and *agudeza*, or cleverness, brought success rather than did true inspiration. These were the qualities that most readily evoked the coveted approbation and proclaimed the winners. To be acclaimed a Poet was to achieve high distinction in the community, and disgruntled losers of these contests occasionally displayed a saltier talent for satirical expression. In 1618, for example, the guild of silversmiths in Mexico City sponsored a poetic tournament intended to signalize the Pope's recent proclamation of the Immaculate Conception, possibly the instigation of as much bad verse as any single theme in Spain's Golden Age. The reluctance of the Dominicans in Mexico to accept this matter of faith precipitated a scandal which rocked the viceregal capital. Members of this order loudly protested the adverse decisions of the judges on their entries in the competition by circulating a series of satirical sonnets and *canciones* which proved far more exciting, if esthetically no more inspired, than the prize-winning poems. The Inquisition was obliged to take a hand in this embarrassing situation and it compiled a record of offensive verses which provide posterity with more entertaining reading than the usual products of colonial *certámenes*.[2]

These functions were an aristocratic pastime, and an event associated with much elegance. Whatever the occasion—reception of a viceroy, an archbishop, or other dignitary, the installation of a university rector, the celebration of a historical incident, or the reiteration of an article of faith—a generous patron invariably underwrote the expense, proud of his role as a collective Maecenas of local poetasters. This philanthropy was often costly, since it included outlays for elaborate decorations, Lucullan repasts, and liberal gratuities as well as valuable prizes, but it was an honor highly esteemed since it bestowed distinction upon gentlemen of wealth otherwise undistinguished. Donors were also titular heads of institutions, ecclesiastical and lay, with ample funds at their disposition.

The patron enlisted the services of experienced functionaries to organize and conduct the tournament in accordance with the best traditions and, if possible, to excel previous performances. These agents were primarily a general secretary, and a panel of respected individuals as judges for the poems submitted. There were other

minor officials but upon the secretary rested the heaviest responsibility, for, as master of ceremonies, he needed to possess gifts of
graceful rhetoric and polite wit as well as administrative talent.
His fundamental task was to devise an *idea,* or symbolic theme,
on which the aspiring members of the local Parnassus might exercise their eager, if meager, genius. This general topic must be
amenable to division into subtopics equivalent to the number of
separate contests contemplated, usually four, each with meters and
strophic forms specifically prescribed. The tournament of 1683,
organized by the University of Mexico to bolster faith once more
in the Immaculate Conception, had the eagle chosen to represent
Mary, and upon its alleged qualities and attributes, fabulous and
otherwise, local wordsmiths fabricated metrical compositions. Each
aspect of the symbolic bird served as a subtopic of an individual
contest and it was suggested by an emblem or allegorical figure
termed *emblema, asunto,* and the like, with verse forms specified
in each case. The collective effusions could then be expected to
result in the maximum glorification of the Virgin.

Hardly less important were the arrangements for processions
and ceremonial functions, for, without the drama of pageantry, the
contests of the muses were incomplete. No effort was spared to
mobilize the very considerable resources of the community in
luxurious raiment, colorful decorations of streets and buildings, and
adornments of man and beast to make the event a gala occasion
for the entire community. A parade marshal prided himself on
bringing out an exhibition of costumes in silk, velvet, and satin,
ornamented with whorls of braid, silver spangles, jewels, and
topped by flowing plumes. Gaily caparisoned horses were an unfailing attraction, mingling with gaudy floats of ingenious symbolism, the whole arranged to endow a familiar spectacle with
desirable variety. The marshal's reward was the coveted privilege
of carrying in the procession the placard of the tournament, an-
nouncing its theme and summoning poets to the lists.

The various units of this column gathered at the marshal's
home, appropriately festooned for the occasion, and took their
place in order of precedence. About midafternoon, after final inspection of uniforms, accoutrements, and details of the floats, the
imposing parade began its slow, measured progress through the
principal streets. Church bells broke into prolonged, rapid, and

discordant clamor, fireworks crackled, and loud reports of mortars strategically placed on corners added to the din. This festive racket delighted the crowds lining the thoroughfares, and intensified their expectancy. Since everyone must revere the Immaculate Conception as a tenet of faith, the procession represented both religious and secular corporations. Friars, monks, and priests marched in their most impressive habiliments, accompanying holy images and sacred insignia, while faculty members of the University in brilliant academic vestments and bearing glittering scepters contributed bright notes to a Baroque symphony of color.

Heralding the approach of the column resounded the shrill trumpets, the rhythmic beats of kettledrums, and martial strains of flageolets, played by gaily uniformed bandsmen. Immediately following on foot and astride horses and mules was a contingent of students in cap and gown, the trappings of their mounts displaying symbols of the scholarly pretensions of the riders. This cavalcade was an overture to the operatic splendor of the lordly gentlemen of the city arrayed in shining livery and mingling with learned doctors of the University in resplendent robes, all riding in stately grace upon restive steeds whose harness glinted in the afternoon sun. This magnificence, contrasting with the more solemn dress of the clergymen, conferred a lofty dignity upon the whole and evoked a feeling of awe in the onlookers.

The climactic feature of the procession was the section that formally announced the poetic tournament and its theme. Leading this group rode the marshal, accompanied by beadles and other University officials, their mounts hardly perceptible under their trappings. Besides a flashing silver mace, and a series of ornate posters with crests, seals, and symbolic devices, this group held aloft an immense *cartel,* or placard, with its grandiose legend. Upon this object the ablest artists had expended their best talent in design, and the effect was dazzling. Surmounted on a staff of solid silver was the *tarja,* a large, filigreed frame of the same metal, which colorfully garbed lackeys kept in balance by holding taut the golden cords strung from its corners. Within it daintily executed lettering set forth its message in excessively rotund diction. Representative of these *carteles* is that of the competition at the University of Mexico in 1683, the involved wording of which is approximately rendered as:

LITERARY PALAESTRA
AND POETIC JOUST
IN WHICH
THE IMPERIAL, PONTIFICAL, AND EVER AUGUST
MEXICAN ATHENS
proposes a design of the triumph of the
MOST HOLY MARY
sketched on a canvas brightened by colors contrived from
a perishable palette, in which
She treads upon the Dragon of Original Sin
at the first Instant of Conception, by summoning the Muses of its Helicon to sing victory
songs celebrating the triumph of the Virgin Birth on
the many-stringed zither of Apollo.
Vergil, the Swan of Mantua, provides the model in verses 71 to 98 in the Third Book of
the Aeneid.[3]

Flanking this dramatic device rode the Secretary and a liveried retinue of assistants and servants. A company of soldiers formed a rear guard, their bright uniforms lending a final touch of color to the procession, and their deftly manipulated pikes providing tacit reminders of the bearers' function as preservers of public order.

In due course the colorful column arrived outside the spacious lecture hall of the University where the Rector, the Viceroy, and other dignitaries were waiting. As the paraders dismounted and moved into the assembly room, the bells of the city accelerated the tempo of their dissonance to a fortissimo. An intricate pattern of decorative detail had transformed the monastic bareness of the auditorium, and the addition of the ornate emblems and devices carried in the procession increased its profusion. As the interior filled with brilliant uniforms and bright costumes, the whole presented a kaleidoscope of color animated by a loud buzzing of conversation and an air of restless excitement.

At last, when a comparative hush fell, the Secretary, with a great show of dignity, slowly mounted the steps of a pulpit at one side of the platform. In a clear, precise voice he began his discourse with high-sounding phrases well studded with Latin quotations. With ponderous aplomb he described the motives of the tournament and announced the specific topics and the particular meters and strophic forms with which contestants should treat them. He also set forth the rules governing the competition and named the judges who would decide on the prize winners. A fortnight was allowed for the final adjudication and the ceremonious awarding of laurels.

Comparatively brief was this introductory rite of the tournament, and the aristocratic audience soon began to disperse, slowly returning to waiting carriages, sedan chairs, and mounts held in readiness by servants and lackies. Many paused to admire at close hand the Baroque splendor of the *cartel* conspicuously affixed at the entrance of the University building. Custom required that the marshal hold a reception at his home and a goodly number of invited guests repaired there to enjoy the rich food and drink lavishly supplied. This gathering of the social elite lasted well into the night. Meanwhile, the less acceptable and more numerous elements of the population, including the students, filled the streets, squares, and *pulquerías,* or bars, where they celebrated the occasion with a boisterousness that permitted little sleep to the more decorous citizens of the neighborhood.

In many a household the days following witnessed intensive activity as aspiring poetasters and wordsmiths laboriously tinkered with tropes, metaphors, and meters in a painful effort to shape them to the prescribed themes. Even if talent had been in greater supply the cramping requirements of the competition gave little play to spontaneity, naturalness, or artistic integrity. The aim was adulation and glorification of the subject matter and it was best achieved by ingenious conceits, by bold juggling of phrases and excessive artifice, together with a pedantic exhibition of classical and scholastic learning. Obscurity was a virtue and a vacuous jumbling of allusions a merit. With the topic in no way disputable, exaggerated panegyrics and bombast were the marks of esthetic excellence.

The frequency of these tournaments had enabled many poetasters to develop techniques for the extraction of acceptable metal from low-grade ores of inventiveness. There were short cuts and easy methods of fitting metrical compositions to specifications against which Secretaries of *certámenes* had to be on guard. They found it expedient to formulate definite laws governing the manufacture of the verbal products submitted to the judges, and they attempted to remove any irritation on the part of contestants by facetious wording. Somewhat typical of this legislation is the following:

I. Prizes must not be limited to a few persons.
   Inasmuch as it is well to restrain covetousness through poetry in persons who, by their profession hardly know what silver is, we decree that two first prizes may not be awarded to one and the

same professor, nor that more than two may be adjudged to anyone else.

II. There must be fitness and propriety in the Glosses.

Inasmuch as it is essential to maintain a proper relation between
the textual verses and the gloss composed upon them, we require
that the words shall be kept in all their proper meanings, and in
the positive sense in which they are employed.

III. There must be no false playing upon words.

Because of the great importance of excluding abuses of Spanish
speech detrimental to good use and poetry in the republic of
letters; we order the elimination, even in humorous passages, of a
false playing on words susceptible of double meaning; only one
meaning may be used, leaving the other implicit in the sound of
the word.

IV. Poets must keep to the highway of their subjects.

Since wandering away from the straight and narrow path of the
subject causes one to fall over verbal cliffs, or lose one's way, we
declare that he who thus loses his bearings also loses prizes.

V. Stolen verses and insincerities of style shall be punished. We
decree exile from Parnassus for those caught on this occasion as
verse pirates or plagiarizers, as manufacturers of empty, pointless
words, of senseless sentences, and of oversubtle and meaningless
metaphors; likewise we ban those who use technical jargon in such
a way as to lack comprehension or reason through misunderstand-
ings that arise from this procedure.

VI. Poems must be submitted in customary form.

We command that poems be submitted signed and sealed, with an
additional copy in a decorated border, on penalty that, in lacking
this adornment, they will not be acceptable in this Parnassus,
inasmuch as we do not concede that poets are too poor to afford
at least a tinted border.

VII. Entries must be submitted on time.

We require the submission of poems to the Secretary of the contest on the specified date. No extension of time will be granted to
anyone, whether major or minor poet.[4]

These rules reveal prevailing practices perhaps more than their
correction, for they did not always apply equally to all contestants.
Literary vanities are among the most susceptible and, in a hierarchy as complex as that of viceregal Mexico, judges of poetic contests often felt it expedient to interpret regulations broadly and
impose them leniently to avoid wounding the pride of highly placed
participants. As a form of insurance against irate reactions of influential contestants a jury of professors, Oidores of the Royal

Audiencia, and other dignitaries of lofty category, lent their support to the appointed referees. As Don Quixote once remarked, "there is no poet who is not arrogant and who does not think that he is the greatest there is," an observation of especial validity in the case of the Creole subjects overseas overly conscious of an inferior status and yearning for recognition. Doubtless of equal pertinence to the tournaments celebrated in the New World centers of culture were the further remarks that the illustrious Knight of the Doleful Countenance addressed to an individual in the throes of contriving verses. "If by chance they are for some literary tournament," he advised, "you should strive to carry off the second prize, for the first is always awarded as a favor to some one of high rank, the second goes to the one who merits first place, and thus the third is, in reality, the second, while the first, by this reckoning, would be third, after the manner of licentiate degrees that are conferred at the universities. But for all that, the first prize carries with it a great distinction."[5]

During the days following the ceremonious announcement of the competition the Secretary received a flood of daintily bordered manuscripts which, in the contest of 1683, totaled more than five hundred metrical compositions. After a preliminary winnowing of the more obvious chaff, he brought these contributions to a meeting of the judges at the home of the patron. This committee attacked the formidable batches of verse, classifying them according to the separate sections into which the *certamen* was divided. A prolonged session doubtless ensued as the judges worked through the welter of strained meters, complicated syntax, and baffling conceits woven into a vast array of ballads, glosses, *décimas*, quintillas, sextets, sonnets, octaves, sapphics, *canciones*, epigrams, and anagrams in Latin as well as Castilian. In making selections they could not ignore the social status of the author, and the application of esthetic criteria was flexible. Despite the Secretary's preliminary sifting, the task was exhausting, and when the committee had finally reached agreement on the prize-winning entries, they gratefully accepted the delicate collation and chilled beverages which the patron had thoughtfully provided. Later, as they rose to leave, their generous host slipped a liberal gratuity into the hands of each, whereupon they departed to their respective homes, doubtless well pleased with their efforts.

The Secretary was a busy man in the time remaining before the public reading of the successful poems. Not only must he supervise the final arrangements for the ceremony, but he must compose a series of brief, witty couplets to recite on bestowing the many awards. Much of the success of the occasion depended upon the deft combination of humor and flattery in these short verses. To amuse the audience and please the vanity of the author required skilful judgment as to the lengths he might go as well as a facile gift of versifying. The Secretary, therefore, devoted much time and thought to this important obligation.

The final, gala event usually occurred about two weeks after the procession proclaiming the tournament. The University auditorium appeared even more brilliantly decorated than before, with draperies of rich cloth, bright bunting, and symbolic insignia veiling its architectural features. The platform, too, seemed more densely crowded, and across its entire width stood a row of large carved chairs; those near the center were surmounted by canopies embroidered with coats-of-arms and other devices, and in front was a massive carved table equipped with writing accessories. The real focus of attention, however, was a large showcase at one side offering a vista of glittering silverware, jewels, and rich fabrics artistically displayed. There were the prizes provided by the patron with ostentatious munificence, among which were trays, vases, salvers, platters, cups and spoons of engraved silver, jewelled snuffboxes and tobacco containers, scented gloves, and lengths of choice silk, satin, velvet and other fine textiles in brilliant hues arranged with graceful elegance. Only with difficulty did the eyes of the audience stray from these objects, and their gaze quickly returned to them with fascinated wonder.

The assembled public represented the most aristocratic and socially pretentious elements of viceregal society who had come quite as much to be seen at an occasion of such cultural importance as to listen to its tedious proceedings. Some were seated but most remained standing, a perfumed mass in polychromatic splendor of bright attire, plumes, and jewelled swords. A noisy chatter of conversations again pervaded the hall as the assembly awaited the arrival of the viceroy and his retinue without whom the ceremonies could not begin. That lordly official regarded a lack of punctuality as a prerogative of his high office and, to keep in a prolonged state of expectancy so distinguished a gathering, was a satisfying demonstration of personal power. All the more theatrical and regal was his eventual entrance after the long period of suspense.

When a flourish of trumpets at last heralded his approach, a quiver of excitement ran through the audience as its eyes turned toward the portal. From the platform descended a procession of professors, doctors, and others of high degree, in cap and gown, bright hoods, and other regalia; it advanced toward the doorway to welcome the highest magistrate in the land and his gentlemen-in-waiting. As the two columns met much ceremonious bowing and posturing ensued, after which a single line formed with the Viceroy and the Judges of the Royal Audiencia at the head, resplendent in court dress, and in a slow, measured step, it advanced to the platform and took designated seats. As a degree of quiet returned, swelling strains of soft music spread through the auditorium, and the Secretary was observed slowly mounting the pulpit to begin the program.

It was a leisurely age which loved variety and punctilio, and it willingly accepted the varied formalities which preceded the reading of poems and the bestowal of prizes. A pious invocation was *de rigueur,* designed, it would seem, to impress the Deity as well as the aristocratic gathering with its rhetorical flourishes, generous sprinkling of quotations from Latin authors, pedantic allusions, and other literary conventions. Verbal genuflections directed at the viceroy and the royal judges and similar salutations then followed. Congenial to the Baroque spirit was a commingling of this ritual-istic solemnity and a mundane humor in public functions of this sort, and the noblest sentiments might rub elbows in democratic fashion with crude satire and witty sallies of dubious propriety. Hence these respectful formalities frequently gave way to comic relief of a graceless nature called *vejámenes.* These were somewhat ludicrous comments which often expressed in jest what jealous rivals were saying of others in private. Oddities of appearance, manners, and conduct attributed to contestants were caricatured in apocryphal anecdotes or verbal sketches little calculated to spare the victim's feelings. The greater his discomfiture the greater the hilarity of the gathering. Usually the object of these mortifying attentions resigned himself to this horseplay, but occasionally sensi-bilities proved tender and tempers flared. In the light of the prevailing *pundonor,* or brittle code of honor, it is curious that these robust jibes and barbs, so offensively personal, provoked so few reprisals of a physical sort. The Secretary read them to the assembly from a sheaf of notes called *cedulillas* as if they were news items, heightening the effects of the quips by his histrionic gifts.

Few commodities are more perishable than current jokes and few things are more transitory than fashions in wit. In reading these sallies of a by-gone age a modern observer wryly grimaces at their tasteless jocularity and marvels at the tumultuous laughter which, apparently, they evoked from the cultured elite of a Baroque society. An example or two will suffice. The first is from a *vejamen* at the University of San Marcos, in Lima, Peru.

"This *cedulilla* declares that when the gentleman taking the doctor's degree was a school boy, his teacher told him one time to take off his shirt. To this request the lad quickly responded: 'I'm not wearing a shirt today because it is a work day. My mother keeps it in her closet for holidays.' "

A second example from the same source depends for its levity upon the chief stock-in-trade of such mid-nineteenth century North American humorists as "Petroleum V. Nasby" and "Josh Billings," that is, colloquialisms and phonetic spelling of words. Hence its feeble wit (by present standards) which, like that of a pun, can hardly find adequate translation.

"This *cedulilla* is a letter to a certain nun, the object of his affections, and it reads: My dear little shorty: this afternoon I'll cum to see you and I'll take you to where we can eat a *yanqui* of sweet potatoes and jerked beef. As a penalty for not cummin' out yesterday afternoon because you were playin' a game of *chueca* I'm sure goin' to giv you a coupla hard raps and the same number of slaps. Your chummy Antuquito, usque ad mortem et infra."[6]

Such drollery often served as the *hors d'oeuvres* of a metrical banquet featured by a surfeit of verbal viands. This act concluded, the Secretary adopted a more unctuous tone as he prepared the public for the feast to follow. In verses of his own composition he lyrically set forth the theme and purpose of the poetic tournament, and followed this overture by a pedantic disquisition in artificial prose on the various symbols around which the competing poetasters had woven their word patterns in the several divisions of the tournament. This discourse did not fail to exhibit the orator's scholastic learning, and his thought hardly emerged from the labyrinthine syntax and the lush foliage of classical allusions and ponderous quotations. However, the listeners knew that the end had come when the Secretary closed with an exhortation to the "Mexican swans to gird the armor of Apollo and go forth to battle the muses." This summons was purely rhetorical, however, for the contestants, having submitted their poems, were already veterans of combats in Parnassus, and the victors were awaiting their laurels. The Secretary then explained the special theme of the first section of the tournament, with its assigned meters, and read the poem ad-judged the best. Its proud author then stepped up to receive the designated trophy, and upon delivery the Secretary recited the punning couplets so carefully contrived beforehand. In a similar manner he dealt with second- and third-prize winners, and suc-cessively through the several parts into which the competition was divided. Even some entries which failed to receive awards were also read—no doubt to ease the disappointment of a sensitive con-testant. These proceedings consumed long hours and their tedious-ness would hardly seem relieved by the witticisms of the master of ceremonies and the interludes of music. Indeed, so wearisome does it all appear that one wonders whether the viceroy, the noble gentlemen of the Royal Audiencia, and many other dignitaries grac-ing the occasion by their presence did not often struggle to repress discreet yawns, and whether their thoughts did not wander into more engaging matters. It is easy to imagine that one or another dozed off for a few merciful moments, for the cloying artificiality and exaggerated conceits must have produced a soporific effect be-yond the power of the Secretary's pleasantries to overcome entirely.

Despite these apparent defects the poetic tournaments remained the most important events of the cultural and literary life of the New World centers of Hispanic civilization through most of the three colonial centuries. The enduring enthusiasm for this esthetic activity was attributable in part, perhaps, to its dual nature. The satisfaction of the participants, at least the successful ones, was twofold. The aspiring author could have his work read aloud to the most select public of society before whom he might appear in the guise of a Poet, a coveted distinction, and in the *relacion,* or chron-icle of the competition published afterward, usually a volume in luxurious format setting forth in prolix fashion the circumstances of the event and reproducing the text of the prize-winning verse, he had almost the sole possibility of seeing his versified lucubrations in the seemingly permanent form of type. There was, then, the double exhilaration of a living audience of contemporaries and the invisible one of posterity. Thus these published records of tournaments became cherished possessions for prominent display in homes and libraries. If most of their contents scarcely deserved embalming in this fashion, they have come down as curious metrical mummies to enliven the excavations of literary archaeologists and to shed light upon the cultural mores of a Baroque antiquity.

For those whom custom obliged to listen patiently during the interminable function the rewards lay, perhaps, in the drama of the spectacle and in the sprightly efforts of the presiding functionary, the Secretary. The humor of his couplets, like that of the *vejámenes,* poorly resists the erosion of time. The chief reliance was on wordplay, in which the Baroque mind developed an extraordinary dexterity. Such legerdemain shares with puns the handicap of being a currency of language rarely convertible into other linguistic coinage, but possibly a single, incomplete example will illustrate well enough the means by which a master of ceremonies sought to excite the risibilities and sustain the interest of an audience. The Secretary of a competition held in Mexico City in 1683 was a well-known scholar who wore spectacles. Exercising a privilege authorized by custom, he had entered a sonnet of his own invention under a pseudonym. The judges, possibly penetrating this disguise without excessive difficulty, had crowned his fourteen-line effort with a first prize. In accepting a silver vase as a fitting tribute to the merit of his brain-child, the recipient, pointing to the glasses he wore, genially declared:

> My sonnet, in its excesses,
> is a most ungraceful monster;
> for, conceived with four eyes,
> it was born with fourteen feet.*

---

* Monstruo de desgracias es
Mi soneto en sus arrojos,
Pues hecho con quatro ojos,
Nació con catorse pies.

# ☙ X

# SOME CURIOSITIES
# OF BAROQUE VERSE

HIGHLY fashionable in the Hispanic world of the seventeenth century was verse writing, a fact the evident addiction to poetic tournaments clearly sustains. An artistic ability of this sort sometimes opened doors to promotion, and the Spanish American Creole, denied higher offices in his own land, eagerly strove for literary distinction as a possible means of breaching the barrier to advancement. Aristocratic prestige, leisure-class dilettantism, and a hunger for material advantage were among other factors which account for the mass production of metrical compositions of all kinds during the Baroque age.

All this outpouring of poesy might have resulted in more creditable art if the overseas subjects of the crown had not succumbed so completely to the literary vices of contemporary Spain. Unhappily, the Baroque retreat from life, with a consequent decline in wit, lightness, irony, and grace of expression, so completely absorbed the Spanish New World that it carried literary abuses to greater extremes. A great poet of Spain, Luis de Góngora (1561-1627), cast so deep a shadow over the artistic expression of the Creole gentry that it extinguished all but the faintest glimmers of light. Much of the early poetry of this bard of Cordoba was strikingly beautiful in clarity and lyric charm but, almost coinciding with Fray García Guerra's arrival at Mexico City, it grew increasingly complex, obscure, and pedantic. The excellence of such highly mannered poems as *Fábula de Polifemo y Galatea* (Fable of

145

Polyphemus and Galatea); and *Soledades* helped to consecrate a cult of the "new poetry" characterized by excessive artificiality, complicated and strained metaphors, invented vocabulary, and syntactical involutions which soon concealed meaning to all but the elect. This involved style paralleled the intricacy already discernible in architectural and sculptural details of Baroque façades and retables. Resembling the euphuism of England, marinism of Italy, and preciosity of France, the new trend in writing, soon referred to as *culteranismo,* or *culto,* or gongorism, descended with blighting effect upon aspiring versifiers of the remote Spanish possessions. A contemporary critic of Góngora had declared that: "Every work, however short, consists of three parts, soul, body, and ornament, that is, subject matter, phrases, and artful expression. . . . Some poets seek only a fanciful exterior, without soul or body."[1] Whatever validity this last statement has with respect to its immediate object, the justice of its application to most writers of verse in Old Mexico is hardly disputable. There, as the poetic competitions have shown, the effort of poetasters to ape the literary habits of the motherland went beyond the models in ridiculous conceits, pomposity, pedantry and other forms of rhetorical flatulence. Destined for a long life in the Hispanic world, this perverse style, with its heavy verbiage and hollow meaning, was still discernible in the writing of the late nineteenth century. An iconoclastic poet of Peru in that period voiced his scorn with characteristic vehemence:

> Thunderous and reverberating Castilian poesy,
> the big drum in the orchestra of Pindar and Homer;
> if hardly dost thou lull souls, surely dost thou deafen ears.

> In the dense foliage of useless words
> grows pallid, the juiceless fruit of thought.
> Oh, speech of Cervantes, thy many-tendrilled vines
> have gigantic leaves and dwarf-like bunches of grapes.*

---

* Atronadora y rimbombante Poesía castellana
  Tambor mayor en la orquesta de Píndaro y Homero,
  Si poco arrullas a las almas, mucho asordas los oídos.

  En el espeso follaje de inútiles vocablos,
  Brota, pálida y sin jugo la fruta de la idea.
  Oh, verbo de Cervantes, en tu viña empampanada
  Son gigantescas las hojas, enanos los racimos
  —Manuel González Prada. *Exóticas*
  (Lima, 1948), p. 41.

Least of all, perhaps, did the New World poetasters appreciate, as a recent critic of Castilian letters puts it, ". . . that no one who cared for vigour and integrity of the language could approve of the principles on which Góngora wrote, however much they might admire the results." And they were indifferent to the fact that "he was leading it away from its fertilizing sources in life."[2] The prize-winning verse of the colonial contests amply justifies these various strictures and deserves even severer ones, for their authors did not stop at meaningless jumbles of artificial expressions and numbing Latinisms, but subjected modes of speech and forms of verse to every form of distortion and wordplay that misguided ingenuity could contrive. Few examples, indeed, were more than a fanciful exterior, without soul or substance, and it would seem that the poetic tournament owed its great revival to a disposition to encourage these aberrations. Competing versifiers delighted to make commonplace the most intricate devices of verbal calisthenics and legerdemain, and an attempt to catalogue the resulting oddities would be an undertaking as difficult as unprofitable. But a few specimens may give a more vivid, if depressing, impression of the esthetic wasteland of much colonial poetry and provide an exhibit of literary phenomena of Baroque inspiration.[3] These curious products often defy translation and some can be represented only in the original Spanish.

One of the least objectionable of these metrical diversions was the gloss. Usually the verses of a quatrain taken in order served as the concluding line of four successive *décimas,* or stanzas of ten lines. The gloss, therefore, did not put as much strain on the inspiration of the author as did most other innovations of the time. Indeed, in the hands of a competent craftsman, it was capable of beauty. Many great figures of Spain's Golden Age had cultivated this form successfully, and its appearance in the overseas domains was certainly not the worst form of literary borrowing. To be sure, Cervantes' hero did not entertain a very high regard for this kind of thing. "A friend of mine," observed Don Quixote, "a man of intelligence, is of the opinion that the writing of poetic glosses is a waste of energy, and the reason he gave me was this: that the gloss almost never can come up to the text but very often, or most of the time, goes beyond the meaning and intention of the original lines. And moreover, he added, the rules governing this form of composition are too strict, they do not permit of interrogations or any 'said he,' or 'I will say'; they do not allow verbs to be turned into nouns or the general sense and construction of the passage to be altered, along with other restrictions by which those who write glosses are bound, as your Grace must know."

The gloss which Don Quixote's interlocutor recited to him on the occasion of these sage remarks is here reproduced from the Putnam version of Cervantes' master work. Requirements of English altered the exact rendition of the lines of the quatrain in the concluding verses of the *décimas*.

> *Oh, could my "was" an "is" become,*
> *I'd wait no more for "it shall be";*
> *or could I the future now but see,*
> *and not this present, dour and glum.*
>
> Gloss
>
> All things must pass away at last,
> and so, the blessing that was mine,
> fair Fortune's gift, it also pass'd,
> ne'er to return, though I repine;
> my skies are wholly overcast.
> Long hast thou seen me at thy feet,
> O Fortune fickle, Fortune fleet;
> but make me happy once again
> and I'd forget my present pain,
> *could but my "was" and "is" now meet.*
>
> No other pleasure do I crave,
> no other palm or warrior's prize,
> such triumph as befits the brave;
> all that I ask: those happier skies
> to which my memory is a slave.
> Woulds't thou but give this gift to me,
> O Fortune, then perchance I'd see
> this fire of mine—O priceless boon!—
> *I'd wait no more for "it shall be."*
>
> Impossible the thing I ask,
> since Time, once gone, none can recall;
> for to accomplish such a task,
> no power on earth but it is too small.
> No more beneath those skies I'll bask.
> Swift doth he come and swiftly flee,

nor doth return, light-footed he!
and well I know it is not right
to seek to stay Time in his flight;
*turn past to present—futile plea!*

My life is anxious, filled with gloom;
and living thus 'twixt hope and fear,
is naught but death's familiar doom;
better to lie upon my bier
and seek the door to pain's dark room.
It seemeth me, it would be sweet
to end it now, thus life to cheat;
but living long and living longer,
the fear within grows ever stronger
*of that dread "shall be" I must greet.*[4]

One of the oldest devices is the acrostic. The Greeks are said to have made use of such combinations, and in every age and language it appears in almost infinite variety. In the seventeenth century its popularity was possibly greatest in the courtly circles of Europe and, consequently, in the literate strata of colonial society. A common form spelled out the name of a person by the initial letter of a succession of lines, but in Old Mexico the acrostic makers were rarely content with anything so simple. They strained their ingenuity to devise novel and complex examples of which a "royal sonnet acrostic," with the technique of a gloss, is symptomatic. The four-line stanza

El bronce y buril
Al valor y el arte
De tan raro Marte
Den aplausos mil.

(Let the trumpet and the engraver's tool give applause a thousand-fold to the courage and art of so rare a martial figure) is spelled out by the initial letters in four vertical columns of words within a sonnet.

| | | | |
|---|---|---|---|
| De a tu | Diestra | Asañoza (que | Excelente |
| Encumbra | Esmaltes | Liberal | Lucida) |
| Zítida | Trompa | Ufana, con | Brunida |
| Aureada | Acción | Aplauso | Refulgente |
| Penetró | Nauta) el | Tabaro hacia | Oriente |
| Lanzó al | Rebelde | Opónese | Zacida |
| Antorcha(a su | Antro | Rasga | Compelida |
| Cereda al | Risco | Andaga lo | Eminente |
| Sojuzgó al | Orgulloso | Empeño | Nculto |
| Otros miden el | Monte | Luego | Bramas |
| Siguiendo | Ayron de | Audaz flechero | Culto |
| Mil laureles | Rozaste en | Rudas | Ramas |
| Tal continuo | Turbión de | Tanto | Insulto |
| Leon, le | Extingues | Esforzado | Llamas[5] |

Another *tour de force* of durable fashion in the poetic contests were the so-called "echoes." The final word of each verse repeated the closing syllables of the penultimate word, thus creating the effect of an echo. The predominance of vowel sounds in Castilian made this trick easier to perform than in English in which a similar effect was achieved more often by repeating the last two or three words of a line as:

> A lampe whose beames are ever bright
> And never feares approaching night.
>        Echo        Approaching night.[6]

A quatrain of a prize-winning sonnet in the 1683 competition exemplifies the Castilian phenomenon.

> Si al alto Apolo la sagrada *agrada*
> Piedad Troyana, a que devida *vida*
> Tanta asegure, que eximida *mida*
> Del veloz tiempo en la jornada *nada*.[7]

As one thing leads to another, so bold spirits ventured still more hazardous feats of cerebration. Such was the "double echo," in which the last three words of a verse re-echoed each other as they dwindled in length. Recalling the mystical words pronounced in the Lenten practice of Ash Wednesday, "reverteris, teris, eris, is," a colonial poet, dwelling upon the inevitableness of death—a theme congenial to the Baroque spirit—wrote a series of quatrains not entirely devoid of substance. Two of these will reveal the technique of the "double echo."

> Todo en la vida es mudable
> y en prueba de su inconstancia
> lo que apreciabas constancia
> *invariable—variable—hable.*
> Mira cuan desconocida
> queda, entre humanas memorias
> la aclamación de tus glorias,
> *pues se olvida—vida—ida.*[8]

(All in life is mutable, and in proof of its inconstancy, it may speak variably about that thou esteemest invariable constancy.
See how the acclaim of thy triumphs remains unrecalled in human memory, for a life departed is a life forgotten.)

"Difficult poetry, both because of the lofty meter and the arduous composition, is that in which every word appears with the same initial letter."[9] This comment which, with equal truth might have included the adjective "useless" as well as "arduous," accompanies a series of octaves fashioned in this manner. Yet alliteration on a large scale was a task of word play often undertaken by colonial wordsmiths. A half octave of doleful feeling will suffice.

> ¡Cielo! ¿Cómo canciones cantaremos
> con corazones casi consumidos?
> con causa conveniente callaremos,
> congojados, confusos, condolidos . . . .[10]

(Heavens! How will we sing songs with hearts almost consumed? Afflicted, confused, and grieved, we shall, with appropriate reason, keep silent . . .)
Separate stanzas shifted in turn to words beginning with A, O, L, and M respectively to voice variations on the same plaint.

The eleven-syllable line, as the meter of the lofty epic, was especially vulnerable to experimentation by manufacturers of macaronic verse. One of the bolder ventures was to force the eight lines to serve the strophic needs of two different verse forms, both of which treated the same theme independently and could be read separately. This feat was accomplished by making the first seven of the eleven

syllables of the eight lines form two roundelays or quatrains, while
the full octave formed the second poem. The following example
illustrates this splitting technique. The quatrains appear in ordinary
type, while the remaining syllables of the octave verses are in
italics.

> O Celebre tu gloria *docta Athenas*
> con digna aclamación, *con voces claras*
> la fama por blazón *de aplausos llenos*
> y el tiempo por memoria *de a tus aras.*
> O seráphico Coro! *pues resuenas*
> oy con manera amante *dichas raras,*
> celebra el puro instante *a Delos pura*
> que haze tu edad de oro *mas segura.*[11]

An approximate translation of the internal quatrains is: "Oh, let
thy glory be celebrated with worthy acclaim, with fame as a
heraldic shield, and time as a record! / Oh, the seraphic Chorus
now hails in fond manner the pure instant that forms thy golden
age." The enfolding octave enlarges on the subject of the Immaculate Conception somewhat as follows: "Oh, may this learned
Athens celebrate thy glory / with worthy acclaim and by clear
words, / and, by its full meed of applause may fame / give time
as a record of thy altars. / Oh, seraphic Chorus, since thou singest
/ now in fond manner of rare bliss, / praise to pure Delos the pure
instant / that makes thy golden age more certain."

Still more taxing to ingenuity than the preceding exercises, it
would seem, were the *poesías retrogradas,* or poems with reversible
lines. The Secretary of the 1683 tournament in Mexico City decreed that the theme of the Immaculate Conception demanded the
most difficult and varied efforts of the contestants. As Aeneas had
found refuge and inspiration on the island of Delos in the Aegean
Sea, so the Spanish monarch, Philip III, "had dropped the anchor
of his hope in the safe harbor" of this article of faith which the
aspiring bards of the viceregal capital should celebrate either by
writing ballads or "quatro dezimas retrogradas." "The latter," he
explained to obviate any misunderstanding, "are composed in such
a manner that, by reading from the last line to the first they will
make sense and deal with the same subject as when read in the
natural order."[12] Owing to the greater syntactic flexibility of Castilian this undertaking was not quite so formidable, perhaps, as in

English, but it clearly subordinated content to ingenuity of form.
A ten-line stanza of a poem crowned with the choicest laurel of
the competition will illustrate.

> Assí el Gran Filipo Amante
> a mejor Delos MARÍA
> con devoción rinde pía
> cultos al primer instante;
> no es mucho, si semejante
> de Eneas la Religión
> grande feliz successión
> a su real casa asegura
> Quando más aplaude pura
> en Delos la Concepción.[13]

Following the normal order, this is approximately rendered:
"Just as the great Philip, devoted / to the best refuge, MARY, / wor-
ships with pious devotion / the virginal Conception / so it is not
too much (to believe that), similar / to Aeneas the Faith / will
vouchsafe a great and fortunate succession / to his royal dynasty /
the more the pure Conception / is praised in Delos." Read in re-
verse the same sentiment emerges.

One of the most abject expressions of the cult of the Spanish
poet, Luis de Góngora, were the *centones* which resembled a crazy
quilt of bits and shreds snipped from the poems of the tutelary
bard (occasionally other poets were thus favored). These frag-
ments, to change the figure, were laid end to end in successive
layers like bricks to form a metrical wall. A Mexican critic aptly
described this bizarre product as "a work as difficult as anti-artistic,
in which neither intelligence, imagination, nor sentiment has a
part; it is a labor so mechanically humdrum that it may be com-
pared to the artisan who does inlay work in wood or forms mosaics
of varicolored stones."[14]

The most diverse materials sometimes went into the fabrication
of centos, including scraps of sacred and profane works, of ancient
Greek and Roman poets, proverbs, apothegms, and even snatches
of popular songs. This game was so fascinating that prose compositions and sermons, and even whole books were similarly constructed. It is said that, during the ceremonies in 1701 honoring
the memory of the recently deceased Charles II, last of the House
of Austria on the Spanish throne, Fray Bartolomé Navarro

preached a sermon stitching together patches torn from the writings of such diverse figures as Vergil, Ovid, St. Paul, Horace, Lucan, Machiavelli, St. John, Euripides, Jeremiah, Terence, St. Matthew, and Martial.[15]

Góngora remained, however, the chief inspirer of cento poems of which the often cited 1683 tournament offers numerous examples. Abuses had crept into this practice and the Secretary was explicit in his instructions. "It is indispensable and the express rule," he warned, "that not two or three, nor even one complete verse be taken to form the new poem. For convenience in checking, the folio number and specific poem, from which half-lines or hemistics are taken, must be indicated in the margins before and after each full verse. And elsewhere the edition, with date and place of publication, is to be cited."[16]

A few lines of one of these prefabricated "poems" will suffice as an illustration.

| | | | |
|---|---|---|---|
| Pan. f. 182 | Propicio albor* Oráculo prudente | Son. f. | 28 |
| Son. f. 37 | El Garzon Phrygio* (quando ya en el puerto) | Can. f. | 39 |
| Can. f. 42 | con naval pompa* de victoria armado | Can. f. | 41 |
| Can. f. 43 | Este jardin* (no pisa con pie incierto) | Com. f. | 189 |
| Son. f. 13 | Oye piadoso* admira reverente: | Can. f. | 39 |

The half lines, separated by an asterisk, have the source and folio number of the first in the left margin, and of the second in the right. The volume used in this instance was the 1654 edition of Góngora's works published at Madrid. Similarly, marriages of half verses continued indefinitely, duly cited, until the diligence of the compiler wearied or until the quota of praises of the theme, in this case, the Immaculate Conception, was complete.[17]

Industry and ingenuity, it is hardly necessary to state, were mistaken for artistic expression, and the perspiration of verbal contortionists had supplanted the inspiration of authentic poets. The inventiveness of puzzle-making, the artful playing of word games, and exhibitions of acrobatic wordplay were the approved ways of deceiving the muses. Especially meritorious was the ability to produce clever puns, rhymed riddles, *paranomasias* (use of words identical in spelling except for a vowel) and similar artifices. The last-named device is illustrated by an example which, in the eyes of contemporary Spanish Americans, possessed the double virtue of wit and patriotism.

> El Inglés, con frascos frescos
> ebrio, con su baba,—beba,
> y haga de la gula—gala,
> que, con él se trata—treta[18]

(Let the Englishman, in his cups, drink with his drool, and let him display his gluttony, for on him one plays one's tricks.)

Another favorite trick was proof of wit. As verses were made reversible, so letters within words were reversed to spell a different word and thus provide an occasion for ingenious manipulation. If "regal" is spelled backwards, it becomes "lager," while "god" and "top," treated in the same manner, became "dog" and "pot" respectively. In Castilian this technique operates with *odio* (hate) and *oído* (ear, hearing) in the following *quintilla*:

> ¿Cómo ha de pintar un hombre
> la Aurora que nunca vido?
> Y más yo (nadie se asombre)
> que de Aurora sólo el nombre
> me despierta odio al oído.[19]

(How is one to depict the dawn when one has never seen it? And how much harder for me in whose ear (don't be astonished) the mere mention of dawn awakens hatred!)

An intriguing game was to write verses ending in letters which, by giving their alphabet sounds, simulated words.

| | |
|---|---|
| Yo soy arriero de R. Q. A. | (recua) |
| y de otros arrieros G. F. | (jefe) |
| y pues he llegado A. U. Z. | (Auzeta) |
| la mala fortuna C. S. | (cese)[20] |

which may be rendered: "I'm a muleteer of a packtrain / and the boss of other muleteers, / and since I've come to Auzeta, / my bad luck has ceased."

But the appeal of these artifices palls and the hour has come to close this museum of literary curiosities, though the exhibits observed by no means exhaust the catalogue. These verbal contrivances are, on the whole, more amusing than the windy pomposity of altisonant verse professing to be serious art, and the glimmers of wit they emit are reminders at least that a sense of humor, however perverted, was not entirely absent in an age which, in retrospect, seems so often dominated by a morbid view of life and a preoccupation with death and decay. The more festive notes, however, in most of the surviving verse of the Baroque period are drowned in the deluge of ponderous artificiality, pedantry, and overly ornate diction that flows like a vast verbal lava over the springs of feeling and beauty. Scholasticism and orthodoxy lay heavily upon speculative thought and its expression, and an anachronistic ideology was stifling the free play of ideas and inhibiting every form of controversy. Hence the frustrated imagination and the repressed mental energy of articulate members of society sought release in an ingenious manipulation of verbal symbols and metrical forms which effectively obscured any latent meanings. To *gongorizar*, with an extravagance of Latinisms, neologisms, syntactical subversions, exaggerated metaphors and tropes, classical allusions, chromatic and musical effects, difficult charades, and the like, was to make a safe detour around the intellectual quicksands of Counter Reformation dogmas and absolutes, and these puerile exercises of wit and ingenuity brought literary distinction well within the range of mediocre talent. With vanity thus gratified, few inquisitive minds were tempted to venture into the risky areas of genuine speculation.

This debasement of the creative impulse was, of course, beneficial to neither the mind of the community nor to its literary expression; it even deflected the imagination from the innocuous beauty of nature to a large extent. Little of the charm of the natural setting of the viceregal capital, or of other scenic parts of the vast realm of Old Mexico seeped into contemporary poetry, and almost no lyric verse of authentic merit remains. That gifted talents were not entirely lacking amid the army of versifiers is certain, for an extraordinarily fine poetess, Sister Juana Inés de la Cruz, a nun in the Convent of St. Jerome in Mexico City, wrote poems of enduring excellence during the last half of the seventeenth century, but the few who possessed genius were too often throttled and thwarted by the ineludible tyranny of prevailing esthetic fashions. Succumbing to these oppressive influences the better endowed spirits were constrained to turn from the cultivation of a more worthy literature to the production of such inanities as have passed in review in the preceding pages.

# ON THE BOOK
# TRADE, 1683

SPAIN had reached the nadir of its political and cultural fortune in the dying years of the seventeenth century. On its troubled throne sat the semi-imbecile Charles II. In 1681 the death of the great dramatist, Calderón de la Barca, rang down the curtain on the Golden Age of Spanish letters and arts, and thus a pall fell upon the peoples of the Hispanic peninsula from which they never emerged completely. But if a sort of nocturnal gloom enshrouded Old Spain in those closing decades, a faint afterglow of the luminous era lit up New Spain. Mexico City, grown more extensive since the days of Fray García Guerra, probably exceeded Madrid itself in physical beauty, and the glittering opulence of its viceregal court now outshone the tawdriness of the royal palace and the aristocratic circles hovering about the degenerate scion of the Hapsburgs.

Within the Mexican city the broad, central streets still looked as if drawn in straight lines by a ruler, and those with parallel waterways now appeared, especially on market days, even more animated than earlier in the century, with products and flowers. The Jamaica canal now rivaled the Alameda as a place of recreation where old and young of every class and caste floated by in blossom-covered barges, their passengers adding gay songs and guitar-strumming to the lively scene. Humble pedestrians strolled along its banks while the well-to-do sat in carriages, both groups

157

consuming the chocolate, *tamales*, *atole*, sweetmeats, and other indigestible viands bought from Indian vendors. Now and then a
larger barge glided past the muddy margins of the brackish water,
its occupants blithely dancing to the melodic rhythms of a stringed
orchestra of *mariachi* players.

In the adobe walls lining the streets were variegated stones and
pieces of *tezontle*, a porous stone, in the form of hearts, circles,
stars, and figured flowers. The low, squat dwellings behind alternated with the more imposing residences which flaunted wide, ornate doorways, and smaller balconies with iron gratings. In every
nook and cranny and in every season flamed garden-boxes of orange
trees, flowering shrubs, and plants veiling the ugliness of congested
living. The unpaved streets were dusty or miry according to circumstances, while the rough cobblestones of other thoroughfares were
scarcely more free of dirt or mud. From Chapultepec, west of the
city and where the viceroys often preferred to live, a long aqueduct,
with its three hundred and sixty-five graceful arches, pointed at
the heart of the capital where lay the central square. This open
space had grown more unsightly in the course of the century because of "more than two hundred fixed and permanent wooden
shops, the majority stocked with large amounts of European and
domestic merchandise. The other booths were not so important as
they dispensed glassware, crockery, groceries, and foodstuffs. The
remainder of the Plaza was covered by Indian stands of reed-grass
and *petates*, in which they sell by day and sleep by night. As a result," wrote a contemporary, "one of the best and most spacious
squares in the world looks to everyone like an ill-assorted village
and a pigsty." The rentals thus provided helped to refill the chroni-
cally empty coffers of the municipality.

Contrasting with this crowded ugliness were the ornate buildings facing the square; the Cathedral, still lacking final architectural details, the City Hall, the viceregal Palace, the Inquisition,
the Audiencia, the University, the mint, the College of Santo Domingo, and the larger emporiums of wealthy merchants. Elsewhere
ecclesiastical establishments had continued to increase since the
time of Fray García Guerra, and at varying distances from the center were scattered some seventeen convents for nuns and a greater
number of monasteries for monks, and some eighty-nine churches
and temples. The city as a whole presented a Baroque sumptuous-

ness, mixed with squalor, hardly rivaled, save for the latter, in contemporary Spain. By moonlight the spires and cupolas gleamed
faintly, casting a ghostly spell over the broken, black masses of the
dwellings in between. On dark nights the lakebound capital lay
under a sable velvet, its somber obscurity scarcely relieved by trembling flickers of lampwicks sputtering beneath images in tiny niches
at domestic doorways.

In 1683 possibly 400,000 souls inhabited Mexico City, which
was then divided into seventeen parishes, five of Spaniards, and the
remaining dozen of Indians and mixtures. Where racial miscegenation had progressed over a century and a half, producing an increasingly complex pattern of pigmented profusion, a total of 72,-
000 passed as of pure European blood. Of these 22,000 were
Spaniards living with their families, and 20,000 more were male
transients. The white female population was reckoned at 30,000.
Permanent Indian residents were estimated at 80,000, with many
more passing in and out of the city continuously. A minority evidently declining in numbers since the days of Fray García but still
conspicuous were the 10,000 or more Negroes and mulattoes,
slave and free, who were domestic servants and petty tradesmen.
Various types of mestizos, or mixed elements comprised the rest of
the inhabitants.[1]

Socially the Creole class was the most powerful, its numbers
and wealth having increased greatly in the course of the century.
The economic depression of the earlier decades had yielded to a
more prosperous period of which the Mexican whites were the
chief beneficiaries. The waning fortunes of the mother country had
enabled many American-born Spaniards to obtain local offices of
government by purchase and other means. If the highest positions
were still out of their reach, the growing economic influence of
this group was making the status of the peninsular Spaniard less
secure and his control less weighty. But this general well-being
was not shared by the proletarian masses who, as their numbers
rose in the city, sank deeper into a morass of misery and alcoholism.
The drinking of pulque, a fermented liquid of the maguey plant,
made drunkenness universal and created fortunes for traffickers in
this beverage. The *pulquerías* were dens of iniquity, and "there is
no quarter, no street, without a public house in which liquor is
sold to the music of guitars, harps, and other instruments, with

rooms in which Negroes, Mulattoes, Mestizos, and many Spaniards meet," wrote a contemporary clergyman.[2] "In the City of Mexico," he went on, "two thousand arrobas of pulque enter every day, and especially on Tuesdays and Saturdays, more than fifteen thousand." Young women were put in charge of these establishments to lure trade, and it was "held for certain that to attract customers these publicans have a provision of persons of both sexes for evil commerce." Moreover, "no royal minister of Justice is allowed to enter the public house to arrest or expel a delinquent." This institution, a fruitful source of corruption, continued to flourish because it brought welcome revenue to an ever-depleted Treasury.

Presiding over the destinies of the sprawling realm in 1683 was the Count of Paredes, the twenty-eighth viceroy, who had held sway for three years amidst a viceregal court perhaps consciously aping the profligacy, luxury, and immorality of the contemporary Versailles of Louis XIV. Though Spain was bankrupt and prostrate, the mines and agriculture of Old Mexico permitted that overseas possession an opulence that even the court of Philip IV in Madrid had scarcely known in its flamboyant period.

A sharply contrasting person and spirit was the newly appointed archbishop (1682-1698), Francisco Aguiar y Seijas, an eccentric clergyman renowned for his puritanical ways, his excessive misogyny, and his extraordinary charities.[3] A twisted Catholic puritan, he had a pathological aversion for women, to whom he imputed all the evils against which the Church inveighed. According to his biographer, he regarded his myopic vision as a special boon since it prevented him from seeing members of the less homely sex. If, through some mischance, a woman crossed his threshold, he promptly ordered the bricks torn up and replaced upon which sacrilegious feet had trod.[4] Lacking entirely, as earlier noted, the taste for worldly pleasures so openly exhibited by his predecessor, Fray García Guerra, he relentlessly campaigned against bullfights, cockfights, gambling, and the theater, and doubtless the fanatic zeal of this mitered bluestocking inspired the Inquisition's renewed energy at this time. Yet his charities were truly munificent, and they even extended to unfortunate elements of despised womanhood. On one occasion he generously supported the efforts of a carpenter and his wife who had taken into their home a demented woman wandering about the streets. So lavish were his benefices that a foreign observer felt that "this ease in finding daily alms is the cause of so many vagrants in Mexico City."[5] Side by side, then, stood the oddly assorted heads of the church-state, each contributing to the indigence of the masses, one by the luxury of a corrupt viceregal court, the other by an exaggerated philanthropy.

Rumors of pirate depredations on both coasts had disturbed the monotony of life in Mexico City from time to time, but in 1683 shudders of alarm shook the capital. News came that in mid-May Vera Cruz had fallen to the dreaded pirate, Lorencillo, whose fierce corsairs sacked the port under the very bastions of the island fortress of San Juan de Ulloa and at a time when the fleet from Spain was hourly expected. In a bold, swift move these buccaneers descended upon the drowsy city, forcing its surprised inhabitants into a parish church. Tightly packed in this narrow space the victims endured for days the horrors of hunger, thirst, heat, and suffocation which must have equalled the torments later experienced in the famous "Black Hole of Calcutta." Children smothered to death and hapless women were dragged out and mercilessly raped, while the invaders threatened to burn the other inmates alive in the building if they did not reveal the hiding places of their wealth. Meanwhile, looting had uncovered a rich haul of silver bars and other treasure awaiting shipment on the incoming fleet. Its imminent approach caused the pirates to hustle their booty and many luckless citizens on board vessels and sail to the nearby Isle of Sacrifices where, without shelter or provisions, they held their victims for high ransoms. Having collected huge sums in this fashion, the buccaneers slipped away almost under the nose of the Spanish ships with the richest plunder ever captured in a port city of the Caribbean.[6]

Another episode which caused tongues to wag furiously that year was the "Case of the Hooded Man." In the midst of the excitement stirred by the sacking of Vera Cruz word reached Mexico City that a mysterious personage known as Antonio Benavides, Marqués de Vicente, was arriving, allegedly as a *visitador,* or royal inspector. The judges of the Audiencia and other viceregal officials, possibly fearing that they would be held responsible for the recent disaster and profiting by the emotional tensions prevailing, chose to regard the newcomer as an imposter. When the latter came to Puebla he was arrested and brought in custody to the capital. Public opinion was sharply divided, some condemning the apparently highhanded imprisonment of the king's representative, and others defending the viceroy's action. The trial of *el Tapado*, or the Hooded Man, as Benavides was called because of the mystery surrounding him, began on June 10, and the population followed its proceedings with eager interest. The effort to wring a confession by judicial torture brought attempted suicide, and feeling ran high during the remainder of 1683.[7] Conservative elements, fearing a threat to their property, believed that the Hooded Man was an agent of the pirates, or that he was bent on inciting revolution in the realm; the more liberal minded espoused his cause and eloquently pleaded for his release. Among these vocal individuals was the remarkable nun-poetess, Sister Juana Inés de la Cruz who, with feminine guile, appealed to the viceroy's clemency by composing a poem on the birthday of his son in which she urged a pardon for *el Tapado*.[8] These efforts, however, were unavailing, for the following year the unfortunate intruder was summarily executed. The enigma of this strange visitor and his mission was never publicly cleared up, and his case long remained a controversial topic of conversation at *tertulias* and social gatherings.

Despite the alarming threats to the security of the realm on the coasts and on the Indian frontiers, cultural life in the capital was vigorous in 1683. It was the year of one of the most elaborate poetic tournaments at the University of Mexico, with its attendant processions, pageantry, oratory, fireworks, and theatrical performances. Plays were written and performed, Sister Juana Inés de la Cruz was composing the best poetry of her time in Castilian, and quantities of books were imported, bought, and read. Indeed, Mexico City was more important than ever as a center of book collections. Religious orders had assembled large libraries, rich in treasures of rare editions and manuscripts. The College of Discalced Carmelites in outlying San Angel, where the famous Spanish novelist, Mateo Alemán, had lived in the days of Fray García Guerra, could boast of ". . . one of the best libraries in America, containing twelve thousand volumes,"[9] and other seminaries and schools were close rivals in this respect. Many collections were semipublic and accessible to interested citizens and scholarly visitors from abroad. Smaller aggregations of books belonged to private individuals, minor officials, lawyers, professors, physicians, merchants, and other laymen who, like Simón García Becerril and

Melchor Pérez de Soto before them, acquired numerous volumes imported regularly through local booksellers, many of which were lighter works of entertainment. In 1683 the rising savant of the University of Mexico, Don Carlos de Sigüenza y Góngora, was busily assembling manuscripts and published materials relating to Indian antiquities, mathematics, astronomy, engineering, history, and philosophy in a collection rated as the finest of the colonial period.

The book-buying public of Old Mexico was so considerable that a surprising number of dealers catered to it. These were usually local printing shops which added large importations to their own products. Probably the most important was that of the Heirs of the Widow of Bernardo Benavides de Calderón. Founded a half century before by a native of Alcalá de Henares in Spain, it had grown rapidly and, in 1683, did much of the local publishing.[10] This success owed much to the business acumen of the widow who assumed management on the death of the founder. Contributing quite as much to the prosperity of the firm, perhaps, was the fact that her six children had all taken orders in the Church, which was an important customer. The eldest son achieved so much distinction by his piety and learning that he was entrusted with high posts, including commissioner of the Inquisition,[11] which possibly accounts for the profitable concession granted to this house for printing and selling primers and catechisms in the realm. One of its annual inventories reveals the large and varied stock on hand in 1683, and this document makes abundantly clear that readers of New Spain could readily enjoy much the same writings as their kinsmen in Old Spain.

Hardly was the Holy Office established in 1571 when the first Inquisitor issued an edict requiring every owner of books to submit a list of them arranged in alphabetical order and with details of title, author, place and date of publication, and the language in which each was printed. While this practice was expected at regular intervals, it was not consistently followed. The advent of a new Inquisitor, a flare-up of heretical rumors, or some other cause occasionally brought renewed enforcement which usually relapsed into extended periods of apathy and indifference. The brief inventory of Simón García Becerril in 1620 preserved in the archive of the Holy Office was, perhaps, the result of censorial activity, momentarily revived. Public booksellers found it expedient to report stock in trade with some regularity, and these documents generally went into the files of the Inquisition without comment. The bookstore of Madame Benavides de Calderón was fairly circumspect in such matters, possibly because of the lucrative concession that her firm enjoyed, and her *memoria de libros* submitted at the end of 1683 rather carefully incorporated the bibliographical data required by the decree of a century before. It thus provides an enlightening glimpse of the varieties of literature carried in stock and presumably in demand. Though invariably listed by short titles— a method to be expected when prolix titles were the fashion— these abbreviations ordinarily permit ready recognition, which is often aided by other bibliographical details present. This inventory lists 276 titles, alphabetically arranged by the author's first name in the awkward practice of the time. Unfortunately it omits the number of copies of each item, thus preventing an analysis of the comparative popularity of individual works, but it provides some revealing insights into the reading preferences and cultural interests of the Mexican public in 1683.[12]

For North Americans the interest of a scrutiny of this booklist of New Spain may be enhanced by a consideration of the literature at the disposal of the New England public that same year. Such a comparison may bring surprises owing to the belief that both the dour Puritans and the inhabitants of Old Mexico shared a deprivation of all light literature, the former presumably by their own choosing, and the latter by the tyranny of the Inquisition. Both communities planted in the North American continent are commonly pictured as spending their slight leisure immersed in prayerbooks and homiletic writings, and eschewing the sensate delights of fiction. An inspection of the booksellers' stock in trade in both regions disproves this misapprehension, and even indicates a curious similarity of taste.

The second half of the seventeenth century had witnessed a rapid expansion of the English colonies, both in population and the area occupied. Massachusetts had prospered mightily and a steady stream of immigration was pouring into it and spreading into its western reaches and neighboring provinces of Rhode Island, Connecticut, and New Hampshire. Its villages and settle-

ments had multiplied, schools were spreading, Harvard College
was training many of its clergy, printing presses were functioning,
and a brisk book trade was developing with regular importations
from England. Boston was clearly the hub of all this commerce
and, though hardly comparable to a metropolis like Mexico City,
it was becoming a center of cultural activity and refinement. In
1683 it counted some 7,000 inhabitants and was a book market
serving 75,000 or more people scattered over New England. Its
leading dealer who, like Madame Benavides de Calderón in Old
Mexico, had several competitors, was John Usher, son of the
founder of the firm whose demise occurred in 1676, "leaving a
goodly fortune." A series of invoices extending from 1682 to 1685
indicates that this Boston merchant had imported 3,421 volumes
from England, and that the books listed were but a part of his
stock. These records show the number of copies of each item,
though they supply fewer bibliographical details than the contemporary Mexican inventory.[13]

The titles on both the Mexican inventory and the Boston invoices tend to fall into overlapping categories of religious writings,
secular nonfiction, and belles-lettres, with a rough equivalence in
the proportions of each. Religion was the dominant thought in
both colonial regions, however far apart they were in doctrinal concerns, and approximately half of the items were of this nature.
Coincidence of specific titles in the assortments of Protestant and
Catholic dealers was, of course, rare, but the common emphasis
was on homiletic writings, sermons, and moral disquisitions. The
absence of bibliographical information in the Boston lists precludes
knowledge of the presses from which the importations came, but
presumably they were all from England. The Mexico City inventory, on the other hand, supplies significant and unexpected evidence that many volumes came from printing establishments
outside of Spain, notably in the Netherlands and France, particularly Antwerp, Brussels, and Lyon.

Since it was the creative writings that enjoyed most popularity
and probably had the widest audience in both regions, it is well,
perhaps, to limit comment largely to items of this class. There is
added significance in dwelling upon this literature of entertainment
owing to a widely held belief that neither the overseas subjects of
the Spanish or the English kings could enjoy the pleasures of light

reading, the former because of the intolerant despotism of orthodox Catholicism, the latter because of the narrow rigidity of Protestant puritanism. For those still holding these traditional convictions, the records of the bookdealers in Mexico City and Boston that benighted year of 1683 provide revelations. These documents not only proclaim the existence of literary entertainment in both communities, but indicate similarities of taste that are more than vague. The Mexican list, to be sure, displays a richer variety and a more eclectic selection, which situation was to be expected in a more sophisticated society. There the assortment tends to fall into four categories: essays, poetry, drama, and prose fiction.

In both cultures the mark of a gentleman was the mastery of the classics and of history, and works in both fields were in evidence in New England and New Spain. Names of Latin and Greek adorn the book lists of each, but the presence of "Greek Testaments" and "Greek Gramers" in modest quantities on the Boston invoices and their absence on the Mexican inventory suggest a possibly greater concern of Englishmen for that language.[14] In a shipment to Mr. Usher the London dealer had apparently sought to promote by free copies the sales of "Siluanus his Theocritus, Lucian, Isocratis, Essopi Fabula and Plutark" with the notation that ". . . the four books of Siluanus are sent as a present to the Chief Schoolmaster in New England being a New Praxis upon some Greek Authors which is well entertained in our Schooles here and much used." But Latin writings abound on both lists; Vergil, Cicero, Martial, Seneca, and Ovid dot the inventory of Madame Benavides de Calderón, and Cicero, Terence, Horace, and Ovid speck the Boston invoices. The forty-two copies of "Bond's Horrace," and especially the twenty-two of "Farnaby's Ovid," and forty copies of "Ouid de Tristibus" strike the eye on Mr. Usher's lists.

Recalling the universal addiction to verse writing in Old Mexico the small percentage of poetry in stock in 1683 is curious, though hardly startling was the presence of the poetical works of Luis de Góngora whose baneful influence was so unmistakable in the tournament held at the University that year. The demand, it would seem, had shifted from the epic and lyric poetry, so artistically memorable in the sixteenth century, to the banal effusions of pietistic *ramilletes*, or garlands of verse, and to the lure of versified comedies, both of which were important staples in the Mexican book trade.

Dramatic literature is conspicuously absent in the Boston market, but the taste for collections of pious rhymes is warmly shared. Paralleling the Spanish *ramilletes*, sacred and profane, are dozens of copies of the English "Jovial Garland, a collection of all the newest Songs and Sonnets used in Court and Country," "The Crown Garland," "Garland of Delight," "The Royall Arbor of Loyall Poesie . . . Triumph, Elegie, Satyr, Love and Drollerie," and the two copies of the doubtfully moral *Poems on Several Occasions* by the Earl of Rochester. These festive effusions hardly comport with the traditional image of Puritan austerity, and they would seem to cancel out the impression of pious rectitude created by garlands of more proper verse. If now and then copies of Milton's *Paradise Lost* and Robert Wild's *Inter Boreale* appeared on the invoices, the esthetically inferior garlands far outnumbered them, much as the trivial *ramilletes* outweighed the works of Castilian bards in contemporary Mexico.

England and Spain were the two countries of Europe that had a great popular theater in the seventeenth century, but it was only in the overseas domains of the Hispanic empire that the enthusiasm for the drama of the motherland was shared. If the Puritans could only view the stage with a certain horror as one of the more conspicuous works of the Devil, hidebound subjects of orthodox Catholic persuasion in the Spanish realms were quite disposed to be indulgent with that satanic manifestation. As already evident, the *corrales de comedias* of Mexico City were crowded daily, while the printed plays delighted the literate. Since 1605 *Partes*, or collections of a dozen comedies each, had brought the works of playwrights in a continuous stream to the eager audience of the Spanish Indies, and for the printers and dealers this kind of reading matter was a bonanza. Madame Benavides de Calderón's inventory amply supplies confirmatory evidence of this enduring vogue. Despite Archbishop Aguiar y Seijas' currently impassioned zeal to suppress the theater in all its forms, she persisted in having in stock a liberal provision of play collections.

Quite properly as the dramatist who so completely conditioned and reflected the enduring essence of the Baroque spirit and who had become the tutelary genius of Spain's decadence, Pedro Calderón de la Barca, so recently deceased, heads the list, represented by the *Fifth Part, or Collection of Comedies*, published in Madrid in 1677. His shorter-lived disciple, Francisco de Rojas Zorrilla

(1607-1648), whose plays often had a more natural and lifelike quality, is present in a two-volume 1680 edition of his *Several Comedies,* and the works of numerous other dramatists were in stock. Likewise plentiful were collections of one-act plays and skits, often witty and satirical, "by various authors."

If the reading of plays was something of a rage in the seventeenth century Hispanic world, it did not entirely supplant prose fiction in various forms. There was a tendency, generally, to inject didactic elements into it and hence it was less diverting than the sparkling, versified *comedias.* Nevertheless the miscellanies of fables, apothegms, legends, novelettes, and full-length novels had a strong appeal to readers. The early sixteenth century *Silva de Varia Lección* (Miscellany) by Pedro Mexia, a potpourri of articles on history, travel, customs, superstitions, mythology, and related topics still retained an interested following. And popular reading fare were the tales of Pérez de Montalbán, the well-known dramatist, while the Mexican public did not fail to appreciate the more admirable *Exemplary Novels* and the *Don Quixote* of Cervantes.

By 1683 it appears that the enthusiasm for the sixteenth century romances of chivalry, still perceptible in the 1655 book list of Pérez de Soto, had at last expired, but no such extinction had overtaken two other sharply opposed types of novels, the ultrasaccharine pastoral fiction and the picaresque narratives distinguished by their racy pungency and sardonic bitterness. Destined for a long life in the Spanish colonies were the recitals of the amours of moonstruck shepherds and lassies, and here an unexpected similarity of taste in seventeenth century New England is observed. That such bucolic ardors had an appeal to Puritan readers in the chillier north can be deduced from the Boston invoices which record a copy of Sir Philip Sidney's *Arcadia,* and fifteen copies of *Argalus and Pathonia,* a poetical romance of kindred nature by Francis Quarles, whose translations of the Psalms and short devotional poems claimed the esteem of the Pilgrim fathers in soberer moments.

As for the contrasting tales of roguery, their vogue would not reach the English-speaking world until the following century when Spanish models would inspire Fielding, Smollett, and others to produce popular novels. But the Mexican public of 1683 was well accustomed to this reading fare and maintained a steady demand for it. The mid-sixteenth century forerunner and classic of the genre, *Lazarillo de Tormes,* still found a ready sale, though the expurgated version, required a hundred years before by the Inquisition and entitled *Lazarillo de Tormes Castigado* (Lazarillo de Tormes Chastised), was the only one available. Many later narratives of this sort figured in the inventory, notably *The Varied Fortunes of Pindar, the Soldier* by Gonzalo de Céspedes, whose particular fancy for eerie episodes with ghosts rising from tombs to assail guilty mortals faintly anticipates the atmosphere of the tales of Edgar Allen Poe. This Gothic character no doubt explains its inclusion in Pérez de Soto's earlier collection. In Madame Benavides de Calderón's stock there were also brief novels and short stories with mingled touches of realism and satire more or less related to the picaresque theme. Many were sketches of manners that, in the nineteenth century, would receive fuller development and serve to revitalize the Spanish novel. Even the more didactic of these fictional narratives were slightly astringent in their satire if less disposed to echo the heavier cynicism of the true tales of roguery. The sardonic humor, sly wit, and wry pessimism of these stories, also apparent in the short plays and skits so avidly bought and read, made them popular in a world of repressed feeling and wearied by an artificial refinement that substituted shadow for substance. Unconsciously readers were seeking an escape from the prevailing *desengaño* and unreality into a derisively imagined reality, and they took a half-grim delight in those writers who dipped their quills in a corrosive ink of frustration and bitterness.

Most symptomatic of this underlying feeling, perhaps, was the presence of the *Works* of Spain's greatest satirist, Francisco de Quevedo (1580-1645) in the 1683 inventory. The most caustic picaresque tale was his *History of the Life of the Buscón,* written when the author was still in his early twenties. "In the whole literature there can be few books showing such a horror and disgust for life written by a man" so young, observes a critic, and perhaps no one in the Spain of his time saw so clearly the seeds of national decadence that were sprouting. His series of lugubrious visions of the Last Judgment and of Hell contained in his *Sueños* (Dreams) are singularly expressive of the profoundly pessimistic and morbid spirit of the Baroque age.

Quevedo's almost pathological attitude toward existence and his preoccupation with infernal tortures had their counterparts in the Puritan soul of the same century, and the writings of such tormented authors were widely acceptable in both the English- and Spanish-speaking world. A work enjoying the status of a "best seller" in the New England of 1683 was the *Day of Doom* by the Reverend Michael Wigglesworth, whose harrowing depiction of sufferings and punishments in the hereafter must have engendered many a nightmare, but nearly every colonial household counted a copy among its furnishings. The affinity of the transplanted Spaniards and Englishmen in such morbid concerns is patent and, as if to confirm this contention, virtually the only Spanish author represented in the invoice of Mr. Usher, Boston bookseller in the 1680's, was this same dyspeptic Francisco de Quevedo, whose atrabilious *Sueños* were present in two copies dressed in English garb as "Quebedo, Visiones Compl, both parts." Unwittingly this splenetic writer of Catholic Spain was fostering self-hatred and a corroding fear in the hearts of New World Christians widely separated by space, language, and doctrine.

Despite its cursory nature the foregoing survey of the stocks in the leading bookstores of Mexico City and Boston pretty well explodes the traditional theory that the inhabitants of those localities were largely denied the pleasures of light reading in the seventeenth century. The Spanish subjects cowering in the awesome shadow of the Inquisition and the Pilgrim fathers sternly reading their Bibles and reproving any frivolity are both stereotypes that have beclouded the vision of posterity. While it is clear that the literate Mexicans in the more populous New Spain had a richer and more diversified assortment of entertaining books from which to choose, it is equally certain that the English settlers in colder New England could indulge mundane tastes in reading with more freedom and delectation than generally realized. The light and slightly immoral verse and at least eleven different romances which the Boston booksellers found sufficiently salable to keep in stock hardly jibes with the alleged austerity of the Puritans. Indeed, it is instructive to glance at a few of these curious narratives that diverted the reportedly inflexible and ascetic New Englanders.

"Their religious interests and concern with demonology stretched pretty far," remarks an observer, "if these were the reasons leading them to buy three copies of *Venus in the Cloyster, or the Nun in* her Smock, and sixty-six copies of *The History of the Damnable Life and Deserved Death of Dr. John Faustus*. And surely no utilitarian interest in shoemaking caused them to buy twenty-nine copies of *The Pleasant History of the Gentle Art. A Discourse containing Many Matters of Delight, very pleasant to read, set forth with Pictures, and Variety of Wit and Mirth*. And what is one to make of the two copies of *The London Jilt, or the Politick Whore; shewing all the artifices and stratagems which the Ladies of Pleasure make use of, for the intreaging and decoying of men; interwoven with several pleasant stories of the Misses' ingenious performances?* Was it material for sermons, or was it only erotica?"[15] And interesting, too, is the London dealer's notation on an invoice of May 29, 1684: "London Jilt is out of print and not to be had."

Other items at the disposal of New England readers were: *A History of Fortunatus*, about a successful young man; *Pharamond, or the History of France. A Fam'd Romance in Twelve Parts*, translated from the French of La Calprenède; *The Most Famous, Delectable and Pleasant History of Parismus, Prince of Bohemia; the English Rogue comprehending the most eminent Cheats of Both Sexes;* which suggests a latent taste for what readers in Old Mexico were enjoying at the moment; *The Famous History of Valentine and Orson; The Most Pleasant History of Tom a Lincoln;* and *Clelia*, a translation of a ten-volume romance of Mlle. de Scudéry. And what interest did a stern Puritan have in purchasing *Scoggins Jests*, with a foreword declaring that "there is nothing beside the goodness of God that preserves health so much as honest mirth"? Strange fare, indeed, is this for a people so easily outraged by the frivolities of a wicked world! It is refreshing to learn that the stiff-necked dwellers on a "stern and rockbound coast" could unbend in lighter moods even if, as seems quite certain, these softer moments were less frequent, less gay, and less spontaneous than those of their distant neighbors in the sunny vales and broad expanses of Old Mexico.

# ❦ XII

# A BAROQUE POETESS

ONE August day of 1667 in Mexico City an attractive, talented girl, still some months short of her sixteenth birthday, entered the sternly ascetic Order of Discalced Carmelites as a chorister. The convent that received her was the one that had been the dream of those earnest nuns, Sister Inés de la Cruz and Sister Mariana Encarnación when they plied the fickle Archbishop García Guerra so assiduously earlier in the century with sweetmeats and seductive music. Though immediate success had eluded these efforts, it will be recalled, patience was triumphant in 1616, and the new religious community came into being. The young lady who, a half century afterwards, gained admittance to its holy precincts was Doña Juana Inés de Asbaje y Ramírez de Santillana, better known as Sister Juana Inés de la Cruz, already mentioned in these pages and famed as the "last great lyric poet of Spain and the first great poet of America."[1] Also musically gifted, her ecclesiastical name was possibly adopted in veneration of the instrument-playing hostess of Fray García Guerra and cofounder of the Carmelite convent, of which she was now a temporary inmate.

In an age when matrimony and religious reclusion were the sole careers open to respectable females, the act of taking the veil was a commonplace event in Mexican society. In most sisterhoods the discipline was not severe, and within the cloistered walls many comforts and amenities of secular life could be enjoyed, including the services of personal slaves.[2] Indeed, for daughters whose matrimonial prospects were not bright, an immured existence of this sort

172

seemed a desirable alternative, and a young woman whose parents or relatives could provide the requisite dowry was regarded as fortunate. But the case of the adolescent Doña Juana Inés de Asbaje y Ramírez de Santillana seemed exceptional, and strangely obscure the reasons for her decision. Here was a maiden "that was far more beautiful than any nun should be,"[3] the darling of the vice-regal court, and the favorite maid-in-waiting of the vicereine. Her personal attractiveness, her nimble wit in penning verse for any occasion, and her amazing knowledge of books, were all very nearly the talk of the town. In fact, the admiring Viceroy himself, on one occasion, had arranged that a group of the leading professors at the University of Mexico should examine the precocious girl in various branches of learning, and when she emerged triumphant from this ordeal, the learned gentlemen marveled at the erudition and composure of a maiden who hardly seemed more than a child.

Her rise and renown in the courtly circle of the capital had been truly phenomenal. A village lass, born in 1651 in a tiny hamlet called Nepantla, "the land in between," that looked up to the snow-crested volcanoes Popocatepetl and Ixtacihuatl, she had begun to read at the age of three, later devouring the small library of her grandfather. When eight years old she went to Mexico City to live with relatives. Soon this pretty child prodigy caught the eye of the vicereine who brought her to reside amidst the luxury and splendor of the viceregal Palace. In this sophisticated environment the young girl rapidly acquired a maturity that quite belied her years, and in the Court she soon found herself envied for her wit by the women and desired for her physical charms by the men.

Social success of this sort in such aristocratic circles was all the more extraordinary in the light of her illegitimate birth, though this circumstance was, perhaps, undisclosed to anyone save her confessor. Her mother, it was later revealed, had had two separate trios of children by as many men, and neither of these unions the Church had hallowed. It was not an uncommon situation at the time, even in families of some distinction, but it was hardly a genealogical asset for any one of patrician pretensions. That this lowly origin influenced the resolve of Juana Inés de Asbaje y Ramírez de Santillana, who thus bore the surnames of her progenitors, to become a nun is likely but, as the sole explanation of her choice, it is unlikely. Her deep passion for study, her stated "total disinclination to marriage," and the promptings of her zealous confessor, the Jesuit *calificador* of the Inquisition, Antonio Núñez de Miranda, had undoubtedly made a life of reclusion seem attractive to her troubled spirit, and finally moved her to abandon the pomp and glitter of the Palace social whirl, of which she was so conspicuously a part.

That this determination was attended by doubts, misgivings, and inner conflict appears evident in the fact that illness caused her to withdraw from the Carmelite order within three months. The transition from a worldly court to the harsh confinement of a convent proved too abrupt and severe. Early the following year, however, she took her first vows in the Jeronymite community, the milder discipline of which was better suited to the sensitive temperament and scholarly aspirations of the poetess. The remainder of her forty-three years of life she spent chiefly within the book-lined walls of her cell, to which she retreated as often as her conventual duties permitted. There she pored over her accumulating volumes, attended to an extensive correspondence within and outside of the broad realm of Old Mexico, and wrote the verses so widely known in her time and that have since won enduring fame.

Her poetry is varied in meter and theme, including love lyrics that occasionally border on the erotic, tender Christmas carols, morality plays, allegorical pieces, and even secular three-act comedies like those performed in the public theaters of Spain and Spanish America. Much of this metrical expression abounded in literary conceits and was clothed in the ornate, florid, and obscure style of prevailing Baroque fashion. Unlike most verse of her contemporaries, however, subtle meaning and profound feeling often lay hidden in the intricate foliage of words and clever figures of speech. The most abstruse and inscrutable of her poems, and the only one that she professed to have written with pleasure, bears the title *Primero Sueño* (First Dream). Consisting of 975 verses of seven and eleven syllables' length, it seeks to reveal the subconscious and organic processes of sleep. In this labyrinthian composition of involved syntax and metaphors this strange nun appears to have outdone her master, Luis de Góngora. For one critic it "is a hymn to the awakening of the spirit of investigation or research, and an unsuspected forerunner of the poetry of the eighteenth century Enlightenment"[4]; for others it seems among the most ultra-Baroque manifestations of colonial verse. Yet many of her sonnets and shorter lyric poems have an almost limpid clarity and an exquisite beauty that mark her as the supreme poet of her time in Castilian.

As time passes the appeal of this Creole nun-poetess increases and the circle of her admirers enlarges. It is not merely the esthetic merit of so much of her verse which brings her this homage— though she is often regarded, as already suggested, as among the greatest poets in the speech of Spain—but, perhaps even more, the complex personality refracted in many of her writings. Her more intimate and spontaneous expression offers glimpses so fleeting and elusive of the inner life of an extraordinary woman that they serve to pique the reader's curiosity rather than to satisfy it. In certain lines her intention seems illumined for a bare moment, like a flash of lightning in the night, only to be followed by an obscurity more impenetrable than before. Thus it is that the enigmatic quality of Sister Juana's verses, even more than the technical perfection of the best of them, inspires a veritable cult and wins for her an expanding audience. Through the heavily embroidered veil of the Baroque conventions are discerned the glimmers of a refined spirit in profound conflict, an ambivalent personality of feminine emotion and masculine intellectuality rent and torn by a series of opposing dualisms. Plainly recognizable are the psychological fissures of a distraught nature, but the contributing tensions remain obscure and the causes unfathomable. Yet not so entirely that they fail to intrigue and fascinate the reader. Many verses appear deliberately opaque, as if the poetess feared to divulge what she longed to express and, half revealing, half concealing, they inevitably invite speculation as to their meaning. Hence the temptation to apply modern techniques of evaluation to her utterances becomes well nigh irresistible, and many critics have succumbed with stimulating, if possibly misleading, results.[5]

It is doubtful that any of the inner struggles externalized in Sister Juana's verses arose from a single origin. More likely they were the outward manifestations of a series of subjective discords inextricably confused and irretrievably blended, and any effort to isolate individual elements is largely vain, since it is likely to result in the distortion of oversimplification. Nevertheless, tentative probings in quest of the reality of the personality behind the verbal curtain of literary conceits have yielded some insights, and further ones will, perhaps, bring similar approximations to truth. In this undertaking it is of interest to focus attention on three sonnets which have been called a "tryptic of variations on the same theme."

In these three poems Sister Juana makes use of a device called *encontradas correspondencias,* or triangular antitheses, and of this peculiarity there are occasional echoes in other poems. Most commentators feel that it is merely an ingenious playing with words, the affected wittiness of a comedy, and the sort of dialectics on the subject of love in which the poets of the time delighted to indulge.[6] Yet the reiteration of these *encontradas correspondencias* in three separate sonnets, presumably written on different occasions, together with hints of similar antitheses elsewhere in her writings, suggests that something more than mere cleverness underlies them. These sonnets have English versions which will serve to illustrate the device employed, though inevitably without exact precision:

> Who thankless flees me, I with love pursue;
> Who loving follows me, I thankless flee:
> To him who spurns my love I bend the knee,
> His love who seeks me, cold I bid him rue.
>
> I find as diamond him I yearning woo,
> Myself a diamond when he yearns for me;
> Who slays my love I would victorious see,
> While slaying him who wills me blisses true.
>
> To favor this one is to lose desire
> To crave that one, my virgin pride to tame;
> On either hand I face a prospect dire.
>
> Whatever path I tread, the goal the same:
> To be adored by him of whom I tire,
> Or else by him who scorns me brought to shame.

> Feliciano loves me constantly;
> Lisardo hates me, who his name adore.
> For the indifferent one my tears will pour;
> I have no taste for him who weeps for me.
>
> To those who tarnish most I give my soul;
> The would-be worshippers I but despise.
> I scorn the man who would my honor prize,
> And favor him who goes away heart-whole.
>
> If I reproach myself with slighting one,
> The other takes offense at my misdeed.
> Between the two I finally am undone;
> They vex me with a torment cruel indeed,

the one asking that of which I've none,
the other lacking that for which I plead.

That Fabio does not love me, when I adore him,
Is an unequaled grief, and hurts my will;
But that Sylvio loves me, though I abhor him,
Is no less penance, if a lesser ill.
Such suffering is hardly to be borne,
When toward my ears ever and ever move
Both the vain arrogance of a man I love
And the irksome sighing of a man I scorn.
If Sylvio's surrender wearies me,
I weary Fabio by surrendering;
By one I keenly seek to be approved,
The other courts my approval eagerly.
Active and passive is my suffering:
I grieve in loving, and in being loved.[7]

The possible inspiration of the Latin poet Ausonius and of the great dramatists, Lope de Vega, and Calderón de la Barca, has been pointed out and the differences of treatment analyzed.[8] But, while it is clear that Sister Juana Inés was often influenced by Spanish and other writers, seldom was she content merely to imitate her models. Generally she borrowed only those forms and ideas which enabled her to pour some essence of herself into them by adapting them to her own peculiar need of the moment. As already suggested, the repeated use of these concepts of unrequited love arouses a suspicion that she selected them because they offered a convenient vehicle to externalize some deep-seated and tormenting conflict of a quite different nature. As one critic puts it, there is no doubt that she wrote these sonnets "with her heart in her pen." What, then, was the struggle afflicting her conscious or subconscious mind? Was it, as the words imply, a reflection of an amorous experience presumably before entering the convent? Possibly, but this interpretation seems much too obvious considering the literary conventions of the Baroque age and the complex personality which she clearly possessed. In the lyric poetry of seventeenth century Mexico the use of the language of love could scarcely be taken at face value any more than the name Silvio, Fabio and Feliciano should be considered those of actual persons. Both practices were then standard, of course, and in some of her verses *de encargo* Sister Juana doubtless used these conventions to please those who had solicited such products of her quill. But in the three sonnets cited one senses a deep, inner disquiet, the mental anguish of a difficult choice that gives no peace. Perhaps the key to this dilemma lies in those lines of Sister Juana which read:

> My soul is confusedly divided into two parts,
> One a slave to passion, the other
> measured by reason.
> Inflamed civil war importunately
> afflicts my bosom. Each part
> strives to prevail, and amidst
> such varied storms, both contend-
> ers will perish, and neither
> one will triumph.*

But within both "reason" and "passion" there is abundant room for varied conflicts producing even more bewildering dilemmas such as the triangular antitheses evident in the sonnets quoted.

Returning to these *encontradas correspondencias,* one may express them schematically as: A loves B, but B does not love A; C loves A, but A does not love C. If A is Sister Juana, whom or what do B and C represent? Having discarded the theory of a personal love triangle, one must dismiss the "whom" and endeavor to analyze the "what" that is symbolized in the names Fabio, Silvio, Feliciano, and Lisardo, or the "B" and "C" of the scheme.

In the multiplying criticism of the life and work of the Mexican nun-poetess there is increasing agreement that her intellectual distinction exceeds her eminence as a poet, and that her preoccupation with ideas was greater than with artistic creation.[9] Without minimizing the deeply emotional and feminine nature of Sister Juana, she was basically a rationalist with a passion for knowledge, and the processes of analysis were stronger and more obsessive than any other of her psyche. Her extraordinary gift as a lyric poet was ancillary to her acutely rational mentality, and her supreme aspiration was the freedom of her mind to roam untrammeled and unimpeded through every realm of thought. To read, to study, to experiment ". . . just to see if, by studying, I might grow less ignorant . . ." was the consuming desire of her existence. Since earliest childhood she had experienced this powerful yearning and

---

> * En dos partes dividida
> tengo el alma en confusión:
> una, esclava a la pasión
> y otra, a la razón medida

later she had begged her mother to permit her to attend the University of Mexico disguised in male clothing. "What is indeed the truth," she wrote in her famous *Reply to Sister Philotea,* a letter of much autobiographical significance, "and which I do not deny (in the first place because it is well known to everyone, and in the second place because, though it may be to my detriment, Heaven has bestowed upon me the blessing of a very great love of truth), is that, ever since the first glimmer of reason struck me, this inclination to learning has been so urgent and powerful . . ." In her young innocence she had desisted from eating cheese in the belief that such food would make her unpolished and uncouth, hence ". . . the desire to know was stronger in me than the desire to eat, even though the latter is so strong in children . . ."[10] This "inclination" triumphed over every other urge, including the sexual—for marriage she had a "total negation" she had declared—and she candidly confesses that her decision to take the veil—her only other choice— was largely influenced by the relatively freer opportunity it promised for study. The more solitary practices of the Carmelites had induced her, perhaps, to select that Order first. She had thought to escape the tyranny of what almost seemed a vice by dedicating herself as a bride of Christ, but ". . . poor, wretched me! I merely brought myself with me, together with my worst enemy, this inclination!" Instead of extinguishing this passion for reading and cogitation she found that, once subjected to her vows, this thirst for learning ". . . exploded like a charge of powder and what took place in me was *privatio est causa appetitus.*"

In the medieval atmosphere of seventeenth century Mexico where women could not dream of independent lives, where it was axiomatic that they possessed inferior intelligence, and where they were scarcely more than chattels of their fathers, brothers, and husbands, intellectual curiosity in Sister Juana's sex was not only indecorous but sinful. It might, indeed, be the workings of the Evil One and, therefore, imperil one's salvation, as her superiors in the convent more than once assured her. Though there were learned women in history, any emulation of them by a nun was not without an attendant sense of guilt. Sister Juana herself had not escaped this feeling, for she wrote: ". . . I have prayed God to subdue the light of my intelligence, leaving me only enough to keep His law, for anything more (according to some persons) is superfluous in a

woman." But, even in these despairing words, one seems to detect
in a parenthetical phrase, in which the masculine form is used, a
veiled rancor against the man-made world of her time. But her
obvious intellectual distinction also aroused the jealousy and antipathy of her companions in the convent, and over the years this
hostility developed in her a persecution complex. Her brilliant,
inquiring mind seemed always a source of vexation. "If my intelligence is my own," she wrote in one of her poems, "why must I
always find it so dull for my ease and so sharp for my hurt?"[11]

This avid curiosity and desire for knowledge, so at odds with her
time, place, and sex, seemed only to bring down upon her head the
criticism and censure of those about her:

> Why, people, do you persecute me so?
> In what do I offend, when but inclined
> with worldly beauties to adorn my mind,
> and not my mind on beauty to bestow?
> I value not a treasure trove, nor wealth;
> the greater measure of content I find
> in placing riches only in my mind,
> than setting all my intellect on wealth.
> And I esteem not beauty, for, when past
> it is the spoils of age's cruelty;
> nor faithless riches carefully amassed.
> Far better nibble, it seems to me,
> at all life's vanities unto the last
> than to consume my life in vanity.*[12]

And again in one of her ballads she asks bitterly why her fondness
for truth must always bring her punishment. "If this fondness I

---

* ¿En perseguirme, mundo, qué interesas?
¿En qué te ofendo, cuando sólo intento
poner bellezas en mi entendimiento
y no mi entendimiento en las bellezas?
    Yo no estimo tesoros ni riquezas,
y así, siempre me causan más contento
poner riquezas en mi entendimiento
que no mi entendimiento en las riquezas.
    Yo no estimo hermosura que, vencida,
es despojo civil de las edades,
ni riqueza me agrada fementida;
    teniendo por mejor en mis verdades
consumir vanidades de la vida
que consumir la vida en vanidades.

have is licit and even an obligation, why should they chastise me because I do what I must?"

These protests, indicating a sensitiveness to sharp disapproval around her, recur so frequently as to suggest a more disturbed state of mind than would result from eminence in the accepted forms of learning of her time, even after due allowance is made for the fact that such pursuits were deemed unsuitable for a woman, and particularly one bound by vows of perpetual submission. This exaggerated feeling of persecution was possibly generated in part by a growing sense of guilt engendered by the *kind* of knowledge that she was seeking and by the *kind* of methods that she was using to acquire it. In short, her learning might appear more secular than ecclesiastical—"What a pity it is that so rich a mind should so debase itself in the petty matters of this world!"[13] the Bishop of Puebla was to chide her—and her procedures more experimental or scientific in the modern way than scholastic and philosophic. Even more reprehensible than mundane knowledge were the unorthodox means of seeking it. "Experimentation tugged at Sister Juana from earliest childhood," comments a student of her life.[14] Here, then, is the possibility of a conflict, intellectual in origin which, given her environment, profession, and sex, would inevitably be spiritual and emotional as well. This inner discord, with its concomitant overtones of heresy and disobedience, could well produce a brooding conviction of guilt and thus, through anxiety, accentuate a feeling of persecution.

About 1600 began a revolution in the minds of western man which ushered in, as earlier discussed, the Age of Science. Kepler and Galileo had simultaneously formulated the principle that natural laws are to be discovered by measurement, and this radical principle they applied to their work. Where the science of Aristotle and the ancients was content to classify and label, the new science now sought to measure, and the quantitative method involved, as one writer puts it, "a new adjustment at many levels in the hierarchy of the human system." And again, "by the sixteenth century the medieval veil between man and nature had fallen, the individual was setting out to express himself through his faculties."[15]

As the seventeenth century advanced, the individual was more and more challenging authority, empiricism was challenging medieval rationalism, and in this process Mathematics was the new tool, as Descartes was demonstrating.

It was Sister Juana's fate to have her being in this age when, even in Old Mexico, though ever so slightly, the long accepted and sole approach to truth was beginning to be threatened by a new way, a new method. Almost imperceptibly the traditional scholastic and authoritarian concepts of revealed knowledge were yielding to the more sensate procedures of scientific observation and analysis. In the Mexico City of her time there was greater awareness of this intellectual revolution than commonly believed, and the capital had a tiny group of savants who were abreast of contemporary thought, even that of non-Catholic Europe. The comparatively free circulation of nontheological books during the sixteenth and seventeenth centuries,[16] the frequent presence in the viceroyalty of transient men of learning from the Old World, and the personal correspondence of local scholars with thinkers abroad, had all contributed to a more vital mental climate in the New World centers than the contemporary dominance of a medieval Church was thought to permit. A small number of Creole *sabios* were already familiar with the ideas and writings of Erasmus, Copernicus, Kepler, and particularly Descartes, whose philosophies they discussed among themselves in comparative freedom and even cited in their published writings.

Most conspicuous of this intelligentsia of New Spain was Don Carlos de Sigüenza y Góngora. He was a professor of mathematics in the University of Mexico, renowned for his studies of astronomy, archaeology, history and natural philosophy, and also an intimate friend of Sister Juana. Living at the Hospital del Amor de Dios where he served as chaplain, he was a frequent visitor at the Jeronymite convent a few blocks away where the nun-poetess had her cell. It appears that these two intellectually gifted and lonely people enjoyed long discussions together in the locutory of the convent. Sigüenza, a very minor poet, was encouraged in these exercises by Sister Juana, while she in turn received his stimulation and training in scientific disciplines. It is likely that she acquired the mathematical instruments and some of the books said to have furnished her cell as a result of this association. Indeed, the attainments of these two figures working together have moved a discerning critic to comment that they were ". . . the first ones (in Mexico) in whom the modern spirit appears or manifests itself."[17] It was Sigüenza who most often brought visiting savants to her convent, including the great mission-founder of the American Southwest, Father Eusebio Francisco Kino. And it was he who initiated the exceedingly intelligent nun into the new methodology propounded by Descartes, of which there are faint indications in her verse.[18] Doubtless it was he who understood her enthusiasm for, and encouraged her in, the performance of such simple experiments in physics as she mentions in her *Reply to Sister Philotea*. And it was he who shared her love for the dawning Age of Enlightenment of which they both were unconscious precursors in Mexico.

The inherent critical capacity of Sister Juana, coupled with omniverous reading, moved her to welcome a more pragmatic approach to truth. Latent in her mind was a healthy skepticism regarding the effectiveness of purely verbal rationalization, and her eager curiosity was insidiously drawn to experimentation and direct observation. A scrutiny of Sister Juana's verse and prose tends to support the conviction that she felt an instinctive distrust of the scholasticism dominating the intellectual life of viceregal Mexico. Her deeper regard for observation and a more scientific analysis seems apparent when, in the *Reply*, she emphasizes the importance of varied studies and methods in throwing light on speculative learning, particularly theology, and her underlying preference is revealed when she adds: ". . . and when the expositors are like an open hand and the ecclesiastics like a closed fist." Her reactions to the specious learning and rhetorical ratiocination around her, characterized chiefly by polemical disquisitions with ostentatious displays of classical quotations and cloudy verbosity, emerge clearly in the ballad beginning with the pathetic verse "Let us pretend that I am happy." The wordy debates of bookish pedants and charlatans of the so-called intelligentsia filling the air about her with their din move her to exclaim metrically: "Everything is opinions and of such varied counsels that what one proves is black, the other proves is white."* And regarding these doctrinaire pundits she would surely have agreed with Alexander Pope's caustic couplet:

---

\* Todo el mundo es opiniones,
de pareceres tan varios,
que lo que el uno, que es negro,
el otro prueba que es blanco.

> The bookful blockhead, ignorantly read,
> with loads of learned lumber in his head.

This universal penchant for splitting hairs in interminable disputes to the neglect of essentials vexes the sound intellect of Sister Juana. "If their soaring rhetoric steeped in false subtleties be not abated, the essential is forgotten in the concern for the accessory."* She seemed to feel that these disputants, to borrow a phrase from Bacon, worked at their endless dialectics ". . . as the spider worketh its web, bringing forth cobwebs of learning, admirable for its fineness of thread and work, but of no substance or profit." The pedantry exhibited in the profusion of Latin and Greek quotations, of classical allusions, and of florid circumlocutions irked the wise nun. "If a trained hand does not prevent the foliage of the tree from becoming too dense, its wild tangle will rob the fruit of its substance."† All this specious erudition moves her to ask: "What silly ambition sweeps us away, forgetful of ourselves? If it is for so short a life, what good is it to know so much?"‡ And in despair she cries: "Oh, if there were only some seminary or school, as there is for knowledge, where they would teach ignorance of such learning!"**

In the *Reply* she comments, with veiled scorn, on the affectation that passed as learning in the excessive number of quotations from authorities: ". . . and I add that their education is perfected (if nonsense is perfection) by having studied a little Philosophy and Theology, and by having a smattering of languages, by which means one may be stupid in numerous subjects and languages be-

---

    * Y si el vuelo no le abaten
      en sutilezas cebado,
      por cuidar de lo curioso
      olvida lo necesario.
    † Si culta mano no impide
      Crecer al árbol copado,
      Quita la sustancia al fruto
      la locura de los ramos.
    ‡ Que loca ambición nos lleva
      de nosotros oluidados?
      Si es para vivir tan poco,
      de que sirue saber tanto?
   ** Oh, si, como hay de saber,
      hubiera algún seminario
      o escuela donde a ignorar
      se enseñaran los trabajos!

cause the mother tongue alone is not room enough for a really big fool." Mindful, likewise, of the self delusion facilitated by the verbalism of scholasticism, Sister Juana believed that everyone should keep within his own mental limitations. If this were so, she tartly exclaims: "How many warped intelligences wandering about there would not be!"

Perhaps the most penetrating stanza of this same ballad is the one in which she puts her finger on the core of true wisdom, the development of sound judgment: "To know how to make varied and subtle discourses is not knowledge; rather, knowledge simply consists of making the soundest choices."*

These and other passages in the writings of Sister Juana reflect a disaffection with the prevailing scholastic methods of thinking in her world and an impatience with an intellectual age which she could not know was passing. She yearned for a newer, freer era of widening horizons, of a differing approach to truth which she did not realize was beginning. But the religious institution, of which she was a part and which was so concerned for her salvation, was wholly identified with the old ways of thinking that did not attract her. Rather, her attachment to the unorthodox kind of thinking became a compulsion against which she struggled constantly, fearful of its implications for her eternal security in its radical departure from ecclesiastical authoritarianism. Her intellectual soul was enamored of this new and scientific approach to truth, but there could be no reciprocation in such a passion for one so closely held in the embrace of medieval tradition as a nun. For her only the concept of knowledge revealed by authority and scholastic methods was proper and permissible. Consequently, she feared this urge to think by unhallowed procedures, and she buried herself deeply in her books in the vain effort to banish such ideas from her mind. Yet this analytical mania obsessed her. "This way of observing everything happened to me and it always happens to me without my having any control in the matter . . . And, continuing on the subject of my cogitations, I must state that this is so constant with me that I do not need any books . . ." When deprived of her reading, as happened for a period, her mind seemed to

---

* No es saber, saber hacer
  discursos sutiles vanos;
  que el saber consiste sólo
  en elegir lo más sano.

accelerate its activity in this manner. "Even though I did not study in books I kept studying everything in God's creation, the individual objects serving me as words and the whole universal scheme as a book. Nothing did I look at and nothing did I hear that I did not speculate on, even the smallest and most material things . . . And so, I repeat, I looked at everything and I wondered about everything . . ." Even in sleep this process operated: ". . . not even in slumber was my mind free of this continuous movement. On the contrary, it seems to operate more freely and unimpeded, bringing out these objects with even greater and more undisturbed clarity than in the daytime."

Thus it appears that Sister Juana found herself not only torn between "reason" and "passion," but also between *two methodologies of reason.* The time-honored dialectics and syllogisms of scholasticism were still entrenched as the accepted means of rationalization in the Church of Christ which held her in its protective arms and to which she was irrevocably bound by vows. This great institution sheltered and loved her, and obedience to its authority and ways was her ineludible obligation. Yet, deep within, she could not reciprocate its love. Instead, she seemed possessed by a way of thinking that threatened to undermine the assumptions on which the Faith rested. On the true object of her affections, the new concept of experimentalism relying on the senses rather than on authority, her benevolent guardian, the Church, severely frowned. Such intellectual exercise might well be inimical to the divine science of theology, and it was potentially, if not actually, heretical. Adherence to such thinking could seriously jeopardize her eternal salvation, which was infinitely precious to her. In her religious play, *The Divine Narcissus,* she wrote: "Behold that what I yearn for I am powerless to enjoy, and in my anxious longing to possess it, I suffer mortal pangs."

In this torturing dilemma Sister Juana, in her long letter to the Bishop of Puebla, sought to rationalize her predilection when she asked how the "Queen of Sciences," that is, Theology, could be understood without knowledge of a series of secular disciplines including Logic, Rhetoric, Physics, Arithmetic, Geometry, Architecture, History, and others. This passage seems a faint echo of the Third Precept of Descartes which reads: ". . . to conduct my thought in such order that, by commencing with objects the simplest and easiest to know, I might ascend little by little and, as it were, step by step, to the knowledge of the more complex, assigning in thought a certain order even to those objects which, in their own nature, do not stand in a relation of antecedence and sequence." But, however cogently she might argue for more pragmatic learning and greater intellectual freedom, the heavy odds of the traditions of her time, place, vocation, and sex were overwhelmingly against her. Inevitably, she fell prey to torturing uncertainty, guilt, and despair, from which she sought release in her more intimate poetry. These inner rendings of her being resulting from the many dualisms of her complex personality became chronic and, in time, made her long for death. In one of her poems appear these words: "I am dying (who will believe it?) at the hands of the thing that I love most, and what is killing me is the love I have for it."* And in a secular play of hers occurs the line: "I am dying for the sake of one who is not dying because of me."

Repeatedly in verse and in prose her guilt complex and torment are revealed by the phrase: "I am my own executioner," which seems a cry of anguish, though "I do not study in order to write, and much less to teach, for that would be unpardonable arrogance in me, but just to see if by studying, I can be less ignorant." In her constricted world with its low, arching dome of heaven, there was no space for her privileged spirit to soar. With deepening despair she knew that such a strange preoccupation with her mind was unseemly in a woman, especially one in religious reclusion; it erected barriers of intercourse with her uncomprehending sisters in the community in which she lived, and their jealousy and envy of her recognized superiority did not grow less. "Let not the head which is the repository of knowledge expect any other crown than that of thorns," she wrote bitterly, for she had known the reprobation of her superiors. Indeed, the chiding letter of the Bishop of Puebla was probably mild and gentle in comparison with the admonitions of her confessor and of the convent sisters. The bishop had reproved her cultivation of "profane letters," by which it was clear

---

* Muero (y quién lo creerá?) a manos
de la cosa que más quiero
y el motivo de matarme
es el amor que le tengo.

that he included her preoccupation with a secular rationalization. He had urged her to confine herself to the exercise of theological scholasticism of which she had given such proof of her skill in her telling critique of the sermon of the celebrated Portuguese Jesuit.

But Sister Juana's mind and heart responded instinctively to a more experimental pragmatism, and she could not bring herself wholly to surrender to the verbal hairsplitting of the intellectual life about her. In many of her poems she used the poetical name "Fabio" as the figure she adored and Silvio, Feliciano and others as the ones she disdained or abhorred. "My will belongs to Fabio, and may Silvio and the world forgive me," are two typical verses. That her preference for "Fabio" stems from its similarity to the Spanish word *sabio*, the wise or learned, is a possibility. Silvio, like other designations, may well refer to the pedants that she could not esteem. But convent-bound in the medieval atmosphere of the ecclesiastical society of Mexico City she could only feel at war with it and with herself. The love and kindliness implicit in the Church's paternalism claimed her gratitude and, of course, her vows compelled obedience to it. Yet the persistent longing for a freer expression of her intuition and for another and more open avenue to truth and to God prevented complete reciprocation and submission in her heart. The sensate experimentalism and scientific methodology of a dawning age beckoned her, while the secular world, which was giving birth to it, was indifferent and unaware of the love of a lonely woman deeply enmeshed in the toils of rigid medievalism. It seemed only to disdain her and, inevitably, Sister Juana's was a blighted love—rejection by the beloved and possession by the unloved—a triangular antithesis. Rarely did she experience even a momentary relief from the incessant conflict within her and, in time, it undermined her health and hastened her death. In this unhappy state of *encontradas correspondencias* she could only externalize her dilemma in verses of obscure symbolism but unmistakable feeling which voiced her suffering repeatedly. In the poignant sonnet, "Who thankless flees me, I with love pursue," the "Who" was, perhaps, experimentalism, a secularized freedom, and a newer age; and in "Who loving follows me, I thankless flee," the "Who" was possibly scholasticism, ecclesiasticism, and medievalism; the first the avenue to salvation by knowledge, the second the avenue to salvation by *faith*.

Who thankless flees me, I with love pursue;
Who loving follows me, I thankless flee;
To him who spurns my love I bend the knee,
His love who seeks me, cold I bid him rue.
    I find as diamond him I yearning woo,
Myself a diamond when he yearns for me:
Who slays my love I would victorious see
While slaying him who wills me blisses true.
    To favor this one is to lose desire,
To crave that one, my virgin pride to tame;
On either hand I face a prospect dire;
    Whatever path I tread, the goal the same;
To be adored by him of whom I tire,
Or else by him who scorns me brought to shame.

As the dawn of April 17, 1695 was casting a wan light over the
troubled City of Mexico the wracked and broken spirit of Sister
Juana quietly claimed its longed-for release from the prison of her
aloneness. "See how death eludes me because I desire it," she had
exclaimed in one of her poems, "for even death, when it is in demand," she had added, "will rise in price." Over the long years of
her short life she had struggled against the viselike prejudices and
incomprehension of her time and place. She had dreamed of a
liberation from the shackles of static traditions and stultifying conventions. She had dared to rebuke the men of her society for their
double standard of morality and had thus struck a first blow for
women's rights.

Which has the greater sin when burned
by the same lawless fever:
She who is amorously deceived,
or he, the sly deceiver?

Or which deserves the sterner blame,
though each will be a sinner:
She who becomes a whore for pay,
Or he who pays to win her?*[19]

---

* Cuál mayor culpa ha tenido
en una pasión errada:
la que cae de rogada,
o el que ruega de caído?

    O cuál es más de culpar
aunque cualquiera mal haga:
la que peca por la paga
o el que paga por pecar?

But more than all else she had struggled for a freedom of thought for all. "There is nothing freer than the human mind," she had proclaimed to a world that could not comprehend these words, or could only hear them as subversive of a God-given truth. Against her the odds were too great and their relentless pressure brought at last a total renunciation of all effort and a complete submission of her intellect. The passionate woman in her capitulated to the devout nun and this surrender left her bereft of life. Physically she survived herself briefly.

To the unhappy nun-poetess during the last four or five years of her existence the world outside must have seemed a projection of her own inner turmoil and affliction. A series of disasters and phenomena were then plaguing the city and its environs, bringing suffering, fear and violence. Heavy rains in 1691 brought successively ruinous floods, crop destruction, famine, and pestilence, while a total eclipse of the sun stirred panic fear. Sullen discontent and mounting tensions erupted into mass riots that nearly toppled Spanish authority in the land. As these sinister events darkened the world without, the storm, so long brewing within Sister Juana Inés, broke.

In 1690 she inadvertently brought to a head the disapproval and hostility of her religious associates slowly gathering over the years. In some way she was induced to write a successful rebuttal of certain views set forth long before in a sermon by a famous Portuguese Jesuit, Father Vieira. Her skill in manipulating the methods of neo-scholasticism evidently pleased the Bishop of Puebla who took it upon himself to publish her paper. At the same time, in the guise of "Sister Philotea," he wrote her a letter chiding her alleged neglect of religious literature and her fondness for profane letters. "You have spent a lot of time studying (secular) philosophers and poets, and now it would seem reasonable to apply yourself to better things and to better books." Clearly, this was a reproof from a superior high in the hierarchy and it could not fail to distress a nun tormented by guilt feelings. Through months of declining health she brooded on a reply to the Bishop's censure. Finally, under date of March 1, 1691, it took form in her famous *Reply* in which, with many autobiographical details and with alternate humility and boldness, she defended herself from the prelate's strictures.

Obscure complications followed this epistolary exchange, chief of which was the withdrawal of her confessor, Father Antonio Núñez de Miranda, who had influenced her decision to enter the convent and had counseled her over the years. Vainly he had urged her to turn from what he considered worldly matters and apply her great talents to things eternal. All her devoted supporters, it seemed to her, were falling away through absence, desertion, or death. And she had never enjoyed the favor of the misogynistic Archbishop Aguiar y Seijas, who had involved her in his frenzied almsgiving. In 1693, as if to remind everyone of her worldliness, a second edition of a volume of her poems, which the vicereine, her friend and patroness, had extracted from her, appeared in Spain, and copies doubtless reached Mexico City soon after. This intended kindness may have hastened her final surrender. On February 8, 1694, using blood from her veins as ink, she indited an abject reaffirmation of her faith and renewed her vows, which she signed: "I, Sister Juana Inés de la Cruz, the worst in the world." She renounced all her possessions, the gifts and trinkets of her admirers, the mathematical and musical instruments that she had so long studied and used, and—the most painful wrench of all—those silent and precious companions of her cell, her beloved books. All were sold and the proceeds given to charity. With this bitter deprivation, she gave herself to excessive acts of penance, self-flagellation, and mortification of the flesh. The coveted death of the body came at last during her tireless ministrations to sisters of her community decimated by a pestilence sweeping the city.

The one kindred spirit that had most nearly understood her, Don Carlos de Sigüenza y Góngora, delivered the funeral oration at her grave. Even his sympathy was denied her in those final, bitter years when his absence on an expedition to Florida, and the preoccupation of public service, private family, and declining health kept him away. The words uttered on the melancholy occasion of her interment are lost but, even more feelingly, they probably echoed sentiments he had expressed in 1680 when both were rising to fame. "There is no pen that can rise to the eminence that hers o'ertops," he had written, and then added, with a sincerity that shines through his pedantic style: "I should like to omit the esteem with which I regard her, the veneration that she has won by her works, in order to make manifest to the world how much, in the encyclopedic nature and universality of her letters, is contained in her genius, so that it may be seen that, in one single person, Mexico enjoys what, in past centuries, the graces have imparted to all the learned women who are the great marvels of history." And he concluded prophetically that the name and fame of "Mother Juana Inés de la Cruz will only end with the world."[20]

# ❧ XIII

# A BAROQUE SCHOLAR

"ON THURSDAY, August 23, 1691, at nine A. M., it was pitch dark, the cocks crowed, and the stars shone, for the sun was in complete eclipse," records a diary. An eerie chill descended with the pall of an unnatural night, bringing superstitious panic upon Mexico City. Amid a pandemonium of shrieking women and children, howling dogs, and braying donkeys the frantic populace fled to the refuge of the Cathedral or the nearest church whose bells clanged a discordant summons for propitiatory prayer. Unnoticed in this frenzied confusion was a solitary, motionless figure who, with strange-looking instruments, surveyed the darkened heavens with a kind of quiet ecstasy. "In the meantime," he wrote soon afterwards, "I stood with my quadrant and telescope viewing the sun, extremely happy and repeatedly thanking God for granting that I might behold what so rarely happens in a given place and about which so few observations are recorded."[1]

These were words of a remarkable scholar of colonial Mexico, Don Carlos de Sigüenza y Góngora, the understanding friend and intellectual companion of Sister Juana Inés de la Cruz. No other incident of his life so well epitomizes the man and his times, for it places in juxtaposition the bold spirit of scientific inquiry which he incarnated and the miasmic atmosphere of ignorance, fear and superstition which he breathed. Intellectual curiosity and independence of mind set him apart from the tradition-bound society of theocratic despotism surrounding him. Yet he remained, nonetheless, an integral part of his milieu and an authentic expression

193

of the Baroque age, for he carefully separated his firm adherence
to religious orthodoxy from his speculative attitude toward secular
studies. He believed, indeed, that the newer methodology would
merely confirm the accepted dogmas of the Faith, and the neo-
medievalism of his environment as strongly conditioned him as the
Middle Ages did the humanists of the Renaissance. But, even more
than the nun-poetess whom he so greatly admired, he symbolized
the transition from the extreme orthodoxy of seventeenth century
Spanish America to the growing heterodoxy of the eighteenth century.

This Creole scholar liked to boast of his ancestry which, from
the times of Isabel and Ferdinand, included men of distinction in
arms and letters. His father, Don Carlos de Sigüenza y Benito, a
native of Madrid, had been, in his youth, a tutor in the royal household. The Mexican-born son was especially proud that his sire
had once instructed the short-lived Prince Baltasar Carlos, upon
whom the dynastic hopes of Philip IV and all Spain had vainly
rested. Why the father chose to renounce this privileged post and
come to the New World is not explained, but the swiftly declining
fortunes of the Peninsula doubtless influenced him to join the
retinue of the newly appointed viceroy of New Spain, the Marqués of Villena. In 1640, in the same fleet that brought the demented Guillén de Lampart who, presently, would proclaim
himself Emperor of Mexico, the elder Sigüenza arrived. If he had
hoped to improve his lot materially by emigration to Spain's richest colony, his expectations, like those of so many others, were
largely defrauded. It appears that he had to content himself with
the modest occupation of a public scribe, though later he became
secretary of a viceregal bureau.

Two years after reaching Mexico City he married Doña Dionisia
Suárez de Figueroa y Góngora, who hailed from Seville, Spain,
and was the daughter of a family of aristocratic pretensions. Her
surnames were distinguished in the annals of Spanish literary history, and her eldest son pridefully attached Góngora to his signature to indicate a blood tie with the Cordoban poet. Nine children
were the fruit of this union, of whom the Mexican scholar was the
second child and the first male. This numerous progeny sorely
taxed the meager income of the former instructor of royalty and,
in time, his more famous son had to assume responsibility for the

family. Whether his brothers and sisters entered the Church, as some did, or acquired mates, all looked to him for economic assistance and counsel.

If Don Carlos, junior, was not so precocious as Sister Juana Inés, his exceptional talents budded early. His experienced father carefully nurtured them, laying a solid foundation for his son's later achievements. For a lad of such promise the Church clearly offered the most distinguished career, and the well-established intellectual distinction of the Jesuits made that Order especially attractive. At the age of fifteen Don Carlos was accepted as a novice and in 1662 he took his first vows. For over seven years he received rigorous training in theology and humanistic studies, but this fruitful period abruptly ended in an episode that seemed to shatter his bright hopes; on the scholar's spirit it left a psychic scar never quite effaced during the remainder of his life.

The proud and impetuous temperament of the young Sigüenza found the Jesuit discipline too severe at times for his independent nature. While his mind enjoyed considerable intellectual latitude, the rigid physical restraints imposed upon his person were galling. A restless impatience with these restrictions finally swept him into a youthful indiscretion which haunted him ever afterward. During his student days at the College of the Holy Spirit in Puebla he yielded to a temptation to elude the vigilance of the prefects and escape from the dormitory to taste the forbidden fruit of nocturnal rambles about the city streets. Discovery of this repeated breach of discipline brought prompt retribution and, on August 15, 1668, he was formally dismissed from the Order. The effect of this disgrace was traumatic, and bitter remorse permanently tinged his nature with a certain melancholy and irascibility. Protesting his repentance, he begged, with tearful earnestness, for reinstatement, but each plea was denied by the implacable Jesuit superiors. In March, 1669, the General of the Order wrote to a Provincial: "Don Carlos de Sigüenza y Góngora also seeks to return to the Company, but I do not grant it to him . . . The cause of the expulsion of this person is so disreputable, as he himself confesses, that he does not deserve this boon . . ." Two years later, a renewed prayer of the contrite youth was refused. "It is not my intention that Don Carlos de Sigüenza shall return to the Company, his case being as you depict it . . ."

Though these rejections seemed definitive the chastened young man never ceased to hope that the Jesuit authorities might relent. Ten years later, in 1677, when his distinction as a professor at the University of Mexico was rising, he again petitioned for reconsideration, trusting, perhaps, that his growing prestige and the passage of time had softened the intransigence of the Jesuit fathers. But another General of the Order, though favorably impressed by Sigüenza's entreaties, was nearly as obdurate. "Don Carlos de Sigüenza y Góngora who, as your Reverence knows, was expelled from the Company, is making a very urgent request for reinstatement on the plea that his salvation would be assured. I am told that he is a person of talent, thirty years old, a professor in the university, and that he can be useful to the Order and that he is most remorseful and repentant. The best that I can do is to absolve him from the impediment of expulsion. I hereby absolve him. Your Reverence will consult with your advisors as to whether it is right to receive him a second time or not. The rest I leave to what comes out of your consultation."[2]

No further progress attended Sigüenza's repeated efforts and the sorrow of his disappointment lay like a shadow on his nature, souring his disposition as the years brought disillusionments and ailments. The zeal displayed throughout his days in intellectual achievement and public service probably arose in some measure from a fervent desire to redeem himself in his own eyes and, conceivably, to bring an awareness to the Jesuit order of the loss sustained in persistently excluding so accomplished a scholar from their ranks. Whether a deathbed reconciliation fulfilled a long-deferred hope still remains uncertain, but the fact that he willed his precious books, manuscripts, maps and instruments to the Company and was interred in a Jesuit chapel points to a final consummation.

Meanwhile, obliged to adapt himself to the painful reality of an apparently irrevocable expulsion, the unhappy Sigüenza was at loose ends in 1668. Clearly, he must make a fresh start in a career outside of his chosen Order. Returning to Mexico City, he resumed theological studies at the University where he began to develop independently the humanistic interests awakened during the years in the Jesuit seminary. Of first importance was mathematics, for which he had a special aptitude. By diligent application, he excelled in this discipline and soon gained recognition as the foremost mathematician in Mexico with a high competence in related sciences.

In 1672 the Chair of Mathematics and Astrology was vacant at the University and Sigüenza decided to compete for it. Two other candidates made a similar decision, one of whom flaunted an academic degree which, he believed, made him solely eligible. Don Carlos, who lacked this accreditation, was unimpressed by his rival's contention, since the University did not grant a bachelor's degree in these particular subjects. Moreover, he tartly reminded the authorities, knowledge of the field was more vital than diplomas; neither of the other aspirants, he declared, had the competence that he possessed who had studied ex-profeso and ". . . was expert in these subjects as is recognized and well known throughout all this Realm because of his two almanacs, one of the preceding year (1671), and the other of the present year which were printed with the approval of Father Julio de San Miguel of the Company of Jesus and of the Holy Office of the Inquisition of New Spain."

These arguments were effective and Don Carlos established his right to enter the competition. The standard practice of selecting faculty members was by a system called *oposiciones*. Each candidate publicly drew texts (*tomar puntos*) from a basic printed authority of the subject matter and, within twenty-four hours, he was obliged to deliver a discourse on the topic thus chosen at random. After the various competitors had each given a rapidly improvised exhibition of erudition, students and degree-holders balloted on the successful contestant, and thus the victor gained the Chair. Elections of this sort were not without fraud, and instances were known when an aspirant had hired a proficient ghost-writer to prepare his lecture for him. Sigüenza professed to suspect a similar intent on the part of the rival who had claimed the sole right to the Chair on the basis of a degree he held, and he demanded that this opponent be placed under the surveillance of two guards during the twenty-four hours allowed for preparing a disquisition. It is indicative, perhaps, of the aggressive and forthright personality of Don Carlos that the University officials acceded to his request. The outcome was a sweeping victory for the blunt young Sigüenza and, on July 20, 1672, he was duly installed as Professor of Mathematics and Astrology.

The University records do not suggest that the Creole scholar was a model occupant of an academic chair, for all too plainly they show frequent petitions for lengthy leaves of absence and for the designation of substitutes to give his lectures. Even more common was his failure to appear in the lecture hall at all, often for weeks at a time. Since university regulations imposed penalties for such derelictions, the fines that Sigüenza paid must have exceeded at times the modest honorarium of one hundred pesos that he received. Immersed in research and, as his reputation grew, in a steady demand for varied public services, routine classroom duties were frequently neglected.

His indifference to these obligations is possibly traceable in part to a lack of regard for the subject of Astrology which, it appears, attracted more students than his beloved mathematics. In an age when that pseudo science retained prestige on both sides of the Atlantic, it is typical of Sigüenza's rugged independence and scientific outlook that he vigorously assailed its false assumptions in his annual almanacs. In a polemic on the nature of comets he gruffly declared: "I also am an Astrologer and I know very well on which foot Astrology limps, and upon what exceedingly weak foundations its structure is reared." And again, in advocating demonstrable evidence in place of the dicta of scholastic authorities—a surprisingly modern attitude in his time—he asked: "What should one infer from them other than that they are all imposed, false, ridiculous, and contemptible, and that astrology is a diabolical invention and, consequently, alien to science, method, principle, and truth? . . ." It is hardly surprising, therefore, that hostile critics saw an inconsistency in this heretical attitude toward a subject that he was paid to teach! But, whatever the causes of his many failures to perform his academic tasks, these omissions sorely troubled his conscience as his last will and testament reveals.

Unlike most of his colleagues on the faculty who were members of religious orders and hence assured of subsistence, Sigüenza had to find means to support himself and assist an assorted family of parents, brothers and sisters, and other dependents. His salary was a nominal fee even when there were no fines to pay and, like many successors in Spanish American universities today, he supplemented his income by varied employments. Over the years these activities brought him titles with various duties and modest emoluments such as: Chief Cosmographer of the Realm; chaplain of the Hospital del Amor de Dios, the most remunerative since it provided living quarters; General Examiner of Gunners; University Accountant; Corrector of the Inquisition, etc., concerning all of which he wryly remarked that they ". . . sound like a lot but are worth very little." He also received remunerated commissions from viceroys for special services of a practical nature and these activities accounted for many absences from his lectures.

When Archbishop Aguiar y Seijas assumed his office in 1682 Sigüenza acquired an influential friend. The comfortable sinecure at the Hospital del Amor de Dios came through this channel which also brought authorization to say mass as a lay priest and thus increase his stipend through fees. As Chief Almoner of the overly generous Archbishop he had onerous obligations which at times he would have been glad to evade. Part of these duties was to distribute one hundred pesos every Monday to the women of the poor whose presence the misogynistic prelate could not abide, and he also gave away large quantities of grain and other cereals at the behest of the philanthropic clergyman.

Sigüenza's gruff spirit and the Archbishop's imperious nature, which contributed to Sister Juan Inés' personal tragedy, occasionally clashed. A contemporary diary reports: "A Controversy: Saturday, October 11th, 1692, Don Carlos de Sigüenza, lay priest, having some differences with the Archbishop, Don Carlos said to the latter that his Illustrious Highness should remember with whom he was talking, whereupon the Archbishop raised the crutch he was using and broke Sigüenza's glasses, bathing his face in blood." Despite these vagaries of temperament the two strongwilled individuals remained close and co-operative friends. Indeed, the veneration of Don Carlos for his assailant increased until, in his mind, the prelate almost acquired the halo of a saint. A clause of the scholar's will reads: "I have in my possession the hat worn by the Most Illustrious and Venerable Don Francisco de Aguiar y Seijas, formerly Archbishop of Mexico. When a number of sick people touched it they recovered from their ailments. Desiring that this practice continue with all veneration, I request that the hat be turned over to Doctor Juan de la Pedrosa and kept in perpetuity in the oratory of Our Father St. Philip Neri."[3] Thus, this Baroque scholar, so modern and clearheaded in many intellectual pursuits, remained the docile child of his age in other respects.

Sigüenza never allowed himself to forget his kinship to the great Luis de Góngora, patron saint of Spanish versifiers in the seventeenth century, and even as a student in the Jesuit seminary he sought to prove worthy of this literary connection. All too plainly his poetic efforts betray a genealogical affiliation, though esthetic degeneracy had set in with this particular descendant. His *Indian Spring*, a fervent hymn to the Virgin of Guadalupe in seventy-nine octaves, faithfully reflects the abuses and excesses of a tired Gongorism. Written while the author was still in his teens and published in 1662, with reprintings in 1668 and 1683, it is more an evidence of a certain precocity than of hereditary genius. His *Evangelical Oriental Planet*, a panegyric of St. Francis Xavier, friend and companion of the founder of the Jesuit order, was printed after Sigüenza's death. This lyric effort was probably composed about the time of his expulsion from the seminary, possibly with the hope of restoring himself to the good graces of the superiors. Never completely satisfied that its artistic merit equaled its lofty subject, he had withheld it from publication. These literary aspirations, which he was reluctant to abandon, were doubtless a topic of many chats with the far more musically gifted Sister Juana Inés in the locutory of her convent. Wisely, he decided to concentrate his energies on scholarly pursuits.

Like the humanists of the Renaissance, no field of investigation was entirely exempt from the workings of his curious mind, but his achievements were most notable in related areas of archaeology and history on one hand, and in mathematics and applied sciences on the other. His studies of the pre-Hispanic civilizations of Mexico which, in time, brought him undisputed authority, he began the year of his dismissal from the Jesuit school. As he mastered the native languages he assembled books, codices, maps, and manuscripts relating to the ancient culture of the aborigines. In the 1670's he acquired a large collection of the papers, notes, and translations which had belonged to Fernando de Alva Ixtlilxochitl, who flourished, it will be recalled, in the days of Archbishop-Viceroy García Guerra. A son of the Indian choncler, Juan de Alva Cortés, held the family estate in San Juan Teotihuacán, not far from Mexico City, which acquisitive officials sought to wrest from him.

Sigüenza, it appears, had successfully intervened to protect De Alva Cortés from this rapacity of the white masters. In gratitude the Indian owner gave the Creole savant a small plantation and, what was even more appreciated, the precious collection of his father's papers. With these documents and other accessions Sigüenza came to possess the richest library of these materials anywhere, much of which he had intended to will to the Vatican in Rome and to the Escorial in Spain. These data, combined with his own archaeological explorations, particularly in the Toltec pyramids at Teotihuacán, were the substance of monographs of probable importance, most of which unhappily survive in name only. Their existence is chiefly known through occasional references and brief descriptions of contemporaries. His difficulties in getting his findings into print were the perennial ones of scholars lacking private means or philanthropic subsidies to defray the costs of publication. With literacy so low and secular investigations so much less esteemed than theological disquisitions, his studies had little hope of finding their way into the more permanent form of type.

Though Sigüenza tried to give a religious significance to his research as, for example, his ingenuous effort to identify the Aztec Quetzalcoatl with the Apostle St. Thomas in his *Phoenix of the West,* the Church, the most likely Maecenas of such erudite endeavors, was apparently unimpressed by this curious thesis. Other monographs, *The History of the Chichimeca Indians, Mexican Cyclography, Geneaology of the Mexican Monarchs, Calendar of the Months and Feast Days of the Mexicans,* and other similar works, likewise failed to win financial support and presently vanished. In the light of sources used and now lost, these studies probably possessed permanent value and their disappearance is a regrettable loss. Toward the end of his life the author's despondency increased regarding the fate of his findings and this mood moved him to put them generously at the disposition of contemporaries more fortunate in being able to publish their own books. Fathers Florencia and Vetancourt have left comprehensive accounts of phases of Mexican history in which they acknowledge indebtedness to Don Carlos, and the Italian traveler, Gemelli Careri, in his *Giro del Mondo,* devoted an extensive chapter to Aztec hieroglyphics, religion, and culture based on materials, including drawings, supplied by the Mexican Creole. For the most part Sigüenza's only recourse was to slip bits of information on Nahuatl lore into the pages of books of unrelated and ephemeral character which, from time to time, he was commissioned to write.

His historical writings on the period since the Spanish Conquest had a similar fate and most are known by title only. Without doubt, valuable data were embedded in such narratives as *The History of the Mexico City Cathedral; History of the University of Mexico,* concerning which he wrote in his will: "I fondly request the Royal University to accept the affection with which I began to write about its history and greatness but which was called off by the *claustro* for reasons unknown to me"; the *Historical Tribunal,* possibly a history of Mexico; *Theater of the Grandeur of Mexico City; History of the Province of Carolina* (Texas); and various others.

Better fortune attended his contemporary chronicles, written in his later years, which were a kind of rudimentary journalism. The Count of Galve, viceroy from 1688 to 1696, leaned heavily during these critical years upon the counsels of the Creole scholar who became a sort of court chronicler. The Madrid government's support was pitifully weak in the last, inglorious days of the Hapsburg dynasty while both the heart and the frontiers of New Spain presented problems of increasing gravity to the viceregal administration in a series of episodes that Sigüenza recorded. These accounts are often more readable than his learned treatises, though his prose suffered from the involved syntax and pompous rhetoric currently fashionable. He liked to think, however, that his style was simple and natural. In the prologue of the *Occidental Paradise,* the story of a Mexico City convent that he was commissioned to write, he declared: "Regarding the style I employ in this book, it is what I always use, whether I am conversing, writing, or preaching because, perhaps, I could not do otherwise even if I tried . . ." Loftily he condemns gongoristic abuses so universal in his time, seemingly unconscious of his own patent derelictions. Yet he sometimes did approach his self-proclaimed lucidity, and occasionally his accounts of current happenings offer instances of vivid reporting. *The Trophy of Spanish Justice* (1691) relates the adventures of a successful military expedition against the French on Santo Domingo; *An Account of What Happened to the Windward Fleet* (1691) tells of the maritime phase of this undertaking; and the *Flying*

*Mercury* (1693) recounts the bloodless reconquest of New Mexico. An interesting piece of reportage on the disastrous corn riot of the Indians in Mexico City on June 8, 1692, is contained in a letter intended for publication but unprinted until 1932.[4]

The most charming of these journalistic narratives is a curious account of the misadventures of a Puerto Rican youth during a journey around the world entitled *The Misfortunes of Alonso Ramirez*. Told in the first person, it purports to relate the story of his capture by English pirates who later set him adrift in a small boat which was finally wrecked on the Yucatan coast where he had a Robinson Crusoe-like adventure. Though Sigüenza slows the pace of his recital with pedantic details, he is writing in the picaresque tradition of Spanish literature and with more than his accustomed verve. Indeed, some literary historians like to classify this curious *relación* as a precursor of the Mexican novel.[5]

The more authentic claim of this Baroque scholar to distinction lies in his scientific writings which provide a better index of his intellectual caliber. Here again, however, most of his significant contributions never achieved the semi-permanence of print and hence are known only by hearsay, but the slight number surviving insure him a high place in the annals of the intellectual history of Old Mexico and, indeed, of colonial Spanish America.

Mathematics received his most constant devotion and represented his greatest competence. If his eminence in this discipline derives from its applied rather than theoretical aspects, it is owing probably to the fact that he shared Descartes' belief in the importance of mathematics as a method of search for knowledge and as a tool for the conquest of truth. In this faith he assembled the best collection of treatises and instruments then to be found in the New World, which he ultimately willed to the Jesuits "in gratitude to, and as an adequate compensation for, the good training and good instruction that I received from the reverend fathers during the few years that I lived with them . . ." Though he applied this skill to engineering projects, civilian and military, his most enthusiastic application was to astronomy.

As early as 1670 he observed the phenomena of the heavens, keeping precise records which he was ever eager to exchange with others. He strove continually to make these data as exact as possible, importing the latest instruments available. In his observations of the total eclipse of the sun in 1691 he used a telescope "of four lens which, up to now, is the best that has reached this city. Father Marco Antonio Capus sold it to me for eighty pesos." Thus it is likely that, in solid learning, technical literature, and efficient instruments, he was the best equipped scientist of his time in the Spanish overseas dominions. Through his extensive correspondence with leading men of science, his reputation spread to Europe and Asia. As early as 1680 his distinction had won him appointment as the Royal Cosmographer of the Realm, and it is stated that Louis XIV, with offers of pensions and special honors, sought to lure the Mexican savant to his Court.

A few of the missing works which were the fruit of his diligence are: *A Treatise on the Eclipses of the Sun,* known by title only; *A Treatise on the Sphere,* described merely as consisting of two hundred folio pages; and a polemical pamphlet inspired by the Comet of 1680 and bearing the Baroque caption: *Mathematical Bellerophon Against the Astrological Chimera of Don Martin de la Torre,* etc. It is briefly described as displaying all the subtleties of trigonometry "in the investigations of the movements of comets, either by means of a rectilinear trajection in the hypotheses of Copernicus, or by the conical spheres of the Cartesian vortices." But already by 1690 this paper had disappeared.

Fortunately, a like fate did not overtake an impressive little volume called *Astronomical and Philosophical Libra,* thanks to the generosity of an admiring friend who subsidized a small edition, of which a few copies survive. It is a polemical treatise on the nature of comets that provides the most substantial evidence of the competence and enlightenment of its author. A spirit of modernity pervades its pages which echo the subversive ideas of Gassendi, Descartes, Galileo, Kepler, Copernicus, and other thinkers still suspect in the late seventeenth century. Curiously blending scientific objectivity and emotional subjectivity, it refracts the tensions of the Baroque age as it reveals glimpses of the proud, sensitive, and touchy personality of the Creole scholar.

The "Great Comet of 1680," which so distressed the ignorant and exercised the best minds on both sides of the Atlantic, was first seen in Mexico City on November 15. Everywhere, and particularly there, this strange apparition stirred dread and foreboding of dire calamities and grave misfortunes to come. For Sigüenza it was an exciting event and an auspicious occasion. As the newly appointed Royal Cosmographer of the Realm, he felt it his duty to allay the groundless fears and widespread uneasiness that it caused generally in Mexican society. He therefore brought forth on January 13, 1681, a pamphlet with the resounding title *Philosophical Manifest Against Comets Stripped of their Dominion Over the Timid.* He was well aware that its subject matter was controversial, but he was hardly prepared for the tempest loosed by his well-meant effort to restore public confidence.[6]

In his treatise Don Carlos sharply disagreed with the ominous import that astrologers attributed to these astral manifestations. While freely acknowledging his ignorance of the true significance of these phenomena, he was sure that they should be venerated as the work of a just God. This mild assertion seemed almost subversive in the superstitious atmosphere of New Spain, and it promptly provoked an astringent reply from a Flemish gentleman living in Yucatan, named Martin de la Torre, in a pamphlet entitled: *Christian Manifest in Favor of Comets Maintained in Their Natural Significance.* Basing himself on astrological data, the author asserted that comets were, in fact, warnings from God Himself of coming calamitous events. Sigüenza, whose combative disposition reacted immediately to opposition, quickly retorted with his well-conceived if pompously styled *Mathematical Bellerophon,* previously mentioned, in which he emphasized the superiority of scientific analysis over astrological lore.

Nearer at hand exploded a more startling response to the original pamphlet. It came from the pen of one of his own colleagues in the University of Mexico, a professor of surgery. Bearing the designation *A Cometological Discourse and Account of the New Comet,* etc., it set forth the proposition that this astral apparition was composed of the exhalations of dead bodies and of human perspiration! Contemptuously Don Carlos declared that he would not deign to reply to such arrant nonsense. Still others entered the fray with their theories and one, whose eminence and prestige were too great to ignore, brought forth a stout rebuttal from Sigüenza in the previously cited *Astronomical and Philosophical Libra.*[7]

The person inspiring this supreme effort was a Jesuit from the Austrian Tyrol who happened to arrive from Europe at the height of the polemic en route to the mission frontier of Old Mexico.

Father Eusebio Francisco Kino, as he is known to history, was about the same age as Sigüenza, well educated in various European universities, and highly proficient in mathematics. Of imposing presence, gifted in languages, and widely reputed for his learning, he had declined a proffered professorship at the University of Ingolstadt in order to devote his life to bringing the light of the Gospel to the heathen in a remote and inhospitable region of the globe. The sacrifice of so many talents to so noble a cause was the supreme idealism of the age, and the most distinguished members of the viceregal society eagerly sought out the newcomer, including Don Carlos, who had an additional motive in their common love for mathematics. Moreover, since Father Kino had taken observations of the Comet of 1680 before embarking at Cádiz, an exchange of data would be illuminating. At the home of the Mexican Creole the two savants indulged in long discussions of their mutual interests.[8]

To the sensitive Don Carlos Father Kino seemed a little supercilious and aloof and there was a sort of tacit air of superiority about him; he did not, for instance, display a proper esteem for the Creole's observations. This indifference probably arose, Sigüenza later commented sourly, because the Mexican scholar had not studied at the University of Ingolstadt and the European could not imagine, therefore, that mathematicians might grow "amidst the reeds and cat-tails on the margins of a Mexican pond!" The highly intelligent Creole scholar was peculiarly prone to the feeling of inferiority which his class experienced in the presence of those born in Europe, for he believed that his own gifts and the lofty lineage that he claimed entitled him to equal consideration. Especially galling was the condescending, sometimes disdainful, attitude that Peninsulars assumed toward the American-born, and foreigners from the Continent did not seem to think their learning entitled to any respect at all. "In some parts of Europe," Sigüenza observed caustically, "especially in the north through being more remote, they think that not only the Indian inhabitants of the New World, but those of us who, by chance, were born here of Spanish parentage, either walk on two legs by divine dispensation or that, even using English microscopes, they can hardly discover anything rational in us!" In the case of Father Kino the sensitivity of Don Carlos was possibly exacerbated by the fact that his guest was a member in high standing of the religious Order from which he himself had been summarily ejected and to which he was repeatedly denied reinstatement.

Father Kino's stay in Mexico City, where he was preparing himself for the mission field, had not been long when rumors reached the Creole professor that this visitor was about to publish a work on the recent comet refuting Sigüenza's contentions. Friends of the Mexican scholar repeatedly warned him that the eminent Jesuit, so recently in contact with German scientists, would be a formidable antagonist in the debate. Father Kino himself gave no hint of these intentions and Don Carlos, confident of the soundness of his stand, allegedly awaited developments with composure. At last one evening, as the missionary was about to depart for Sinaloa to begin his work, he paid the Mexican ex-Jesuit a farewell call in his lodgings. In the course of the conversation the visitor casually handed his host a copy of a treatise *Astronomical Exposition,* just off the press. His manner was patronizing, or so thought the hypersensitive Creole scientist, as he suggested that the latter might peruse with profit this book that he had written, for it might give the worthy Mexican-Spaniard something to think about. Don Carlos interpreted these words as a challenge to an intellectual duel and the *Astronomical and Philosophical Libra* was his answer!

The fact that Father Kino did not anywhere mention Sigüenza by name did not lessen the conviction of the thin-skinned Creole that the statements were aimed at him. When he read, for example, that comets were really dire omens and harbingers of evil and that the opposite opinion was contrary to what all mortals were aware, the high, the low, the noble and plebian, the learned and unlearned, Don Carlos was certain to whom this comment alluded. "No one knows better where the shoe pinches than he who wears it and, since I assert that I am the object of his invective, everyone may believe that, without question, it was I." Since the rational view of these natural phenomena was held by no one, according to Father Kino, the implication was that Sigüenza was nothing! And when the Jesuit missionary concluded that the ominous portent of comets was evident to all ". . . unless there be some *trabajosos juicios* (dull wits) who cannot perceive it," the Mexican professor exploded: "Those who understand the Castilian language well know that, in telling someone that he is a 'trabajoso juicio,' it is the same as calling him crazy. Since this is the case, as it undoubtedly is, long life to the Reverend Father for the exceedingly rare praise with which he honors me!"

In this fashion the Mexican scholar vents his choler in the opening chapter, after which he settles down to a methodical discussion of the problem, setting forth a geometrical analysis of the movements of comets, their paralaxes, refractions, etc., accompanied by carefully executed diagrams. The offended Creole scientist struggles to keep his exposition on the dispassionate plane of reason but, despite himself, throughout the text mica-like glints of sarcasm and resentment shine amid the solid substance of his discourse, and he is unable to resist here and there a sardonic thrust at his opponent.

No attempt will be made to follow this very technical discussion. It is enough, perhaps, to point out its underlying significance in the intellectual history of colonial Mexico. The great struggle between the authoritarianism of neo-scholasticism and the empiricism of experimentalism, hardly initiated in the days of Fray García Guerra, but which so troubled the brilliant mind of Sister Juana Inés, had now reached a break in the work of her friend and intellectual companion. Less shackled by sex and religious vows than the poetess, Don Carlos had succeeded in divorcing secular concerns from the tradition of authority, thus enabling his thoughts to soar unhampered in such matters. Though a lay priest, he had no solemn pledge of submission to monastic superiors to respect, and he was freer to separate his rationalism in natural philosophy from the immutable dogma of theology than the convent-bound nun. This fact suggests a curious paradox in the lives of these two superior individuals; if Sister Juana Inés' secret sorrow was the impossibility of escaping into a world of wider horizons, Sigüenza's private grief was the impossibility of returning to the strict rule of a religious community.

What emerges perhaps most clearly from a reading of the *Astronomical and Philosophical Libra* is the heterodoxy of its author in the pursuit of truth in nature. His radical disposition is apparent in a bluntly expressed disrespect for authority in learning, in his belief in methodical doubt, in his conviction of the necessity of demonstration, and in his reliance on mathematics as a means of measuring natural phenomena. The direct influence of Descartes is obvious in the occasional references to that philosopher by name and the citations of his works. The Mexican thinker is disposed to strip away the long-standing prejudices still inhibiting his contemporaries in Europe as well as in Old Mexico. For the moment timeworn superstitions and shallow delusions assume material form in the person of the ungrateful and haughty Father Kino, the very embodiment of the spiritual ideal of his culture and the image of his own lost hope. With unconcealed venom the Creole ex-Jesuit assails the dogmatic utterances of his opponent on the significance of comets and he decisively disposes of the validity of authority in such matters. ". . . I hereby point out that neither his Reverence, nor any other mathematician, even if he is Ptolemy himself, can set up dogmas in these sciences, because authority has no place in them at all, but only proof and demonstration. . . ." Here, plainly, is the modern spirit lighting up the darkness of neomedieval thought. The problems and doubts that the spectacle of nature presents to mankind, he went on, could never be resolved by merely searching through old texts to find out what the ancient authorities of classical learning had said on the subject. "What would I say to satisfy one who affirmed," he exclaimed, "that, in a subject open to discussion, it is necessary to accept what others say when clearly no one, with a mind and reasoning power, is ever guided by authorities if these authorities lack congruity . . ." "And would it be wise," he asks, promptly adding that it would be unwise, "to assert in these times that the heavens are solid and unchangeable just because most ancient authors state that they are? That the moon is eclipsed by the shadow of the earth and that all comets are semilunary merely because these authorities so advise? Would it be creditable to the intelligence to accept the teachings of others without looking into the premises on which their ideas are based? . . ." This kind of skepticism was rare in the Baroque world of seventeenth century Mexico, and it was a little subversive in a culture in which Theology, as the "Queen of Sciences," still reigned supreme.

This unequivocal flouting of the sacrosanct principle of authority, which most contemporaries did not dare to challenge, foreshadowed an intellectual scuffle destined to enliven the academic halls of Old Mexico and of Spanish America nearly two generations later, namely, the dethronement of Aristotle as the high priest of knowledge. As early as 1681 Sigüenza had proclaimed his heresy. ". . . even Aristotle, the avowed Prince of Philosophers who, for so many centuries, has been accepted with veneration and respect, does not deserve credence . . . when his judgments are opposed to truth and reason. . . ." Here, indeed, was a sharp break with the past and an utterance that the Jesuits, by whom he so longed to be accepted, would hardly have condoned. Indeed, soon after the death of Don Carlos the members of that intellectually advanced Order were reminded that they must teach Aristotelian philosophy only, and that they must eschew the "erroneous propositions of Cartesian thought."[9]

Such, then, was the bold thinking which the sensitive and highly intelligent Mexican savant revealed in his carefully reasoned rebuttal of Father Kino's assertions and insinuations. Every page of the *Astronomical and Philosophical Libra* discloses a logical and erudite, if somewhat atrabilious, mind well versed in the ideas of thinkers such as Conrad Confalonier, Athanasius Kircher, Pico della Mirandola, Juan Caramuel, Kepler, Gassendi, Oldenburg, Descartes, and many others cited in the text and in the footnotes. It is plain that this isolated and lonely worker was more than dimly aware of the currents of scientific thought flowing more strongly in contemporary Europe and that he was in the ranks of those exalted spirits who strove to slip the bandage of ignorance and superstition from the darkened eyes of his fellowmen. In the closing pages of this small but impressive treatise its author effectively demolishes the astrological misapprehensions of Martin de la Torre and records his own observations of the controversial comet from January 3 to January 20, 1681.

Ten years elapsed before this remarkable little volume found its way into print, though the necessary license was obtained at once. This delay doubtless stemmed from the inability of the impecunious author to defray the cost of publication of so technical a work for so limited a readership, and it owed its final appearance to the generosity of an admiring friend. Sigüenza was immensely proud of this effort and upon especially distinguished visitors passing through Mexico City he was wont to bestow a copy. When the famed Italian traveler, Gemelli Careri, dropped into the Creole scholar's quarters at the Hospital del Amor de Dios, he departed with the *Astronomical and Philosophical Libra* along with much other data that the learned professor supplied for the forthcoming book about his tour of the world. Whether Father Kino ever took any particular notice of the treatise which his own work had called forth does not appear. Explorations and mission-building in the northwestern provinces of Old Mexico absorbed his energies and interests and no indications are available that he renewed acquaintance with the oversensitive Creole on the one or two widely spaced visits that he subsequently made to the viceregal capital.

The closing years of Sigüenza's life coincided with those of the seventeenth century and of the Hapsburg dynasty on the Spanish throne, and the cancerous ills of the Empire had their counterparts in the body of the Mexican humanist. Marked physical decline was already visible in 1694, and it accelerated in the years following. He suffered intensely from stones in the kidney and ". . . . one in the bladder the size of a large pigeon's egg according to the statement of the surgeons who have felt it." Walking, even a short distance, was difficult and painful. As the specter of death loomed, beloved relatives and associates succumbed to it, accentuating the grief and despondency of the dying scholar. The year 1695 deprived him of a favorite brother, and about the same time he sustained an equally poignant loss in the final release of the tormented mind and spirit of Sister Juana Inés. As he delivered a funeral oration at her grave, an acute realization of his own desolate aloneness fell upon him. In succession his aged father, ex-tutor of the long-dead Prince Baltasar Carlos, the viceroy, Count of Galve, and the Archbishop Aguiar y Seijas, his most influential patrons, passed away. The prelate's decease probably ended Don Carlos' remunerative employment as Chief Almoner and, along with his health, his economic circumstances deteriorated, though the demands of numerous relatives remained unceasing. Abruptly the office of University Accountant with its perquisites was taken from him, and his status of professor emeritus had come only after vexatious delays owing to his less than faithful performance of its duties. In this near penury he accepted the post of Corrector for the Inquisition and to the tedious scrutiny of suspected books he devoted his waning vigor—a task singularly uncongenial to his enlightened spirit and a misapplication of his talents.

His last year was clouded by an episode that hastened his end, for it touched a most sensitive part—his integrity as a scientist.

Back in 1693, at the urgent request of the Count of Galve, he had made his longest journey and undertaken his most momentous mission. French intrusions in the Gulf of Mexico, which threatened the coast of Texas, Louisiana, and Florida, had frightened Spanish authorities into a belated effort to occupy effectively that part of the Gulf region. Among other measures they sent an expedition to reconnoiter and map the promising bay of Pensacola. Leaving his quiet, comfortable study he embarked on his only sea voyage and explored and charted that Florida inlet.[10] A recommendation for immediate occupation by the Spaniards only met procrastination owing to the grave uncertainties of an expiring dynasty and the feeble resources of the empire until French aggression brought tardy action. In 1698 Andrés de Arriola, an officer famed for his voyage to and from the Philippine Islands in record time, reluctantly accepted a commission to plant a settlement at Pensacola Bay. When a French vessel made its appearance at its mouth Arriola scuttled back to Vera Cruz and the Mexican capital and brought a highly critical report of the locality, challenging the accuracy of Sigüenza's earlier survey.

The ailing scholar reacted sharply to these aspersions with more than his customary acerbity, promptly accusing the returned officer of deserting his post and falsifying the findings of 1693. The offended Arriola then demanded that the viceroy—no longer Sigüenza's loyal friend, Count of Galve—require the scholar to go back to Pensacola with him and prove his contentions by a new survey. The fact that Don Carlos was obviously too ill to travel did not deter Arriola from insisting, and Viceroy Moctezuma felt constrained to oblige Sigüenza to comply or give a satisfactory explanation.

Mustering his failing strength the Creole professor drew up a masterful reply, bringing into play the dialectical skill and biting sarcasm that had left their marks on opponents in other polemics. With analytical precision he broke Arriola's statement into its component parts which, one by one, he battered with merciless cogency and unassailable logic. "I am not one who has to unsay what he has once said," he proudly declared. If the viceroy insisted on a journey to Pensacola, he was ready to comply despite his precarious health and crippled state, but he would impose his own conditions. If his body was frail, his spirit was as stout and pugnacious as ever. So confident was he of the correctness of his earlier report that he would wager his dearest possession, his library, on the favorable outcome of a new survey. This collection "is the best of its kind in the realm" and, "together with his mathematical instruments, telescopes, pendulum clocks and valuable paintings, the total is appraised at more than three thousand pesos," and this he would bet "against an equivalent sum posted by Arriola . . ." on the rightness of his earlier findings. But, he stipulated, the viceroy must send them on separate ships to the Florida coast, otherwise there would be no lack of occasions, he stated grimly, "either for him to throw me into the sea or for me to throw him."[11]

This second voyage by Sigüenza never occurred, partly because his health rendered it impracticable, but more probably, because he had effectively refuted his opponent's allegations. The incident did not fail, however, to deepen his despondency, and it had called forth his last revealing communication. In a measure it was the counterpart of Sister Juana Inés' remarkable *Reply*, for both documents symbolize a crisis in the lives of the writers. Both are answers to criticism of their activities; both contain intimate personal data; both are a defense against imputations on the use of their intellects; both are carefully meditated and subjective records; and both herald the disintegration and decease of their authors. While Sister Juana Inés' *Reply* is clearly more moving and significant, the exceptional character and unique personality of both ill-starred individuals are poignantly etched in the phrases of their lengthy depositions. For the nun the pace of death was slower; for the scholar it was speedier. A little more than a year after signing his rejoinder his troubled spirit and tormented body found rest. August 22, 1700 brought liberation.

In character and attainments this Baroque scholar resembled the humanists of the Renaissance whose curious, encyclopedic minds laid the foundations of modern science and learning. Like them he confronted the task of keeping in balance the increasing independence of the human spirit and the unquestioned authority of the Church. His rugged mind, methodical doubt, and sturdy pragmatism in secular matters were exceptional in the Baroque time and place in which he lived. In religious dogma and pious faith he remained ever submissive and devout, accepting implicitly ecclesiastical authority and the validity of the tenets of orthodox Catholicism. This dichotomy of his mental life is nowhere more apparent than in his last will and testament prepared in the final

weeks of his existence. There, in curious juxtaposition, is the testimony of his unquestioning and naive acceptance of miracles and
of things supernatural, and there also he proclaims his unswerving
devotion to the luminous spirit of scientific investigation and to the
enlightened service of mankind. One testamentary clause attests to
the thoroughly modern attitude that infused his being and epitomizes a lifelong dedication.

"Inasmuch as the physicians and surgeons attending me in my
long and painful illness relating to the urine have been unable to
determine whether it is due to gallstones or the bladder and, since
there is apparently no known remedy for the exceedingly severe
pain and torment that I am enduring, it is my desire that whoever
may have a similar disease may regain health or, at least, obtain
some relief through learning the cause of this ailment. Without
this knowledge or experience no relief can be found, nor any
medicine applied which will reach it. Therefore, since my body
must return to the clay from which it came, I request, in the name
of God, that, so soon as life has departed from me, my body shall
be opened by any physicians or surgeons desiring to do so, and
that the right kidney, the bladder, the small end of which is to
deprive me of life, and the arrangement of the organisms shall all
be examined carefully. I request that whatever deductions are
made shall be revealed to other physicians and surgeons so that
they may have data to guide them in administering to other sufferers. I ask in God's name that this be done for the common
good, and I command my heir not to interfere, for it matters little
that this be done to a body which, within a few days, must be
corruption and decay."

An executor of the will reported: "His command was carried
out, and, after opening him, they found a stone the size of a peach-
stone in the right kidney where he had said that he felt pain."[12]
Thus, in an age when among his class human remains were
deemed sacred and dissection was still counted a desecration, this
consecrated savant of seventeenth century Mexico demonstrated,
in his last act, a desire to seek truth and to serve mankind even beyond the boundary of life. His spirit clearly foreshadowed the end
of the Age of the Baroque and the beginning of the Age of Reason
in Hispanic America.

# ❧ XIV

# A SUMMING UP

IN THE seamless fabric of time the year 1700 seems to mark a visible conjunction of two centenary epochs of changing events and shifting patterns in the history of the western world. The civil, religious, and dynastic wars of the Baroque age that had so long wracked Europe were evolving into struggles of colonial and commercial rivals. The emerging national states of the early seventeenth century had acquired, or had occupied more effectively, overseas possessions which transformed these political entities into competing empires. The chief contenders were Portugal, Spain, Holland, France, and England, but by 1700 the period of active growth of the first three was past, leaving the last two to lock horns in the eighteenth century like titans in a contest for supremacy on the high seas, in North America, and in India, as well as in continental Europe. And thus the era of "world wars" was ushered in, transferring the parochial strife of nationalistic peoples from a regional stage on the western fringe of the Eurasian land-mass to a global theater.

An inadvertent catalytic agent of this development was Spain, owing to the inglorious end in 1700 of nearly two centuries of Hapsburg rule through the death of the childless Charles II. The magnitude of the Spanish empire still gave the Peninsula an impressive semblance of might and, in the age of absolute monarchs who reckoned territories as personal possessions, the extinction of a royal line exposed a rich estate to the cupidity of claimants of all shades of legitimacy. Such pretensions, however, were increasingly encumbered by grave considerations of a "balance of power," and, whoever the successful contestant might be, the award of this grand prize would inevitably create an inequilibrium in the international affairs of Europe. When the dying Charles II changed his will in favor of Philip of Anjou, grandson of Louis XIV, the "Grand Monarch," the preponderance of power clearly lay in Bourbon hands. A coalition led by Great Britain challenged this French hegemony in the War of Spanish Succession, and from 1702 to 1713 military campaigns on a larger scale than ever before devastated the Continent, including Spain, and this conflagration spread to North America in the so-called Queen Anne's War. With the Bourbon heir finally confirmed on the Spanish throne as Philip V, Spain had entered a new era.

Old Mexico could not remain untouched by these events and a few inhabitants were dimly conscious that the year 1700 signified a crossing into an epoch of disruptive consequences. Up to then the belief persisted that New Spain was far removed from the ideological conflicts and bloody strife rending Europe, which had scarcely known seven years of peace in an entire century. It almost seemed as if Mexico was reserved by God for a more perfect realization of His plan which was a static, peaceful order, and for this fulfillment the mother country had, in part at least, bled itself white despite liberal transfusions from the silver veins of the New World. Sheltered and remote the broad realm of Old Mexico hardly comprehended the inevitability of change and the futility of Spain's ideal.

But to many officials entrusted with the direction of its affairs the advancing decades had brought a slow awareness of the delusion engendered by a fancied isolation. Even before Fray García Guerra arrived in 1608, jealous rivals of Spain had encroached upon its imperial preserve in America. Bold adventurers of England, France, and Holland had seized neglected islands of the Caribbean, and even portions of the mainland. During the rule of the Archbishop-Viceroy Dutch activities in this island-strewn sea seriously threatened the approaches to the treasure-yielding realm. In the course of the century this nibbling at the edges of empire grew more aggressive and seriously disturbed Spanish authorities. The important islands of Barbados, the Bahamas, and Jamaica fell like plums into the English lap, and the strategic entrepôt at the isthmus of Pan-

ama suffered brutal destruction by the piratical Morgan. Hardly
less ominous were the French gains in the West Indies: Marti-
nique, Guadeloupe, Guiana, and the western end of Santo Domingo,
the island on which the Spaniards had planted their first settlements and which would become the richest overseas possession
of France in the eighteenth century.

Menacing as these losses were to viceregal Mexico, the silver
mines of its northern regions still seemed immune to attack, and
the re-enforced convoys of treasure fleets generally managed to
elude the enemies lodged in the islands. But the closing decades of
the century brought alarming indications that remoteness no longer
guaranteed the security of this mineral wealth. Far to the north
on the mainland the English settlements in Virginia and New England were expanding until, in 1688, their populations numbered
three hundred thousand. Bold representatives were pushing southward from the Carolinas and presently they would carve out a
region from the vacant, vaguely delimited spaces of Spanish Florida
and name it Georgia. So imperfect was the geographical knowledge of the Spaniards concerning this general area that the fancied
proximity to the northern mines of these intrusions caused deep
anxiety.

But far more corroding was the fear inspired by French activities.
The settlers of New France in the "northern mystery," though less
numerous than the English, were more widely dispersed in regions
along the St. Lawrence river, Lake Superior, and the Ohio river.
During Colbert's rule they had increased three hundred per cent
in a score of years. In 1682 Sieur de la Salle had paddled down the
Mississippi and claimed its great basin for France, naming it
Louisiana in honor of the king. Two years later he led an ill-fated
expedition of four vessels and three hundred colonists to the Gulf
of Mexico to plant a settlement at the mouth of the great river as
a base of operations against the northern frontier of New Spain.
Miscalculations landed him on the bleak coast of Texas where
disaster ended his enterprise. But the news of this undertaking
startled Spanish officialdom from a troubled somnolence, and frantically they dispatched expedition after expedition to seek out the
rumored colony and pre-empt any desirable ports on the neglected
northern Gulf coast. As a scientific observer and map-maker,
Sigüenza y Góngora, it will be remembered, had shared in these

efforts, visiting Pensacola and Mobile bays, and entering the mouth of the Mississippi.

The Treaty of Ryswick in 1697 brought a truce to the intermittent warfare of Spain and France which merely freed the latter country for more aggressive acts against Spanish possessions in America. Soon Iberville was on his way to occupy Louisiana and link it with New France, thus driving a formidable wedge between Spanish Florida and the silver region of Mexico. The intent of France was unmistakable. "La grande affaire est la decouverte des mines," ran the orders of the French leader,[1] and Mexican authorities shuddered at the implications of this intrusion. The splendid isolation, which had so long facilitated a static order and Baroque brilliance in New Spain, was ending.

If relatively few within Mexico were fully aware of these external developments, many more were acutely conscious of internal events which filled them with a strange, *fin de siècle* uneasiness as if all things were coming to a close. In 1691 heavy rains brought flash-floods that hurled masses of water through parched ravines, destroying homes, barns, mills, and cattle of Spaniards and Indians alike. Even churches, shrines, and convents were swept away as the torrents charged through villages and hamlets. The downpour caused the canals of the capital to overflow and Lake Texcoco, its great expanse nearly dry normally, was soon capable of floating ships of heavy burden, while the causeways leading across it to the city became impassable; packtrains could not bring supplies to relieve the starving inhabitants. Adobe houses disintegrated in the excessive moisture and formed mounds of viscous mud which slithered into the watery streets and squares, leaving wretched occupants without shelter, food or fire. In the surrounding country the cloudbursts transformed fields into a water-logged morass, which ruined crops completely. When at last the rains diminished, a blight, spreading with the rapidity of a conflagration, attacked the wheat and corn in outlying districts and, for long months, famine and deprivation stalked the land.

Dread phenomena of Nature, such as had attended Fray García Guerra's demise earlier in the century and seemingly had ushered in the Baroque era, now repeated themselves as if to herald the approaching end of that age. The superstitious masses interpreted an eclipse of the sun as a dark indication of divine displeasure which spawned hysterical fears slow to dissipate. It was the same phenomenon that Sigüenza y Góngora had observed with his telescope and which he pronounced "not only a total eclipse but one of the greatest that the world has ever seen." In this atmosphere of wretchedness, misery, and panic all the hidden resentments, the gnawing injustices, and repressed hatreds came to the surface and a sullen mood of restiveness pervaded the city. The apprehension of the privileged minority turned to fright as rumors of impending riots and public disturbances hardened into facts. On June 8, 1692 mounting tension exploded into mob violence which burned the viceregal palace and other important buildings and made a bloody shambles of the cluttered square in front of the Cathedral. The viceroy luckily escaped from the frenzy of the rioters, but the complete overthrow of the Spanish government was barely averted. For long months a nervous expectancy of further uprisings agitated the entire realm.

Hardly did this state of alarm subside when a pestilence of high mortality swept through the viceregal community, exacting a heavy toll from every caste and class. Even when the force of the plague was spent death, with remorseless insistence, continued to select its victims among the illustrious and powerful, including the viceroy, and the Archbishop. These somber happenings accentuated the Baroque concern with dissolution and decay and, in the hearts of the inhabitants, the conviction strengthened that the end of the age, indeed of the world itself, was imminent.

If the eighteenth century was to witness the beginnings of a breakdown of the orthodoxy so carefully imposed by Spain on its overseas possessions, the seventeenth century had placed an almost ineffaceable seal upon the character and personality of embryonic nations. The fluidity of the earlier age of conquest and settlement had given way to the rigidity of a fixed pattern after Spain's expansive effort ground to a virtual halt in 1600. The mounting repression of the Counter Reformation had slowed movement and facilitated the consolidation of a neomedieval civilization and culture. Circumstances were propitious to this development in Old Mexico and they produced perhaps its most complete manifestation. An accelerated fusion of varied human elements favored an intricate hierarchy of class and caste, and this ethnic diversity tended toward a social immobility that left the dominant whites unchallenged in a permanent position of privilege. It thus created a societal design nearly immune to the erosion of time and modernity. Economically these heterogeneous constituents formed a proletarian mass largely deprived of the fruits of its toil. If the *encomienda,* a semi-feudal system of lord and serf, or master and slave, implanted in the sixteenth century, was breaking down in the Baroque age, already replacing it was a harsher system of debt peonage, destined to linger on into twentieth century Mexico and plunge that nation into the anarchy and chaos of social revolution.

Inherent in the colonial order was an arbitrary, monolithic state headed by a vice-sovereign with nearly absolute authority who functioned essentially as an overseer of the enormous estate of its absentee owner, the king of Spain. The royal master wished to derive the maximum income from his property but, as a Christian monarch, his attitude was usually paternalistic and he believed that he was benefiting his subjects by often enlightened decrees. Vast distances and slow communications nullified most of these good intentions, and his Majesty's representatives often were little less than unrestrained despots. Exercising judicial, executive, and even lawgiving powers, they were unassailable and omnipotent; their will took on the semblance of statutes and their persons an aura of infallibility. Surrounded by an obsequious bureaucracy they were accessible only through a fawning adulation or the influence of favorites. Few viceroys and governors of the seventeenth century were men of more than mediocre talent and character who could hardly help but feel transformed into demigods by such unlimited authority. This haughty importance, so gratifying to vanity, fostered a tradition of personalism and dictatorship fated to haunt the political life of the later republic.

The same period witnessed the planting of the seeds of *caciquismo,* or political boss rule in local communities, an evil which flourished in all its malignity when the right of suffrage under republican institutions provided the illusion of popular sovereignty. The provincial *corregidores* and *alcaldes mayores* were district magistrates who often usurped absolute authority within their jurisdiction. Enjoying unchallenged sway, they easily enriched themselves through a monopolistic sale of salt, seeds, tools, and other necessities to the defenseless Indian peasantry. And these corrupt agents of government were seldom averse to accommodating aristocratic families of the locality by abusing their prerogatives to coerce the wretched peons into wageless service to them and by suppressing any latent restlessness of the exploited. Thus a pattern of petty despotism and personal rule in local government hardened and became virtually immune to the subsequent attrition of political experience.

Clearly evident in the seventeenth century was the consolidation of the power and wealth of the Church. Theoretically subordinate to the State, its influence was felt in every aspect of secular life. In many ways it acquired a predominance in human affairs rivaling that of the medieval Church in Europe, and this tradition it was slow to relinquish. Its dual task of converting the native population and preventing backsliding among the faithful was sufficient warrant to justify the accumulation of material wealth and the constant enlargement of the staff of clergymen. Well before the close of the sixteenth century its immense holdings of land identified its interests with those of the landed aristocracy, and its equalitarian ardor soon cooled. The leisurely life of many churchmen made an ecclesiastical career attractive, and monasteries, convents, and churches rapidly multiplied to accommodate the increasing numbers of the religious community. Vast resources of treasure and real estate, permanently retained by a system of mortmain, soon transformed the Church, particularly the various Orders, into the chief fiscal agencies of the realm. Fiduciary activities such as moneylending, mortgages, leases, rentals and the like, were highly lucrative and, as an important supplier of capital, it exercised a powerful influence on the colonial economy. This abundant wealth and an easy command of artisan and manual labor enabled the Church to transform cities and hamlets, especially in the core region of Mexico, into an immense museum of Baroque architecture and art which remains a patrimony of the modern nation. These rich resources, coupled with an unquestioned spiritual authority, bestowed upon the institution a tremendous weight in every phase of social, cultural, intellectual, and even political life of the people with lasting effects. Through its secular arm, the Inquisition, it brooked no criticism or dissidence in public opinion while it exerted severe restraint upon private behavior. Thus the Church acquired a position, particularly in the seventeenth century, that became almost impregnable and highly resistant to the corrosive effects of modern secularism.

An agrarian capitalism was the underlying economic ideology of this neomedieval, semifeudal order, the prosperity of which rested mainly on the ownership of land and its products. Hence of paramount importance to the ruling groups was the absolute possession of these productive means and the despotic control of the peasantry. A system of latifundia readily solidified, and this concept of social organization involving large estates owned by a select few, and a vast proletariat, provided a pattern which endured into the twentieth century. The Baroque age witnessed an oppressive development of this order owing to the relatively limited amount of arable soil, the inefficient methods of cultivation, the deteriorating effects of sheep-raising and pastoral pursuits, and the insatiable acquisitiveness of landholders who generally preferred to live in the cities. European invaders had early taken up the best tracts which their descendants expanded, often by absorbing the communal lands of Indian villages. This procedure reduced the aboriginal owners to a condition of debt peonage, and in one fell swoop, increased acreage and a labor supply for the white masters. It was a method which achieved its fullest efficiency under the Díaz regime of the late nineteenth century.

The rewards of proprietorship were psychological as well as material. Extensive holdings of land brought a coveted social prestige and, for elevation into a seigneurial position, an enormous estate was often a valid substitute for a lofty lineage of aristocratic distinction. Many an adventurer was thus able to overcome the handicaps of an undistinguished origin and bequeath an honored name to his family. Patrician pride quite as much as economic advantage contributed to the perpetuation of hereditary ownership through the institution of *mayorazgos,* or primogeniture, which flourished well into the republican period. In the course of the seventeenth century the Creole class became predominantly the landholders, and they tended to adopt a less paternal attitude toward their Indian serfs than the Spanish Peninsulars whom they supplanted. The ultimate abolition of the controversial *encomienda* had thus brought no improvement to the unenviable lot of the Indians, and the persistence of *latifundismo,* with all its evils, was guaranteed by the tradition of mortmain preserved by the Church and of primogeniture retained by the aristocracy. Much later this rigid order would expire belatedly in the fury of social revolution.

With slight modification, then, a neomedieval civilization sank deep roots into the Mexican soil during the seventeenth century. The privileged minorities of the State, Church, and landed proprietors, aided and abetted by a small but influential group of merchants and entrepreneurs chiefly engaged in the extractive industries, collaborated to preserve a fixed and constant order in a world of accelerating change. The long decades of this middle century saw the solidification of Hispanic culture in its most orthodox form in a semifeudal society of class and caste based on a system of latifundia directed by an absolute State and an even more arbitrary Church. The aim of this civilization was immobility, spiritual, intellectual, cultural, social, political, and economic. In this static order inspiration, imagination, and ingenuity could have free play only within the accessory and not the formal or essential aspects of life and reality. The repressed vitality of a heterogeneous but enormously creative people was consequently denied a fruitful outlet and was forced to expend itself for the most part in dramatic trivia and excessive ornamentation—a heritage of the Baroque age still not wholly extinguished.

This formative era of Old Mexico did not, of course, begin with the Spanish Archbishop-Viceroy, Fray García Guerra, nor did it expire with the intellectually curious Sigüenza y Góngora, but these two figures symbolize, in a measure, important stages in its evolution. The Baroque period, which they represent, clearly does not offer the abundant external history of the days of the Conquistadors nor that of the times that immediately preceded the War of Independence, yet it was not wholly static. Behind its heavily embroidered veil there was movement, for the Baroque spirit sought to reconcile a bold modernism in form with an extreme oldness in content. This effort, which evaded issues and avoided the concrete, resulted in some changes of an inner nature during the century that suggest a vague polarity in the contrasting times and personalities of Fray García and Don Carlos de Sigüenza.

The earlier figure epitomizes the neomedieval ideal of the Spanish Counter Reformation with its fusion of ecclesiastical and secular authority, its theological learning, and its reliance on verbalism in the quest of truth, and Fray García seemed a nearly perfect embodiment of this spirit. If at that moment the resolute endeavor of Spain to preserve orthodoxy in religion and thought in Old Mexico from the schismatic differences of contemporary Europe seemed successful, considerable seepage of ideas regarded as subversive had occurred when Sigüenza y Góngora began his studies. Just as the weakening monarchy of the Peninsula could not prevent foreign encroachment on its New World territories, so it was unable to prevent the encroachment of foreign ideas there. Doctrinal rigidity, backed by Inquisitorial censorship, may have kept them to a mere trickle, but it did not exclude them altogether; and, if the colonial mentality seemed parched, it did not cause newer concepts to evaporate entirely. Receptive minds such as that of Sigüenza y Góngora were quietly initiating a shift from the semantic ambiguities of scholasticism as a means of explaining everything to the more precise language of mathematics as a means of explaining natural phenomena. Where Fray García was singleminded in his approach to all problems, Don Carlos discriminated between those relating to things eternal, which he left to traditional rationalization, and those temporal, to which he applied the new methodology of observation and measurement. Where Fray García did not question the authority of Aristotle in secular disciplines Don Carlos, two generations or more ahead of his time in Mexico, was vigorously anti-Aristotelian. He and, to a lesser degree, his contemporary, Sister Juana Inés de la Cruz, were precursors of the Enlightenment that presently reached their *patria*.

In less abstruse matters the interval between Fray García and Don Carlos was likewise a transition. The Archbishop-Viceroy, a Peninsular Spaniard, came to Mexico City with the absolute power of a proconsul to administer the affairs of a federated kingdom of an empire consciously aping the ancient Roman system. For the provincial subjects, and especially the Creoles, the boon of imperial citizenship was enough, and they acknowledged the distant grandeur of the Hapsburgs with pride and awe. As the decades passed this attitude remained outwardly unchanged, but inwardly the Creoles had grown restive, and their antagonism increased toward the Europe-born Spaniards who continued to occupy the highest offices. These American-bred whites had risen in numbers and, through interlocking family interests that gave them a certain cohesion, their power was consolidating. The fact that the declining fortunes of the mother country and its perennial bankruptcy enabled the Creoles to acquire many minor offices by purchase served only to sharpen their resentment at an exclusion still main-

tained by the crown from the major offices. Since common griev-
ances suffered often unite more closely than common blessings
shared, the Creoles thought of themselves more and more as Mexican Americans and sought compensatory pride in their homeland.
Though the feeling was not without conflicts and insecurity arising out of the friction of races and a morbid sense of cultural
inferiority, an embryonic nationalism was emerging. By 1700 the
Spanish Americans were obtaining a firm grip on the affairs and
management of their country.

This nascent Mexicanism crops out occasionally in Sigüenza's
writings as in his frequent allusions to "mi Patria," his reference
to the supercilious indifference of Europeans, and his claims of
Mexican equality with the Old World in artistic and even intellectual potentialities. All this was no more, probably, than a manifestation of regionalistic loyalty characteristic of Hispanic peoples
everywhere, and it is doubtful if Sigüenza's conception of his
"Patria" extended much beyond his own class or far beyond the
bounds of the populous vicinity of Mexico City.

To him, as to those of his social milieu, his conceptions were in-
separably associated with things Spanish. Yet it is significant that,
perhaps more than anyone of his time, he also included in this
national consciousness the aboriginal heritage of his land. His lifelong dedication to the Indian antiquities bears witness to this fact.
Great Spanish scholars such as Sahagún and Torquemada had
earlier given their lives to these studies, but in the Mexican Creole's
work one senses a greater identification with this ancient lore.
From the age of twenty-three he collected books, codices, maps, and
paintings relating to pre-Hispanic native life until he had assembled the richest assortment of archaeological and historical materials on the Aztec civilization then in existence. Mastering various
Mexican languages, he compiled scholarly monographs, practically
none of which survive. "If there were someone in New Spain who
would pay the cost of printing. . . . there is no doubt that I would
bring forth several works, in the composition of which I have
been stimulated by the great love I have for my country . . ." he
wrote, and mournfully added, ". . . these and other data require
large volumes, and so they will probably die with me (for I shall
never be able to publish them because of my great poverty)."[2]

Another incident reveals a certain Creole boldness in the face

of Spanish authority as well as the scholar's disposition to count
the indigenous culture as a component of his Mexicanism. A new
viceroy, Marqués de la Laguna, came from Spain in 1680 and, as
was customary, elaborate arrangements were made for his ceremonious entry into the capital. An important feature was invariably
an Arch of Triumph with appropriate allegorical decorations and
emblematic designs. Nearly always in these devices the organizers
made use of myths and legends of Greek and Roman antiquity
shaped to please the vanity of the vice-sovereign. Sigüenza y Góngora was commissioned on this occasion to select the topics and
execute the designs, and he chose to break rather sharply with
tradition. Ignoring the standard models of ancient classics, he represented pictorially and with suitable inscriptions the Aztec gods
and emperors, each of whom embodied a virtue or trait deemed
desirable in rulers. In his *Theater of the Political Virtues Apper-
taining to a Prince as Noted in the Ancient Monarchs of the Mexican Empire,* a volume commemorative of the occasion and written
in the turgid, indigestible prose of Baroque scholarship, Sigüenza
sets forth in much detail the remarkable character and accomplish-
ments of the aboriginal kings scorned and despised by the Spaniards.[3] As European Christians could find inspiration in the pagan
culture of Greeks and Romans so, this Creole scholar seems to
imply, Mexican Christians could derive similar understanding from
an American past, and with warmth and enthusiasm he exalts the
qualities and achievements of the heathen magistrates of his native
land. In all this one senses that, in a subtle fashion, the highly intelligent Sigüenza wished to remind a proud Peninsular that the
realm over which he had come to preside was no mere adjunct of
the Spanish empire but a land with a rich heritage of its own.
And it is likely that, in praising the integrity and political acumen
of the pre-Hispanic rulers of Mexico, he artfully sought to in-
struct the new appointee of the king of Spain in matters of states-
manship and right government for his Creole *patria.*

In this intention, so carefully veiled in Baroque fashion by a
welter of detail and heavy verbalism, is evident a dawning Mexicanism which the more articulate Spanish American expressed on
more than one occasion. In his description of the *mascarada* at
Querétaro, it will be remembered, he had seized the opportunity to
expatiate on the virtues of the rulers of pre-Cortesian Mexico and

also on the military potentialities displayed by his countrymen in that parade. Open expression of such sentiments marked an advance in national consciousness, for it is doubtful that in the times of Fray García Guerra even the most discontented Creole would have had either the appreciation of the Indian past or the effrontery to draw upon it for an allegorical theme to honor the accession of the king's vicar in the realm. Indeed, to have held up the pagan chieftains of the Aztec barbarians as models for instruction and emulation of the haughty conquerors would have seemed scarcely less than *lèse majesté*. In the closing decades of the century, however, the Creole class was conscious of its growing strength and cohesion and increasingly disposed to assert itself, though still with discreet restraint. Moreover, in the course of the century the complex and involuted pattern of the transplanted Spanish Baroque had absorbed elements of indigenous history and feeling as well as Indian motifs in art and architecture, thus imbuing sentiment and artistic expression with a hybrid character distinct from that of Spain and, in a measure, unique. As ethnic fusion had advanced in the progressive mixing of the races, an amalgamation in the sphere of esthetics and psychology had paralleled it.

During the decades that followed the seventeenth century little change appears in the Baroque spirit save, perhaps, its tendency to intensify a predilection for exaggeration, extravagance, hyperbole, and superlatives which sometimes carried artistic and literary expression to even more grotesque extremes. These manifestations were, perhaps, the products of the sustained repression of an inner vitality which was about to explode. The prolonged crisis in the "eternal order of theology" had built up tensions that orthodoxy and tradition could not contain much longer. The long incubation of expanding pressures was to release the revolutionary ideologies of eighteenth century rationalism and nineteenth century republicanism. Yet when they came and violent as the resulting convulsions were, they failed to shatter completely the Baroque matrix which the long years of Spanish domination had tempered to a granitic hardness. Its indelible imprint remained etched upon the personality and civilization of Spanish America everywhere. Indeed, to sum it all up, so pronounced is this peculiar legacy today that it has moved a discerning critic and distinguished citizen of that area to comment recently: "The Baroque was one of the most profoundly rooted elements of tradition in our culture. In spite of nearly two centuries of encyclopedism and modern criticism, we Hispanic Americans have not yet fully emerged from its labyrinth. It still heavily influences our esthetic sensibility and many complex aspects of our collective psychology."*

* "Sin embargo (lo Barroco) fué uno de los elementos más prolongadamente arraigado en la tradición de nuestra cultura. A pesar de casi dos siglos de enciclopedismo y de crítica moderna, los hispanoamericanos no nos evadimos enteramente aun del laberinto barroco. Pesa en nuestra sensibilidad estética y en muchas formas complicadas de psicología colectiva." Mariano Picón Salas. *De la conquista a la independencia. Tres siglos de historia cultural hispanoamericana* (Mexico City, 1944; 3rd Ed., 1958), p. 107.

# NOTES

1. Cf. José A. Calderón Quijano, *Historia de las fortificaciones en Nueva España* (Seville, 1953), pp. 15 ff.
2. Juan Diez de la Calle, *Noticias sacras i reales (1657-1659), Manuscritos de América* 3023 (Madrid, Biblioteca Nacional).
3. Cf. A. P. Newton (ed.), *Thomas Gage, The English American. A New Survey of the West Indies, 1648* (London, Guatemala City, 1946), chap. 5.
4. These details and most of the account of Fray García Guerra given in this chapter are derived from Mateo Alemán, *Sucesos de D. Frai García Gera Arçobispo de Mejico* . . . (Mexico, 1613). Critical edition of Alice H. Bushee. Reprinted in *Revue hispanique,* 25 (New York, Paris, 1911), pp. 1-99.
5. Francisco Sosa, *El episcopado mexicano. Biografía de los Excelentísimos Señores arzobispos desde la Época Colonial hasta nuestros días* (Mexico City, 1939; earlier ed. Mexico City, 1877)
6. "Letter of Don Carlos de Sigüenza y Góngora to Admiral Andrés de Pez Recounting the Incidents of the Corn Riot in Mexico City, June 8, 1692," Appendix B of Irving A. Leonard, *Don Carlos de Sigüenza, A Mexican Savant of the Seventeenth Century* (Berkeley, University of California Publications in History, vol. 18, 1929). The original text from a contemporary copy in the Bancroft Library of the University of California, Berkeley, appears in a critical, annotated edition by Irving A. Leonard. *Alboroto y motín de los indios de México del 8 de Junio de 1692* (Mexico City: Museo Nacional, 1932), and in more abbreviated form in Manuel Romero de Terreros (ed.), *Carlos de Sigüenza y Góngora. Relaciones históricas* (Mexico City: Biblioteca del estudiante universitario, 13, 1940).

7. Newton, *op. cit.*, p. 90.
8. Cf. Artemio de Valle-Arizpe, *El Palacio Nacional de México* (Mexico City, 1936), chap. iii, *passim*. Sosa, *op. cit.*, appendix, quotes this anecdote taken from *Reformas de los descalzos de Nra Señora de Primitiva Observancia*, vol. 1, chap. xxvi.
9. Andrés Cavo, *Los Tres Siglos de México durante el Gobierno Español hasta la Entrada del Ejército Trigarante* . . . (Mexico City, 1836-1838), 4 vols., entry of June 10, 1611.
10. *Ibid.*, entry of December 25, 1611.
11. Sosa, *op. cit.*, pp. 87 ff., gives detailed description of funeral obsequies.
12. Vicente Riva Palacio, *México através de los Siglos* (Barcelona, 1888-89), 5 vols., vol. II, p. 561.

CHAPTER II

1. Americo Castro, *The Structure of Spanish History* (Princeton University Press, 1954), p. 191.
2. G. R. G. Conway (ed.), *Friar Francisco Naranjo and the Old University of Mexico* (Mexico City, 1939), pp. 37-38.
3. This discussion is indebted to Ernest Nagel in chapter 8 of *Chapters in Western Civilization* (New York: Columbia University Press, 1954).
4. Darnell H. Roaten and Federico Sánchez y Escribano, *Wolfflin's Principles in Spanish Drama, 1500-1700* (New York: Hispanic Institute in the United States, 1952), pp. 7-12.
5. Cf. Guillermo Díaz-Plaja, *Historia de la literatura española* (Barcelona, 1953), 2 vols., vol. I, pp. 220-23.
6. Roaten and Sánchez y Escribano, *op. cit.*, p. 168, n. 2.
7. Pál Kelemen, *Baroque and Rococo in Latin America* (New York, 1951), p. 14.
8. *Ibid.*, p. 22.
9. A stimulating discussion of the Baroque in Colonial Spanish America, to which this description owes much, is found in Mariano Picón Salas, *De la Conquista a la Independencia. Tres Siglos de Historia Cultural Hispanoamericana* (Mexico City, 1944), chaps. v, vi.
10. Carl J. Friedrich, *The Age of the Baroque, 1610-1660* (New York, 1952), chap. v.
11. Brooks Adams, *Law of Civilization and Decay* (New York, 1955), chap. x.
12. Friedrich, *loc. cit.*

CHAPTER III

1. Salvador de Madariaga, *The Fall of the Spanish American Empire* (London, 1947), pp. 3-4.
2. Cf. Pedro Henríquez Ureña, "Observaciones sobre el español en América," *Revista de filología española*, 18 (Madrid, 1931), pp. 122 ff.
3. Madariaga, *op. cit.*, chap. x, *passim*.
4. Bernal Díaz del Castillo, *The Discovery and Conquest of Mexico, 1517-1521*, Introduction by Irving A. Leonard (New York, 1956), p. 267.
5. Alberto M. Carreño (ed.), *Gonzalo Gómez de Cervantes. La vida económica y social de Nueva España al finalizar el siglo XVI* (Mexico City, 1944), p. 124.
6. Irving A. Leonard, *Don Carlos de Sigüenza y Góngora, A Mexican Savant of the Seventeenth Century* (Berkeley, 1929), p. 240.
7. A. P. Newton (ed.), *Thomas Gage. The English American. A New Survey of the West Indies, 1648* (London and Guatemala City, 1946). A newer edition is: *Thomas Gage's Travels in the New World*, edited by Eric S. Thompson (Norman: Univ. of Oklahoma Press, 1958).
8. Newton, *op. cit.*, p. 42.
9. Jorge Juan and Antonio de Ulloa, *Noticias secretas de América* (Madrid, 1918), Part II, chap. viii.
10. Newton, *op. cit.*, p. 84.
11. José Antonio Saco, *Historia de la esclavitud de la raza africana en el Nuevo Mundo* (Barcelona, 1879), p. 62. New edition (Havana, 1932), 2 vols.
12. Hubert Herring, *A History of Latin America* (New York, 1955), p. 101.
13. Saco, *op. cit.*, p. 130.
14. *Ibid.*, p. 164.
15. Newton, *op. cit.*, pp. 119, 164-65.
16. Irene Diggs, "Color in Colonial Spanish America," *Journal of Negro History*, 2 (1953), pp. 405-27.
17. Cf. Hensley C. Woodbridge, "Glossary of names used in colonial Latin America for crosses among Indians, Negroes, and Whites," *Journal of the Washington Academy of Sciences*, 38, no. 11 (Nov. 15, 1948), pp. 353-62.

CHAPTER IV

1. Cf. Woodrow Borah, *New Spain's Century of Depression*. Ibero-

Americana series, 25 (Berkeley: Univ. of California Press, 1951), *passim.*

2. Chapter xiii of *Repertorio de los tiempos* quoted in Francisco de la Maza. *Enrico Martínez, cosmógrafo e impresor de Nueva España* (Mexico City: Sociedad Mexicana de Geografía y Estadística, 1943).

3. Gerald Brenan, *The Literature of the Spanish People* (New York-Cambridge, 1951), p. 173.

4. Printed in Dorothy Schons, *Notes from Spanish Archives.* Book I (Ann Arbor, Mich., 1946), p. 17.

5. Francisco Rodríguez Marín, *Documentos referentes a Mateo Alemán y a sus deudos más cercanos* (1546-1607) (Madrid, 1933), pp. 52-53.

6. *Ibid.,* p. 52, note; Francisco Rodríguez Marín. *Discursos leídos ante la Real Academia Española . . .* (Seville, 1907), p. 37.

7. Cf. Irving A. Leonard, "Mateo Alemán in Mexico: a Document," *Hispanic Review,* 17, no. 4 (1949), pp. 316-27.

8. Rodríguez Marín, *Documentos . . . ,* pp. 54-55; José Gestoso y Pérez, *Nuevos datos para ilustrar las biografías del maestro Juan de Malara y de Mateo Alemán* (Seville, 1896), pp. 16-22.

9. Printed in Leonard, *op. cit.,* pp. 327-30.

10. José Toribio Medina, *La Imprenta en México (1539-1821)* (Santiago de Chile, 1907-1912: 8 vols.), vol. 2, p. 43.

11. Brenan, *op. cit.,* p. 171.

12. Antonio Castro Leal, *Juan Ruiz de Alarcón, su vida y su obra* (Mexico City, 1943), p. 29; Dorothy Schons, "The Mexican background of Alarcón," *Publications of the Modern Language Association,* 57 (1942), pp. 89-104.

13. Cf. Francisco Pérez Salazar, "Dos nuevos documentos sobre D. Juan Ruiz de Alarcón," *Revista de Literatura Mexicana,* 1, No. 1 (1940), pp. 154-65.

14. Francisco de Icaza, *Sucesos reales que parecen imaginados de Gutierre de Cetina, Juan de la Cueva, y Mateo Alemán* (Madrid, 1919), pp. 253-63.

15. William A. Kincaid, "Life and Works of Luis Belmonte Bermúdez (1587-1650?)," *Revue hispanique,* 74 (1928), pp. 1-260.

16. Cf. Alfonso Méndez Plancarte, *Poetas novohispanos.* Biblioteca del estudiante universitario, 33 (Mexico City, 1942), pp. xxx-xxxi.

17. Cf. Emilio Carilla, *El Gongorismo en América* (Buenos Aires, 1946), chaps. ii, iii, iv, for a general discussion.

18. Pedro Henríquez Ureña as quoted in Méndez Plancarte, *op. cit.,* p. xxxiv.

19. Cf. John Van Horne, *Bernardo de Balbuena. Biografía y Crítica* (Guadalajara, 1940), *passim.* Also José Rojas Garcidueñas, *Bernardo de Balbuena: La vida y obra* (Mexico City, 1958), pp. 139-72.
20. De la Maza, *op. cit., passim.*

CHAPTER V

1. A. P. Newton (ed.), *Thomas Gage. The English American. A New Survey of the West Indies, 1648* (London and Guatemala City, 1946), p. 62.
2. Antonio Vázquez de Espinosa, *Nueva España en el Siglo XVII* (Mexico City, 1944), pp. 117 ff.
3. Artemio de Valle Arizpe, *Calle vieja y calle nueva* (Mexico City, 1949), p. 25; Fernando Cepeda y Fernando Alonso Carillo, *Relación universal legítima y verdadera del sitio en que está fundada la muy noble, insigne, y leal Ciudad de México . . . lagunas, ríos, montes que la ciñen y rodean, calzadas que la dividen y azequías que la atraviesan . . .* (Mexico City, 1637), *passim.*
4. Trent Elwood Sanford, *The Story of Architecture in Mexico* (New York, 1947), p. 180.
5. Details for this description are derived from various sources, including A. P. Newton, *op. cit.;* Vázquez de Espinosa, *op. cit.;* Valle-Arizpe, *op. cit.;* Luis González Obregón, *The Streets of Mexico,* trans. by B. C. Wagner (San Francisco, 1937); Bernardo de Balbuena, *La Grandeza Mexicana,* Edición y pról. de Francisco Monterde, Biblioteca del estudiante universitario, 23 (Mexico City, 1941; also 1954).
6. Marcelino Menéndez y Pelayo, quoted in Alfonso Méndez Plancarte, *Poetas novohispanos. Primer siglo, 1521-1621.* Biblioteca del estudiante universitario, 33 (Mexico City, 1942), p. xli.
7. Translation of Thomas Walsh in *Hispanic Anthology: Poems Translated from Spanish by English and North American Poets* (New York, London, 1920). Regarding Miguel Guevara and the famous sonnet, see Alberto M. Carreño, *No me mueve mi Dios para quererle. Consideraciones nuevas sobre un viejo tema* (Mexico City, 1942), *passim;* Victor Adib, "Fray Miguel de Guevara y el soneto a Cristo crucificado," *Ábside,* 13, no. 3 (1949), pp. 311-26.
8. This inventory is reproduced in Irving A. Leonard, "One Man's Library, Mexico City, 1620," *Estudios Hispánicos,* Homenaje a Archer M. Huntington (Wellesley, Mass., 1952), pp. 327-34.
9. Francisco Javier Sánchez Cantón, *La Librería de Juan de Herrera* (Madrid, 1941).

234    *NOTES TO PAGES* 81-88

10. This author's work "en todo idioma," as well as the novels and *Labyrinth of Love* of Boccaccio are listed in the *Índice último de los libros prohibidos y mandados expurgar para todos los reynos y señoríos* . . . (Madrid, 1790).

11. Irving A. Leonard, "Un envío de libros para Concepción de Chile, 1620," *El Bibliófilo Chileno* (Santiago de Chile), vol. 2 (1948), pp. 1-7.

12. Robert Stevenson, "The Distinguished Maestro of New Spain: Juan Gutiérrez de Padilla," *Hispanic American Historical Review,* 35 (1955), pp. 363-73.

13. James D. Hart, *The Popular Book. A History of America's Literary Taste* (New York, 1950), p. 4.

CHAPTER VI

1. The original inspiration of this chapter came from a pamphlet by the Marqués de San Francisco (Manuel Romero de Terreros y Vinent) entitled *Un Bibliófilo en el Santo Oficio* (Mexico City: Librería de Pedro Robredo, 1920). While in Mexico City in 1932 I had a typescript made of the "Inventario de los libros que se hallaron a Melchor Pérez de Soto, vecino desta Ciudad, y obrero mayor de la Santa Iglesia Catedral della, los cuales se metieron en la Cámara del Secreto deste Santo Oficio (1655)," (Archivo General de la Nación. *Inquisición,* tomo 440), a manuscript of 107 folio pages, with the intention of making a detailed analysis of a colonial book list of such exceptional interest. (Professor Julio Jiménez Rueda published it in 1947 without commentary in *Documentos para la historia de la cultura en México,* Mexico City, as one of a series of publications under the auspices of the Archivo General and the Universidad Nacional Autónoma de México.) As other matters intervened I finally turned the typescript over to my student Donald G. Castanien, who made the projected analysis a doctoral dissertation under my direction. This thesis is now available in microfilm at the Library of the University of Michigan. Dr. Castanien published a summary of it as an article entitled "The Mexican Inquisition Censors a Private Library," in the *Hispanic American Historical Review,* 34 (1954), pp. 374-92, and the account in this chapter is indebted to both of these works.

2. Juan José de Eguiara y Egurén, *Prólogos a la Biblioteca Mexicana,* Ed. de Agustín Millares Carlo (Mexico City, 1944), p. 121.

3. Cf. Julio Jiménez Rueda, *Herejías y supersticiones en la Nueva España. Los Heterodoxos en México* (Mexico City, 1946), *passim.*

4. *Ibid.,* pp. 214-25.

5. James D. Hart, *The Popular Book. A History of America's Literary Taste* (New York, 1950), p. 9.

CHAPTER VII

1. R. E. Schultes, "The Appeal of Peyote (*Lophophora Williamsii*) as a Medicine," *American Anthropologist*, 40 (1938), pp. 698-715; R. E. Schultes, "Peyote, an American Indian Heritage from Mexico," *El Mexico antiguo* (Tacubaya, 1938), 5, nos. 5-6; W. LaBarre, *The Peyote Cult* (New Haven, 1938).

2. *Ramo de Inquisición*, tomo 289, Archivo General de la Nación, Mexico City. Original text and translation in Irving A. Leonard, "Peyote and the Mexican Inquisition, 1620," *American Anthropologist*, 44, no. 2 (1942), pp. 324-26.

3. *Libro primero de votos de la Inquisición de México*, 1573-1600. Introducción de Edmundo O'Gorman. Archivo General de la Nación (Mexico City, 1949), *passim*.

4. Francisco Pérez Salazar, "Las obras y desventuras de Pedro de Trejo, *Revista de literatura mexicana*, 1, no. 1 (1940), p. 124; Julio Jiménez Rueda, "Poesías sagradas y profanas de Pedro de Trejo," *Boletín del Archivo General de la Nación* (Mexico City), 15 (1944), pp. 209-312.

5. Charles Henry Lea, *The Inquisition in the Spanish Dependencies* (New York, 1908), chap. 6.

6. Luis González Obregón, *D. Guillén de Lampart. La Inquisición y la Independencia en el siglo XVII* (Mexico City, 1908), pp. 73-235; Gabriel Méndez Plancarte, "Don Guillén de Lampart y su Regio salterio," *Ábside*, 12, no. 2 (1948), pp. 125-92; no. 3 (1948), pp. 287-372.

7. José Ortega y Gasset, "Notes on the Novel," in *The Dehumanization of Art, and Other Writings on Art and Culture*, Anchor Book A72 (Garden City, N. Y., 1956), p. 67.

8. Juan Francisco Gemelli Carreri, *Viaje a la Nueva España* (Mexico City, 1927), pp. 101, 179.

9. Joseph de Buendía, *Vida del . . . P. Francisco del Castillo, S. J.*, (Madrid, 1633), fol. 444.

10. Antonio de Molina, *Antigua Guatemala* (Guatemala City, 1943), pp. 28-30.

11. Everett W. Hesse, "Calderon's Popularity in the Spanish Indies," *Hispanic Review*, 23, no. 1 (1955), pp. 12-27. A very useful compendium of the colonial theater is José J. Arrom, *El teatro de Hispanoamérica en la Época Colonial* (La Habana, 1956).

12. George W. Bacon, "The Life and Dramatic Works of D. Juan Pérez de Montalbán (1602-1638)," *Revue Hispanique*, 26 (1912), pp. 1-474.

13. An account of this controversy is given in *ibid.*, pp. 24-51.

14. Irving A. Leonard, "Pérez de Montalbán, Tomás Gutiérrez and Two Book Lists," *Hispanic Review*, 12, no. 4 (1944), p. 278.

15. Text of this play is available in James Fitzmaurice-Kelly, *The Nun Ensign* (London, 1908).

16. Joaquín María Ferrer, *Historia de la Monja Alférez, Doña Catalina de Erauso, escrita por ella misma e ilustrada con notas y documentos* (Paris, 1829), pp. 113-19.

17. C. Bravo-Villasante, *La Mujer vestida de hombre en el teatro español. Siglos XVI-XVII* (Madrid, 1955), *passim*.

18. The copy of the play used is a photostat from the University of California (Berkeley, *Osuna*, tomo colecticio 132, folios 273-90v.)

19. Dorothy Schons, "Some Obscure Points in the Life of Sor Juana Inés de la Cruz," *Modern Philology*, 24, no. 2 (1926), p. 153.

20. These proceedings are preserved in manuscript at the Archivo General de la Nación, Mexico City, *Ramo de la Inquisición*, tomo 667, no. 14, fojas 233-36, with the title: "Autos en raçon de Vna Comedia Titulada El Valor perseguido y traicion Vengada del Dor Juan Perez de Montalban y el entremes Titulado del Sacristan. Su Autor Pedro Bezerra." Cf. Irving A. Leonard. "Montalbán's El Valor Perseguido, and the Mexican Inquisition, 1682," *Hispanic Review*, 11 (1943), pp. 47-56.

CHAPTER VIII

1. Luis González Obregón, *México Viejo* (Paris, Mexico City, 1900), p. 254.

2. Antonio de Robles, "Diario de sucesos notables," *Documentos para la historia de México*, Series 1, vol. II and III (Mexico City, 1853), vol. II, p. 31.

3. Robles, *op. cit.*, vol. III, pp. 60-61; Irving A. Leonard, *Don Carlos de Sigüenza y Góngora, A Mexican Savant of the Seventeenth Century* (Berkeley, 1929), p. 219.

4. A. P. Newton (ed.), *Thomas Gage, The English-American. A New Survey of the West Indies, 1648* (London and Guatemala City, (1946), p. 165.

5. Gregorio Martín de Guijo, "Diario de Sucesos notables," *Documentos para la historia de México*, 1 series (Mexico City, 1853),

vol. I, p. 224; Robles, *op. cit.*, vol. III, pp. 289, 290; vol. II, p. 123.

6. Guijo, *op. cit.*, vol. I, p. 395-96.

7. Robles, *op. cit.*, vol. II, p. 224.

8. González Obregón, *op. cit.*, p. 252. A compilation of notices referring to *máscaras*, largely taken from the Robles and Guijo diaries, is given in Vicente Riva Palacio, *México através de los siglos* (Barcelona, 1888-1889), 5 vols, vol. II, pp. 722-23.

9. *Glorias de Querétaro en la Nueva Congregación Eclesiástica de María Santíssima de Guadalupe* . . . (Mexico City, 1680). Reprinted by Ediciones Cimatario, (Querétaro, 1945).

10. The text is available on pp. 47-51 of the 1680 edition, and pp. 50-54 of the 1945 reprinting. It also appears, with notes on Aztec terms, in Irving A. Leonard, "A Mexican *Máscara* of the Seventeenth Century," *Revista de estudios hispánicos*, II, no. 2 (1929), p. 163-67.

CHAPTER IX

1. The description of the formalities of a poetic tournament (*certamen*) given in this chapter is a composite one derived from notes compiled from many contemporary printed accounts of these competitions occurring during the seventeenth and early eighteenth century in Mexico City, Lima, Bogotá, and other centers of Colonial Spanish America. While basically all such functions were conducted in the manner set forth, differences of detail were present, of course, in most of them from time to time and from place to place. With the Baroque preoccupation with the elaboration of form, diversity in an artistic activity of this sort is clearly to be expected. In many years of investigation of the cultural and literary history of colonial Hispanic America I have not come across any systematic effort to describe the practice of a custom as complete in detail as the one here undertaken. While the data presented are drawn from many contemporary descriptions, usually quite brief, it should be acknowledged that a large measure of reliance was placed on the record of these two tournaments held in Mexico City in 1682 and 1683 contained in the *Triunfo Parténico* of Carlos de Sigüenza y Góngora, published in that city in 1683 and reprinted there in 1945 in the Biblioteca Mexicana de Libros Raros y Curiosos (Ediciones Xochitl), with a prologue by José Rojas Garcidueñas. Of incidental interest is Francisco Pérez Salazar, "Los concursos literarios en Nueva España," *Revista de literatura mexicana*, 1, no. 2 (1940), pp. 290-306.

2. "El certamen de los plateros en 1618 y las coplas satíricas que de él se derivaron," *Boletín del Archivo General de la Nación* (Mexico City), 16, No. 3 (1945), pp. 343-84.

3. Carlos de Sigüenza y Góngora, *Triunfo Parténico* (Mexico, 1945), p. 137.

4. These regulations are taken from Pedro de Peralta Barnuevo, *El Cielo en el Parnaso, cartel del certamen que . . . la Real Universidad de San Marcos de Lima . . .* (Lima, 1736), no pagination. They are reproduced in José Toribio Medina, *La imprenta en Lima* (Santiago de Chile, 1904), 4 vols., vol. II, pp. 386-87.

5. Part II, chap. 18. Quoted from the Putnam translation with the permission of the Viking Press, Inc., New York.

6. Luis Antonio Eguigurén, *El paseo triunfal y el vejamen del graduando,* Biblioteca del cuarto centenario de la fundación del la Universidad Major de San Marcos (Lima, 1949).

CHAPTER X

1. Juan Martínez de Jáuregui, *Discurso poético* (Madrid, 1624).

2. Gerald Brenan, *The Literature of the Spanish People* (New York, Cambridge, 1951), p. 252.

3. Irving A. Leonard, "Some Curiosities of Spanish Colonial Poetry," *Hispania,* 15, no. 1 (1932), pp. 39-54.

4. Part II, chap. 18. Quoted from the Putnam translation with the permission of the Viking Press, Inc., New York.

5. Reprinted in José Toribio Medina, *La Imprenta en Lima* (Santiago de Chile, 1904), 4 vols., vol. III, pp. 463-64.

6. From "The Sea Nymphes Dittie," in R. Warwick Bond, *The Complete Works of John Lyly* (Oxford, 1902), 3 vols., vol. I, p. 443.

7. Carlos de Sigüenza y Góngora, *Triunfo parténico* (Mexico City, 1945), p. 216.

8. Ricardo Palma, *Flor de academias* (Lima, 1899), p. 289.

9. Quoted in Medina, *op. cit.,* vol. II, p. 503.

10. *Ibid., loc. cit.*

11. Sigüenza y Góngora, *op. cit.,* p. 230.

12. *Ibid.,* p. 206.

13. *Ibid.,* p. 213.

14. Francisco Pimentel, *Historia crítica de la literatura y de las ciencias en México* (Mexico City, 1885), p. 140.

15. Vicente Riva Palacio, *México através de los siglos* (Barcelona, 1888-89), 5 vols., vol. II, pp. 751-52.

16. Sigüenza y Góngora, *op. cit.,* p. 216.

17. *Ibid.,* p. 219; Irving A. Leonard, "Some Góngora Centones in Mexico," *Hispania,* 12, No. 6 (1929), pp. 568-69.

18. Ricardo Palma, *op. cit.*, acta décima cuarta.
19. *Ibid.*, acta décima sexta.
20. *Ibid.*, p. 258.

CHAPTER XI

1. These details are drawn from the description by Leonel Waffer entitled "La Ciudad de México en 1678," in Artemio de Valle-Arizpe, *Historia de la Ciudad de México según los relatos de sus cronistas* (Mexico City, 1939), pp. 453-57. Also useful was the Fer map of 1715 reproduced in Luis González Obregón, *México Viejo* (Paris, Mexico City, 1900), opposite p. 579. A key to the streets and buildings indicated on the Fer map is given in the appendix of the same work.
2. Agustín de Vetancourt, quoted in Salvador de Madariaga, *The Fall of the Spanish American Empire* (London, 1947), p. 53.
3. Francisco Sosa, *El episcopado mexicano* (Mexico City, 1877), p. 150.
4. Joseph de Lezamis, *Vida del Apóstol Santiago el Mayor* (Mexico City, 1699). This work contains a prefatory biography of Aguiar y Seijas, without pagination.
5. Francesco Gemelli Careri, *Giro del mondo parte sesta* (Naples, 1721), p. 150. There are good modern Spanish translations of this interesting account.
6. Vicente Riva Palacio, *México através de los siglos* (Barcelona, 1888-89), 5 vols., vol. II, chap. xv.
7. *Loc. cit.*
8. Ezequiel A. Chávez, *Ensayo de psicología de Sor Juana Inés de la Cruz* (Barcelona, 1931), p. 452.
9. Gemelli Careri, quoted in Valle-Arizpe, *op. cit.*, p. 377.
10. Cf. José Toribio Medina, *La imprenta en Mexico, 1539-1821* (Santiago de Chile, 1907-1912), 8 vols., vol. I, p. cxxviii; Francisco Pérez Salazar, "Dos familias de impresores mexicanos del siglo XVII," *Memorias de la sociedad científica Antonio Alzate* (Mexico City), 43 (1925), pp. 447 ff.
11. Sigüenza y Góngora gives a highly laudatory account of this individual in the fragment of his *Piedad heroyca de don Fernando Cortés* in Francisco Pérez Salazar (ed), *Carlos de Sigüenza y Góngora. Obras* (Mexico City: Sociedad de Bibliófilos Mexicanos, 1928), pp. 331-40.
12. This inventory is in the Archivo General de la Nación, Mexico City, *Ramo de la Inquisición*, tomo 661, fol. 40-47v, and is reproduced in Irving A. Leonard, "On the Mexican Book Trade, 1683," *Hispanic American Historical Review*, 27, no. 3 (1947), pp. 419-35.

This document, which I discovered and photographed in 1940, is not included in the interesting collection of similar book lists assembled by Edmundo O'Gorman and published as "Bibliotecas y librerías coloniales, 1585-1694," in *Boletín del Archivo General de la Nación* (Mexico City), X, no. 4 (dated 1939, but published subsequently), pp. 663-1006. Document XD of this collection is a 1655 *memoria* (1,126 titles) of the bookshop of the Viuda de Bernardo Calderón, as is Document XVI (1,239 titles), a *memoria* of the year 1660.

13. These and the following details relating to the Boston book trade are gleaned from Thomas G. Wright, *Literary Culture in Early New England, 1620-1730* (New Haven, 1920), and Samuel E. Morison, *The Puritan Pronaos. Intellectual Life of New England in the Seventeenth Century* (New York University Press, 1936).

14. Tom B. Jones, "The Classics in Colonial Hispanic America," *Transactions of the American Philological Association*, 70 (1939), pp. 37-45.

15. James D. Hart, *The Popular Book. A History of America's Taste* (New York, 1950), p. 16. Quoted with permission of the Oxford University Press, Inc., New York.

CHAPTER XII

1. Arturo Torres-Ríoseco, *New World Literature, Tradition, and Revolt in Latin America* (Berkeley, 1949), p. 40. There are numerous biographical studies of the nun-poetess; perhaps the best to date is Anita Arroyo, *Razón y pasión de Sor Juana Inés de la Cruz* (Mexico City, 1952).

2. Interesting data on life in colonial convents are given in Josefina Muriel, *Conventos de monjas en la Nueva España* (Mexico City, 1946).

3. Frederick B. Luquiens, "Spanish American Literature," *Yale Review Quarterly*, XVII, no. 3 (1928).

4. Francisco López Cámara, "El cartesianismo en Sor Juana y Sigüenza y Góngora," *Filosofía y letras* (Mexico City), no. 39 (1950).

5. Particularly interesting in this connection are: Ezequiel Chávez, *Ensayo de Psicología de Sor Juana Inés de la Cruz* (Barcelona, 1931); and Ludwig Pfandl, *Die zehnte Muse von Mexico Juana Ines de la Cruz. Ihr Leben, Ihre Dichtung. Ihre Psyche.* (Muenchen, 1946).

6. Julio Jiménez Rueda, *Sor Juana Inés de la Cruz en su época (1651-1951)* (Mexico City, 1951), p. 76.

7. Original text of the sonnets:
    Al que ingrato me deja, busco amante;

al que amante me sigue, dejo ingrata;
constante adoro a quien mi amor maltrata;
maltrato a quien mi amor busca constante.

Al que trato de amor hallo diamante;
y soy diamante al que de amor me trata;
triunfante quiero ver al que me mata
y mato a quien me quiere ver triunfante.

Si a éste pago, padece mi deseo:
si ruego a aquél, mi pundonor enojo:
de entrambos modos infeliz me veo.

Pero yo por mejor partido escojo
de quien no quiero ser violento empleo,
que de quien no me quiere, vil despojo.

. . . . . . . . . .

Feliciano me adora y le aborrezco;
Lisardo me aborrece y yo le adoro;
por quien no me apetece ingrato, lloro
y al que me llora tierno, no apetezco:

a quien más me desdora, el alma ofrezco;
a quien me ofrece víctimas, desdoro;
desprecio al que enriquece mi decoro
y al que le hace desprecios enriquezco;

si con mi ofensa al uno reconvengo,
me reconviene el otro a mí ofendido
y al padecer de todos modos vengo;

pues ambos atormentan mi sentido:
aquéste con pedir lo que no tengo
y aquél con no tener lo que le pido.

. . . . . . . . . .

Que no me quiera Fabio al verse amado
es dolor sin igual, en mi sentido;
mas que me quiera Silvio aborrecido
es menor mal, mas no menor enfado.

¿Que sufrimiento no estará cansado,
si siempre le resuenan al oído,
tras la vana arrogancia de un querido,
el cansado gemir de un desdeñado?

Si de Silvio me cansa el rendimiento,
a Fabio canso con estar rendida:
si de este busco el agradecimiento,

por activa y pasiva es mi tormento,
pues padezco en querer y ser querida.

. . . . . . . . . .

Translation of the first sonnet is by Pauline Cook in *The Pathless Grove* (Prairie City, Ill.: Decher Press, 1951), and is quoted with her permission; the second by S. G. Morley in Torres-Ríoseco, *op. cit.*, p. 218, and is quoted by permission of the University of California Press; and the third by Peter H. Goldsmith in Thomas Walsh, *Hispanic Anthology: Poems Translated from the Spanish by English and North American Poets* (New York, London, 1920).

These sonnets and other poems cited in this discussion are available in Alfonso Méndez Plancarte, *Obras Completas de Sor Juana Inés de la Cruz* (Mexico City, 1951-57), 4 vols., vol. I, Lírica Personal. Edición, prólogo y notas de . . . Poems are indexed by the first verse.

8. *Obras completas*, vol. i, p. 531; and especially Carlos González Echegaray, "Sor Juana y Frey Lope," *Boletín de la Biblioteca Menéndez y Pelayo*, 24 (1948), pp. 281-89.

9. Pfandl, *op. cit., passim*; Arroyo, *op. cit., passim*; José María de Cossío, "Observaciones sobre la vida y la obra de Sor Juana Inés de la Cruz," *Boletín de la Real Academia Espanola* (Madrid), 32 (1952), pp. 27-47; *see also* Jose María Pemán, "Sinceridad y artificio en la poesía de Sor Juana Inés de la Cruz," *ibid.*, pp. 55-72.

10. The text of this *Respuesta* is in vol. IV of the *Obras completas*.

11. *Obras completas*, vol. I, p. 6, verses 57-60.

12. Translated by Pauline Cook, *op. cit.*, p. 25, and quoted with her permission.

13. The text of this letter of the Bishop of Puebla, Manuel Fernández de Santa Cruz to Sor Juana Inés is reproduced in *Sor Juana Inés de la Cruz. Carta Atenagórica. Respuesta a Sor Filotea.* Edición, prologo, y notas de E. Abreu Gómez. Clásicos Mexicanos (Mexico City, 1934), pp. 46-48.

14. Cossío, *op. cit.*, p. 36.

15. Lancelot Law Whyte, *The Next Development in Man* (New York, 1950), pp. 106, 107.

16. Cf. Irving A. Leonard, *Books of the Brave* (Cambridge: Harvard Press 1949), *passim*. Regarding works in Sister Juana's library, see E. Abreu Gómez, *Sor Juana Inés de la Cruz. Bibliografía y Biblioteca.* Monografías Bibliográficas Mexicanas, 29 (Mexico City, 1934), *passim*.

17. López Cámara, *op. cit.*, p. 129.

18. *Ibid.*, pp. 122-23. Sigüenza cites Descartes in his *Libra astronómica y filosófica* (Mexico City, 1690).

19. Translation of Robert Graves, in *Encounter*, no. 3 (December, 1953), and quoted with his permission.

20. Carlos de Sigüenza y Góngora, *Teatro de virtudes políticas*, in Francisco Pérez Salazar, *Obras de Carlos de Sigüenza y Góngora* (Mexico City, 1928), p. 38.

CHAPTER XIII

1. This and numerous other quotations in this chapter are from the long letter of Sigüenza y Góngora addressed to Admiral Andrés de

Pez in Madrid. It was entitled *Alboroto y motín de los Indios de México del 8 de Junio de 1692*, a contemporary copy of which is preserved in the Bancroft Library of the University of California (Berkeley). A translation appears as Appendix B of Irving A. Leonard, *Don Carlos de Sigüenza y Góngora, A Mexican Savant of the Seventeenth Century* (Berkeley, 1929). From this copy an annotated edition by Irving A. Leonard was made in 1932 and published by the National Museum, Mexico City. In 1940 (again in 1954) it was reprinted in shortened form in Manuel Romero de Terreros (ed), *Carlos de Sigüenza y Góngora. Relaciones históricas.* Biblioteca del estudiante universitario, 13 (Mexico City). On the life of this Creole scholar the biography of Leonard cited above still remains the fullest treatment. A shorter life is that of José Rojas Garcidueñas, *Don Carlos de Sigüenza y Góngora, erudito barroco.* Vidas Mexicanas 23 (Mexico City, 1945).

Sigüenza's verse is available in *Carlos de Sigüenza y Góngora. Poemas.* Recopilados por Irving A. Leonard. Estudio preliminar de E. Abreu Gómez. Biblioteca de Historia Hispanoamericana (Madrid, 1931).

2. Cf. Edmundo O'Gorman, "Datos sobre D. Carlos de Sigüenza y Góngora, 1669-1677," *Boletín del Archivo General de la Nación de Mexico*, 15, No. 4 (1944), pp. 593-612, and E. J. Burrus, "Sigüenza y Góngora's efforts for readmission into the Jesuit Order," *Hispanic American Historical Review*, 33 (1953), p. 387.

3. This interesting will of Sigüenza is printed in Francisco Pérez Salazar, *Biografía de D. Carlos de Sigüenza y Góngora, seguida de varios documentos inéditos* (Mexico City, 1928), pp. 161-92.

4. *The Trophy of Spanish Justice* and the account of the Windward Fleet are reprinted in Pérez Salazar (ed.), *Obras de Carlos de Sigüenza y Góngora.* The *Mercurio Volante* or *Flying Mercury* was published by the Quivira Society in facsimile with a translation and introduction by Irving A. Leonard, *The Mercurio Volante of Sigüenza y Góngora. An Account of the First Expedition of Don Diego de Vargas into New Mexico in 1692* (Los Angeles, 1932). Regarding the corn riot of the Indians, see note 1.

5. The text of *Infortunios de Alonso Ramírez* is available in vol. 20 of the *Colección de libros raros y curiosos que tratan de América* (Madrid, 1902), and in Manuel Romero de Terreros, *Relaciones Históricas de Carlos de Sigüenza y Góngora* (Mexico City, 1940, 1954).

6. This exceedingly rare pamphlet is reprinted in modernized form in *Universidad de Mexico*, 11, No. 11 (1957), pp. 17-19.

7. There is no modern edition of this important treatise. The text here used was a photostatic copy in the Bancroft Library of the University of California (Berkeley), from an original preserved in the John Crerar Library of Chicago, Ill.

8. Concerning Father Kino, see Herbert Eugene Bolton, *Rim of Christendom* (New York, 1936).

9. Gerard Decorme, S. J., *La obra de los jesuitas mexicanos, durante la Época Colonial, 1572-1767* (Mexico City), vol. 1, p. 231.

10. For a full account, see Irving A. Leonard, *The Spanish Approach to Pensacola, 1689-1693*, Quivira Society Publications, vol. 9 (Albuquerque, 1939).

11. This letter, dated May 9, 1699, is printed in Pérez Salazar, *Biografía*, . . ., pp. 119-60. A detailed account of the Pensacola project as a whole is given in William E. Dunn, *Spanish and French Rivalry in the Gulf Region of the United States, 1678-1702*, University of Texas Bulletin, No. 1705 (Austin, 1917), and of Arriola's part in Irving A. Leonard, "Don Andrés de Arriola and the Occupation of Pensacola Bay," in *New Spain and the Anglo-American West*, Historical Contributions Presented to Herbert Eugene Bolton (Los Angeles, 1932), 2 vols., vol. 1, pp. 81-106.

12. Antonio de Robles, "Diario de sucesos notables," *Documentos para la historia de México*, Series 1, vols. II and III (Mexico City, 1853), vol. III, p. 262.

CHAPTER XIV

1. Pierre Margry, *Decouvertes et etablissements des Français dans l'ouest et dans le sud de l'Amerique Septentrionale, 1614-1756* (Paris, 1879-1888), 6 vols., vol. IV., p. 351.

2. Carlos de Sigüenza y Góngora, *Parayso Occidental* (Mexico City, 1684), prologue.

3. *Teatro de virtudes politicas que constituye un principe: Advertidas en los monarcas antiguos del Mexicano Imperio* . . . (Mexico City, 1680), reprinted in Francisco Pérez Salazar, *Obras de Carlos de Sigüenza y Góngora con una biografía* (Mexico City, 1928), p. 1-148. See also Francisco López Cámara, "La Conciencia criolla en Sor Juana y Sigüenza," *Historia mexicana*, 6 (1957), no. 3, pp. 350-73. Hermenegildo Corbató, "La emergencia de la idea de nacionalidad en el México colonial," *Revista Iberoamericana*, 6 (1943), pp. 377-92.

# A BRIEF BIBLIOGRAPHY

Alemán, Mateo. *Sucesos de D. Frai Garcia Gera Arcobispo de Mejico* . . . Critical edition of Alice H. Bushee, *Revue hispanique* (New York-Paris, 1911), vol. 25, pp. 1-99.

Andrade, Vicente de Paula. *Ensayo bibliográfico mexicano del siglo XVII* (Mexico City, 1899).

Arróm, José J. *El teatro de Hispanoamérica en la Época Colonial* (Havana, 1956).

Arroyo, Anita. *Razón y pasión de Sor Juana Inés de la Cruz* (Mexico City, 1952).

Balbuena, Bernardo de. *La grandeza mexicana.* Biblioteca del Estudiante Universitario, 23 (Mexico City, 1954).

Bancroft, Hubert Howe. *History of Mexico* (San Francisco, 1883-88), 6 vols.

Bolton, Herbert Eugene. *Rim of Christendom* (New York, 1936).

Borah, Woodrow. *New Spain's Century of Depression.* Ibero-Americana series, 25 (Berkeley, 1951).

Carilla, Emilio. *El gongorismo en América* (Buenos Aires, 1946).

Carreño, Alberto (ed.). *Gonzalo Gómez de Cervantes. La vida económica y social de Nueva España al finalizar el siglo XVI* (Mexico City, 1944).

Cavo, Andrés. *Los tres siglos de México durante el gobierno español* . . . (Mexico City, 1936-38), 4 vols.

Cepeda, Fernando, y Carrillo, Fernando Alonso. *Relación universal legítima y verdadera del sitio en que está fundada la muy noble, insigne, y leal Ciudad de México* . . . (Mexico City, 1637).

Chávez, Ezequiel A. *Ensayo de psicología de Sor Juana Inés de la Cruz* (Barcelona, 1931).

Conway, G. R. G. (ed.). *Friar Francisco Naranjo and the Old University of Mexico* (Mexico City, 1939).

Cuevas, Mariano, S. J. *Historia de la Iglesia en México* (Tlalpam, D. F., Mexico, 1921-24), 3 vols.

Diggs, Irene. "Color in Colonial Spanish America," *Journal of Negro History*, 2 (1953), pp. 405-27.

Friedrich, Carl J. *The Age of the Baroque, 1610-1660* (New York, 1952).

García, Genaro (ed.). *Documentos inéditos o muy raros para la historia de México* (Mexico City, 1905-11) 35 vols.

Gemelli Careri, Juan Francisco. *Viaje a la Nueva España* (Mexico City, 1927).

González Obregón, Luis. *The Streets of Mexico*. Translated by B. C. Wagner (San Francisco, 1937).

———. *D. Guillén de Lampart. La Inquisición y la independencia en el siglo XVII* (Mexico City, 1908).

———.*México Viejo* (Paris, Mexico City, 1900).

Guijo, Gregorio Martín de. *Diario de sucesos notables*. Documentos para la historia de México (Mexico City, 1853).

Jiménez Rueda, Julio. *Herejías y supersticiones en la Nueva España. Los heterodoxos en México* (Mexico City, 1946).

Kelemen, Pál. *Baroque and Rococo in Latin America* (New York, 1951).

Lea, Charles Henry. *The Inquisition in the Spanish Dependencies* (New York, 1908).

Leonard, Irving A. *Don Carlos de Sigüenza y Góngora, A Mexican Savant of the Seventeenth Century* (Berkeley, 1929).

———. *Alboroto y Motín de los indios de México del 8 de junio de 1692* (Mexico City, 1932).

———. *The Spanish Approach to Pensacola, 1689-1693*. Quivira Society Publications, vol. 9 (Albuquerque, 1939).

Madariaga, Salvador de. *The Fall of the Spanish American Empire* (London, 1947).

Marroqui, J. M. *La Ciudad de México* (Mexico City, 1900-1903: 3 vols.).

Maza, Francisco de la. *Enrico Martínez, cosmógrafo e impresor de Nueva España* (Mexico City, 1943).

Medina, Baltasar de. *Crónica de la Santa Provincia de San Diego* (Mexico City, 1682).

Medina, José Toribio. *La Imprenta en México (1539-1821)* (Santiago de Chile, 1907-1912), 8 vols.

Méndez Plancarte, Alfonso. *Poetas novohispanos. Primer siglo 1521-1621*. Biblioteca del Estudiante Universitario, 33 (Mexico City, 1942).

Méndez Plancarte, Alfonso, and Alberto G. Salcedo. *Obras completas de Sor Juana Inés de la Cruz* (Mexico City, 1951-57), 4 vols.

Morison, Samuel E. *The Puritan Pronaos. Intellectual Life in New England in the Seventeenth Century* (New York, 1936).

Muriel, Josefina. *Conventos de monjas en la Nueva España* (Mexico City, 1946).

Newton, A. P. (ed.). *Thomas Gage. The English American. A New Survey of the West Indies, 1648* (London, Guatemala City, 1946).

Pérez Salazar, Francisco (ed.). *Obras de Don Carlos de Sigüenza y Góngora* (Mexico City, 1928).

———. *Biografía de D. Carlos de Sigüenza y Góngora, seguida de varios documentos inéditos* (Mexico City, 1928).

Picón-Salas, Mariano. *A Cultural History of Spanish America: From Conquest to Independence.* Translated by Irving A. Leonard. (Berkeley, 1962, paperback edition, 1963).

Pimentel, Francisco. *Historia crítica de la literatura y de las ciencias en México* (Mexico City, 1885).

Rangel, Nicolás (ed.). *Cristóbal de la Plaza y Jaén. Crónica de la Real y Pontificia Universidad de México . . .* (Mexico City, 1931), 2 vols.

———. *Historia del toreo en México: Época Colonial, 1529-1821* (Mexico City, 1924).

Riva Palacio, Vicente. *México através de los siglos* (Barcelona, 1888-89), 5 vols.

Rivera, Juan Antonio. *Diario curioso de México.* Documentos para la Historia de México, series 1, vol. 7 (Mexico City, 1854).

Rivera Cambas, Manuel. *Los gobernantes de México* (Mexico City, 1872-1873), 2 vols.

Robles, Antonio de. *Diario de sucesos notables.* Documentos para la historia de México, series 1, vols. 2, 3 (Mexico City, 1853).

Rojas Garcidueñas, José. *Don Carlos de Sigüenza y Góngora, Erudito barroco.* Vidas mexicanas 23 (Mexico City, 1945).

———. *Bernardo de Balbuena: La vida y la obra* (Mexico City, 1958).

Romero de Terreros, Manuel. *Carlos de Sigüenza y Góngora. Relaciones históricas.* Biblioteca del Estudiante Universitario 13 (Mexico City, 1957).

Schons, Dorothy. *Notes from Spanish Archives.* Book I (Ann Arbor, Michigan, 1946).

———. *Book Censorship in New Spain* (Austin, Texas, 1949).

Sigüenza y Góngora, Carlos de. *Glorias de Querétaro en la nueva congregación eclesiástica de María Santísima de Guadalupe* (Mexico City, 1680; 1945).

————. *Triunfo parténico* (Mexico City, 1683; 1945).

————. *Teatro de virtudes políticas* . . . (Mexico City, 1680; 1928).

————. *Poemas.* Recopilado por Irving A. Leonard. Estudio preliminar de E. Abreu Gómez (Madrid, 1931).

————. *The Mercurio Volante.* Facsimile. Translation, Introduction, and Notes by Irving A. Leonard. Quivira Society Publications, vol. 2 (Los Angeles, 1932).

————. *Parayso occidental* (Mexico City, 1684).

————. *Libra astronómica y philosóphica* (Mexico City, 1690).

Sosa, Francisco. *El episcopado mexicano. Biografías de los excelentísimos señores arzobispos desde la Época Colonial hasta nuestros días* (Mexico City, 1939).

Valle-Arizpe, Artemio. *El Palacio Nacional de México* (Mexico City, 1936).

————. *Historia de la Ciudad de México según los relatos de sus cronistas* (Mexico City, 1939).

————. *Calle Vieja y Calle Nueva* (Mexico City, 1949).

Vázquez de Espinosa, Antonio. *Nueva España en el siglo XVII* (Mexico City, 1944).

Vetancourt, Augustín de. *Teatro mexicano* (Mexico City, 1698; 1870-1871), 4 vols.

Wright, Thomas G. *Literary Culture in Early New England, 1620-1730* (New Haven, 1920).

# INDEX

This index does not include the documentary references which are assembled on pages 229-44. Except in certain proper names, including titles of books, the definite and indefinite articles, whether in Spanish or English, are disregarded in alphabetizing subject matter.

# SELECTED ANN ARBOR PAPERBACKS

*works of enduring merit*